Total Transformational Thinking in Academic Leadership

A New DNA

Edited By

Professor Mohamed Zairi

European Centre for Best Practice Management
PUBLISHING HOUSE

Total Transformational Thinking in Academic Leadership
A New DNA

1st Edition 2009

ISBN 978-1-906993-09-2

9 781906 993092 >

Published by:

European Centre for Best Practice Management

Holly House | Spring Gardens Lane | Keighley | BD20 6LE | UK

Tele: +44 (0) 1535612060 | Web: www.ECBPM.com

Cover Design

Nidhi Narula

European Centre for Best Practice Management

Printers

Inprint + Design Ltd

WB07 Richmond Building | Carlton Street | Bradford | BD7 1DP |UK

Tele: +44 (0) 1274 235757 | Web: http://www.inprintdesign.com/

Contents

List of figures

List of co-contributors

Dr. Simmy Marwa

Mr. Sultanul Chowdhury

Acknowledgements

No book is ever written alone and no research endeavour is ever carried out in solitude.

First and foremost, my greatest appreciation has to go to my research teams past and present, and in particular, the individuals involved in these compilations and whose research projects I have enjoyed leading and closely supervising. In particular, my sincere thanks and deep appreciation go to my co-contributors: **Dr. Simmy Marwa & Mr. Sultanul Chowdhury** for making the book on *Total Transformational Thinking in Academic Leadership: A New DNA* possible.

My sincere thanks also go to my support teams, past and present, who make our work possible every day of the week, all months of the year and who have helped sustain our focus and our determination to continue pioneering.

Lastly, my thanks and appreciation go to my wife Alweena and my children Adel, Bilal and Nadir for their unconditional love and unwavering support.

Dedication

But when I searched, I found no work so meritorious as the discovery and development of the arts and inventions that tend to civilise the life of man. (Francis Bacon)

This book is dedicated to all the men and women whose mission in life is to pioneer, validate and enlighten others with knowledge and the discovery of facts and the truth. It is also dedicated to all those who can help by developing solutions to problems and finding answers to enquiries. Dr Joseph Juran once said: 'My job of contributing to the welfare of my fellow man is the great unfinished business.'

It is therefore hoped that the content of this book will help move forward the human thinking capacity, will assist in the development of the enquiry mind and will support future quests for knowledge and advancement of theory and practice in the field of Total Quality Management and related topics.

Our biggest thrill would be to see that the content of this book is used, the knowledge presented consumed and the various ideas applied. It may of course be wishful thinking but we remain hopeful that the efforts made in putting this text together are not futile and that there will be some positive use of the various concepts presented.

As Rita C. Richey (October, 1999) wrote:

Ideas often take a substantial amount of time to be appreciated, and even for those few that attract attention quickly, there is an assumption that one needs the perspective of hindsight to determine their lasting value. Consequently, an intellectual inheritance is usually determined by the survivors rather than by the donor, and the labels that describe the merit of one's ideas are affixed by subsequent generations.

Introduction

It is very hard for leaders to come to grips with the notion of Excellence, particularly that in the 21st century we are often referring to a moving target. Excellence in a modern context is the attainment of a relative state of achievement and performance. The relative state of performance is however appropriate and applicable to any organisation, operating in any sector of the economy and being at any state of competitiveness. Excellence could mean on the one hand being able to fulfil the requirements of customers and stakeholders that are current, clearly defined and predictable since they are representing an ability to replenish, to do more of the same and to be reliable and consistent in dependability.

Excellence on the other hand could mean the ability to stretch, close performance gaps and become 'better' at doing current things with new ideas, solutions and methods. In this context it could also be the ability to fulfil undefined and therefore unfulfilled needs with innovation and new thinking. Finally excellence could truly mean shooting ahead of the duck and not missing a moving target. In this sense, it is about stimulating new thinking, surprising customers and stakeholders with delightful products and services and building a brand reputation through innovation and uniqueness. This state of excellence is dependent on innovation driving the value chain and breaking the mould, using out of the box thinking and not clinching onto a safety net by depending heavily on the past and the present.

Steve Ballmer said: "We can believe that we know where the world should go. But unless we're in touch with our customers, our model of the world can diverge from reality. There's no substitute for innovation, of course, but innovation is no substitute for being in touch, either."

Steve Forbes on the other hand argues that: "The real source of wealth and capital in this new era is not material things.. It is the human mind, the human spirit, the human imagination, and our faith in the future."

Innovation will remain the true predictor of the future, whilst Excellence will be the foundation on which to build a future state. It is therefore imperative for leaders of the 21st century to build sustainable excellence based on the following principles which are depicted in the Model proposed below:

- The Constancy of Purpose, a sense of purposefulness will define what contribution, impact and legacy leaders can leave behind. Excellence n the 21st century is not about 'getting there' but more importantly is about 'continuity' and the assurance that the journey will continue after they have gone;
- Excellence is of course subject to the old maxim 'horses for courses'. It has to be defined to give true meaning to the entity that 'owns' the challenge, the dream and aspiration. Furthermore, Excellence is to be driven, guided, nurtured and grown
- Excellence is about tangible impact and outcomes
- Excellence as stated previously is about developing the momentum for continuity, the potential for growth, the predictability of performance, the dependability on capability, the confidence in the next journeys and what they bring.
- Excellence is similar to a living cell and its nucleus where the DNA gets determine is represented by the culture and work environment that is shaped and created.

This book seeks to examine The Concept of Excellence from the point of view of what academic leaders must do in a '21st century style' to attain and sustain commanding positions in terms of performance and esteem. In particular, the book will focus on the following:

- Exposure to 'super-leadership' principles and practices
- Appreciating the true meaning of 'constancy of purpose' and the task of guiding excellence
- Developing competency in defining and driving sustainable excellence
- Building sustainable performance capability
- Defining an Innovation driven excellent organisation
- Appreciating the importance of culture and excellence in terms of work climate.

The book is presented through 5 parts which are linked through a cycle of:

- Conceptualisation (exposure to new concepts)
- Contextualization (relevancy to Higher Education Institutions)
- Competence (The opportunity to apply some of the ideas in 'own university setting')
- Communication (the opportunity to explore issues and analyse current state in 'own university')
- Confirmation (using the ideas for generating wider commitment for developing actions)

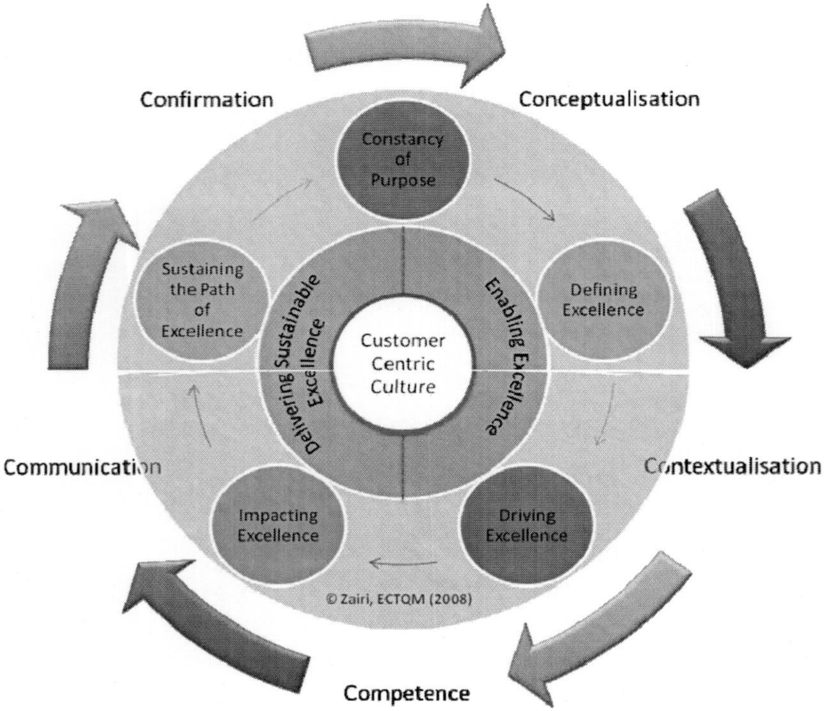

Figure 1: Customer Centric Culture

Becoming a Leader in an Academic Environment – The New DNA

Excellence does not happen by itself, but it has to be achieved through visionary leadership and a continuous drive of value, high quality standards and superior performance outcomes. The role of leadership in an academic context is therefore not dissimilar to the one that takes place in the private sector or in other public sector contexts. Not only do universities and other institutions of higher learning need to focus on identifying the critical factors that are required for developing a vision for excellence, driving it and delivering its outcomes, they also need to create a continuum of leadership roles at various levels so as to ensure a total engagement, a total alignment and a high impact visionary effort.

In addition to knowing what type of leadership universities must have, it is also important to understand what the key attributes are of an effective leader in an academic environment. The knowledge of how to develop an effective academic vision is an essentiality together with the requirements of academic leaders in mentoring and creating effective team work environments, motivating their colleagues and being passionate about academic excellence in its wider context.

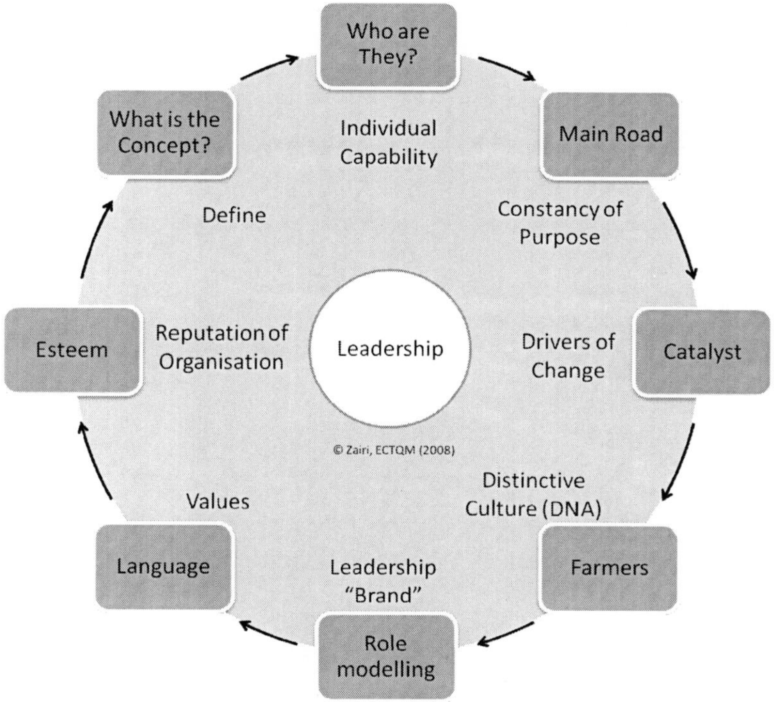

Figure 2: Becoming a Leader in an Academic Environment – The New DNA

Creating an Effective and Conducive Academic Environment

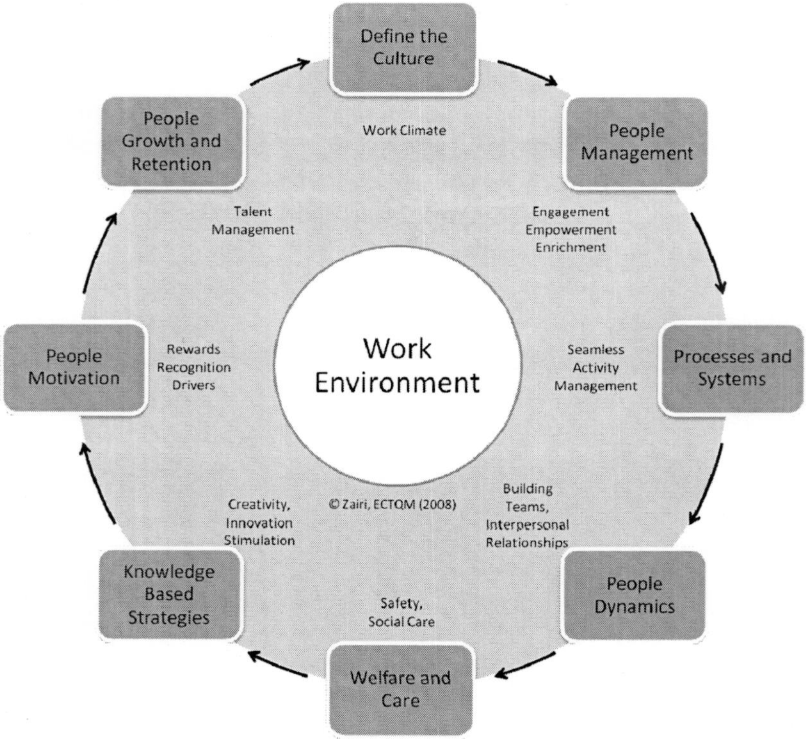

Figure 3: Creating an Effective and Conducive Academic Environment

Excellence as a generic concept can only grow and prosper in environments where high levels of interactions between people is encouraged, where value added contributions are appreciated, measured and recognized and where a seamless approach is built to deliver high value to key stakeholders such as students, employers, and other stakeholders. The fuel that enables academic institutions to ache8ive excellent standards is the creative potential and the exchange of ideas at all levels. In order to build such a climate and work environment, universities need to engage and motivate individual employees particularly scholars and academicians. They also need to harness the explicit and tacit knowledge that exists and they also need to build synergy through teamwork. The creation of opportunities for the growth and development of academic staff in particular is essential for instance; emphasis on conferences, the role of research centres, internal and external exchange opportunities is a useful mechanism. In addition, through the use of the open system perspective, synergy can be further enhanced by having mechanisms for the exchange of ideas and the transfer of know how. Such an environment that creates academic excellence must be supported by world class infrastructure such as IT and facilities plus resources.

Driving Excellence in Academia

In order to achieve excellence status the institutions of higher learning a fresh approach is required, which is heavily dependent on building ambitious strategies that are translated into smart goals and objectives and effectively deployed through developing key performance indicators and embedding the impetus of quality and continuous improvement in all aspects of academic life.

By relying on total integrated management systems such as generic excellence models, universities will be able to create the necessary capabilities for achieving excellence standards and also they are able to build a culture of continuous measurement and optimization. The European Excellence Model for instance is a useful approach for driving and building sustainable excellence in an academic environment.

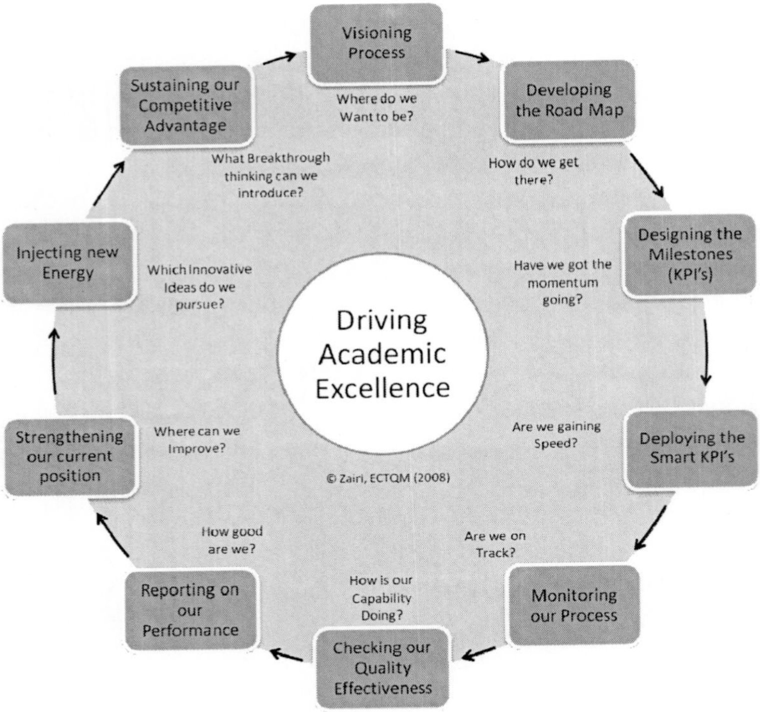

Figure 4: Driving Excellence in Academia

Assessing Academic Excellence

It is useful to understand the methodologies and processes that are used to evaluate quality of programmes and their management. In seeking to gain credible recognition from international accreditation bodies and in order to comply with national accreditation requirements institutions of higher learning have to do a lot of building, development and implementation of best practice applications covering all the facets associated with programme delivery and management, infrastructural support and integrated performance evaluation and follow up.

It is possible therefore that quality tools and techniques such as Six Sigma, the balanced scorecard, and benchmarking and continuous improvement philosophy are used for steering and supporting academic excellence. The assessment of academic excellence can cover QAA, EQUIS, and AACSB etc.

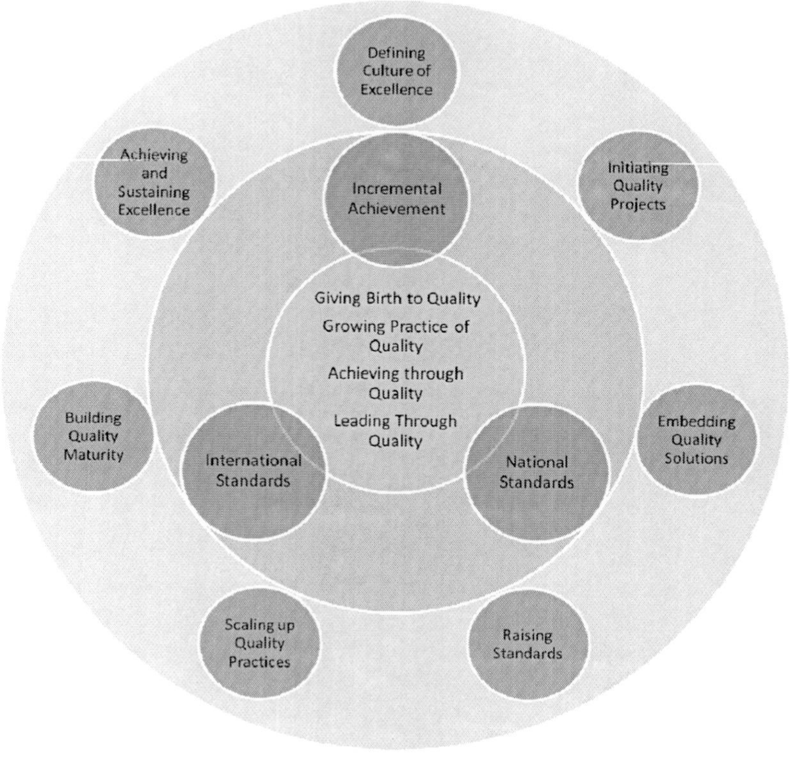

Figure 5: Assessing Academic Excellence

Creating A World Class University

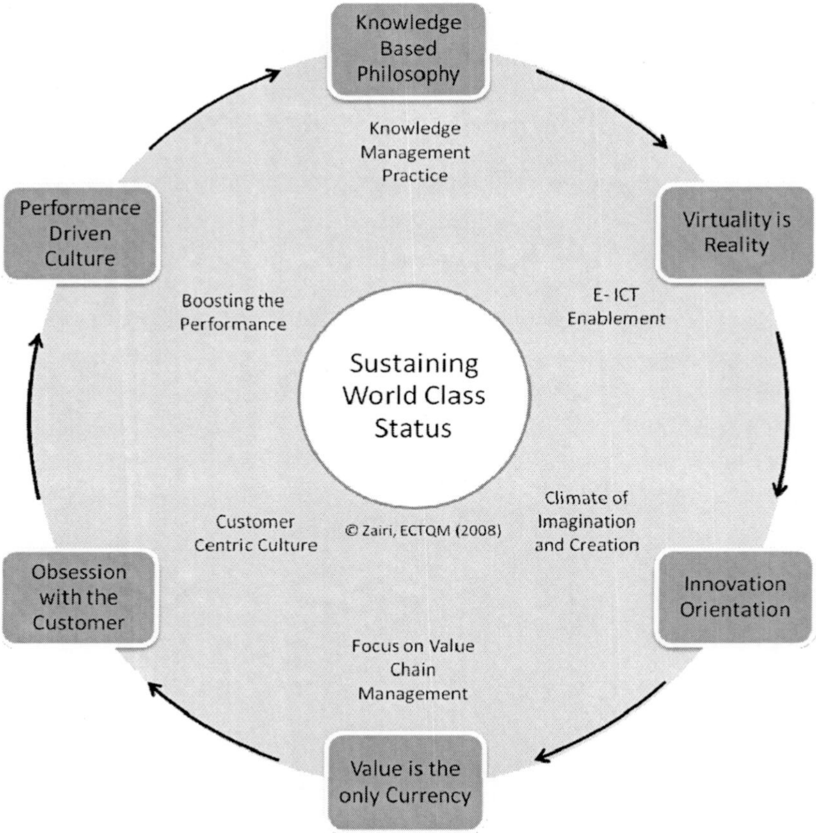

Figure 6: Creating a World Class Status

The future role of universities can only be built if they adopt what might be referred to as an open system approach. Indeed, universities of the future will need to interact continuous with the external environment, develop close partnerships, leverage from similar institutions and centres of excellence and develop closeness to their customers and key stakeholders. Such a task requires all the confidence and capability that are necessary for achieving their aspirations. Without for instance, good reputation, quality ability and being customer centric, being exposed to an open system environment may harm rather than benefit universities. The prerogative therefore is to emphasize on sustaining excellence through accreditation, assessment, measurement and follow up and building a culture that drives excellence through innovation and learning and where the transfer of knowledge and best practice is the fuel for success.

Various research projects have established the critical factors of success associated with effective academic leaders. These, amongst others include their personal characteristics such as their flair, imagination, their passion for innovation, their ability to take risks and absorb complex challenges with the ultimate goal of creation and a belief that innovation is the driving force, and their measure of success of course is to see ideas flourish and turned into useful innovations and measured ultimately by financial success.

Professor Mohamed Zairi
Executive Chairman Zairi Institute
Juran Chair in TQM

Chapter 1
Becoming a Leader in an Academic Environment – The New DNA

Introduction

"Leadership is not magnetic personality—that can just as well be a glib tongue. It is not 'making friends and influencing people'—that is flattery. Leadership is lifting a person's vision to higher sights, the raising of a person's performance to a higher standard, the building of a personality beyond its normal limitations."

Peter F. Drucker

"Managers muddle - leaders inspire. Leaders are people who inspire with clear vision of how things can be done better. "What we are looking for are leaders at every level who can energize, excite and inspire rather than enervate, depress, and control."

Jack Welsh – Ex-CEO & Chairman, GE

Leadership is essential in all organizations and educational institutions are no exceptional, but the concept of academic leadership is unique in higher education and, arguably, is concerned with leadership that extends beyond the organization into the wider world that higher education institutions seeks to serve (Rowley, 1997).

In higher education leadership has been variously defined as: meticulously shifting the attention of the institutions through the mundane language of management systems. It is altering agendas so that new agendas get attention. It is being visible when things go awry and invisible when they are working well. It is building a loyal team that speaks more or less with one voice. It's listening carefully most of the time – its being tough when necessary, and it's the occasional naked use of power – or the subtle accumulation of nuances, a hundred things done a little better (Peters and Waterman, 1982).

Rowley argues that this complex definition incorporates a number of different facets of leadership namely:

- *Leadership is concerned with a sense of direction and vision and imparting of that vision,*
- *Leadership involves working with others*, probably in teams and the maintenance of a relationship,
- *Leadership is a careful and relentless process* that involves attention and details.

In an academic environment, typical leadership roles and/or areas within an institution in which leadership might be exhibited might include:

- *Module leadership* – designing learning outcomes of a module and ensuring that those outcomes are achieved,
- *Course leadership* – operational management concerned with ensuring that courses are delivered successfully on a day to day basis,
- *Research project leadership* – identification of appropriate projects and framing of research questions, selection of research methodologies, and appropriate directions for achieving valuable contributions to knowledge,
- *Head of department* – tactical management concerned with the creation of vision concerning excellence in relation to specific subject areas, and the allocation of resources to pursue each of these individual agendas. Facilitation and interfacing with institutional systems,
- *Senior Management* – includes vice chancellors, deputy vice chancellors /pro-vice chancellors, deans, directorates ...etc. These basically operate at strategic leadership level and are

Similarly, Teelken and Bosch (2000) describe models of leadership in HEIs as:

- *Segmental organization* – characterised by extensive subdivision of the education organization into sections, each of which has one person in charge. Professors each have their own subjects and are responsible for its organization content and design. Segmented organizations functions best in a stable environment, where the emphasis is on subject based teaching. When segmental organizations grow, hierarchic rules within the segments govern internal relationships.
- *Collegiate organization* – is a response to un-sustainability of the hierarchical relationships within separate segments of the organization. These come under two types of pressures: rapid growth due to demographic trends and external democratisation of education and the demand for a more democratic internal organization.
- *The line management organization* – are a response to the circumstances where the conditions under which segmental organization can thrive are increasingly at a premium. It is related to the organization's need to adapt to more and more rules imposed from outside the organization, the desire to develop a distinct profile and the need to interdisciplinary collaboration.
- *Process organization* – characterised by high degree of participation of those involved and high sensitivity to environmental factors.

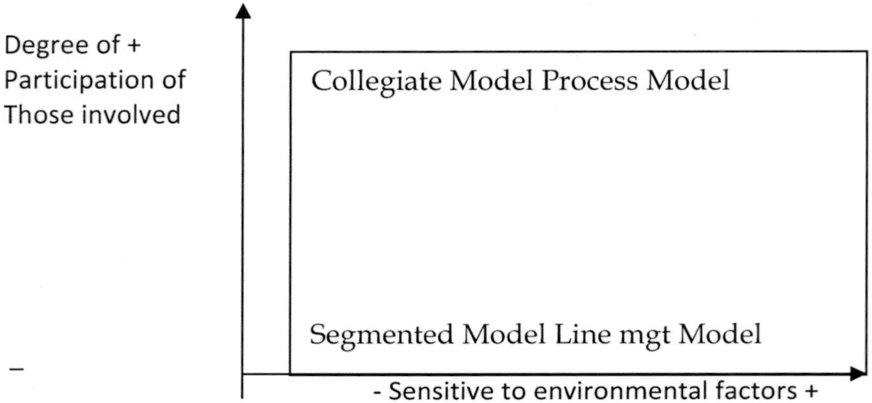

	Primary role of Professor	Primary role of Mgmt
Segmental model	Individual subject specialists	Creating pre-conditions
Collegiate model	Members of department	Process manager
Line management organization	Employees of an organization	Policy maker
Process organization	Members of group with specific responsibilities	Coach

Pedler, Boydell and Burgoyne (1988) contend that universities have to be learning organizations; organizations which facilitates the learning of all its members and continuously translates itself. Mumford (1980) suggests that managers (and by extension academic managers) who are good developers of their staff have the following characteristics. They:

- *Draw out strength and weaknesses of their staff rather than suppressing them;*
- *Reward their people both materially and psychologically for the risks that they take in attempting to develop themselves,*
- *Positively seek to identify learning opportunities for staff,*
- *Give personal time to the development of staff – for example in reviewing and analysing activity associated with learning,*
- *Involve their subordinates in some of their own tasks and do not simply delegate tasks that they do not wish to do themselves,*
- *Share some of their problems and anxieties with their staff as one way of enhancing staff development,*
- *Listen rather than talk,*
- *Do not seek to shape individuals as replicas of themselves,*
- *Take the risk of their departments in pursuit of relevant learning opportunities for their people.*

Given the centrality of leadership in today's HEIs the issue of leadership can no longer be relegated to the backyard, but must be central to continuity and the spring board to excellence. It is with that view in mind that we herein suggest a leadership model hereafter (Figure 1) fit for 21st Century HEIs, aspiring to be world class institutions for possible adoption. The constituent dimensions of this model are dealt with so as to give an overall appreciation of the model, particularly its all embracing dimensions, continuous improvement and robustness to spur growth and sustain super leaders desperately in short supply in the academia.

Figure 7: 21st Century Leadership Model for HEI's

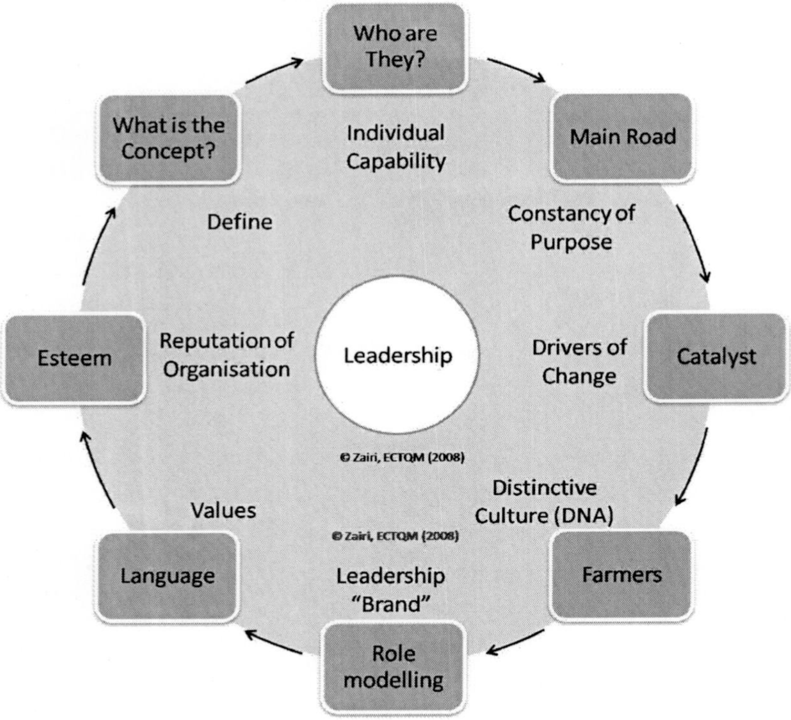

Academic Leadership Defined

"Leadership is not about grand gestures or personal greatness, but about detailed everyday activities and it is available to everyone"
Alison Piasecka

Lees et al. 1994 argues that leadership in HEIs is an influential relationship between the leader and the follower, the emphasis being on empowering the follower for personal and professional success rather than on exclusive mutual reciprocity. Good leadership also emphasized a leader's positive behaviours that inspired followers to achieve specific organizational goals. The leader's behaviour support also fostered shared ownership in a common purpose for the institution. The leadership (Figure 2) may thus be expressed as an equation:

Figure 8: Leadership Equation

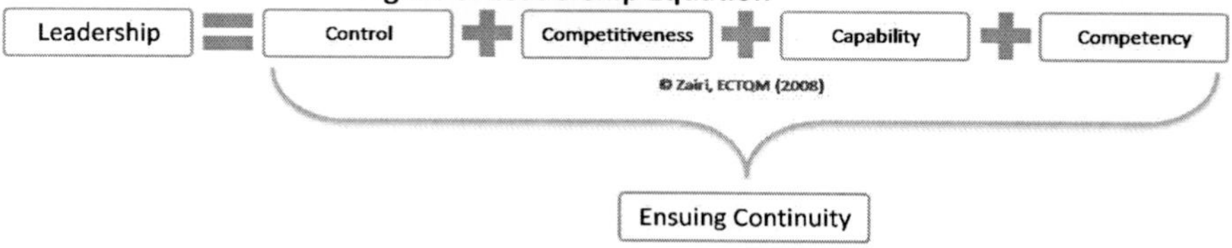

Piasecka (2000) argues that building leadership capability is about sustaining behaviour and performance, which is an art in miniature, rather than grand landscape painting. It's about persistence and detail, as well as flexibility and favours. It's about recognizing that leadership is a construction of planned and opportunistic actions and behaviours that create clarity and meaning for others – and that construction requires the close support of a coaching relationship to bring it alive. Simply put, leadership is about three things: Doing, Building and Being (Figure 3).

Figure 9: Essence of Leadership

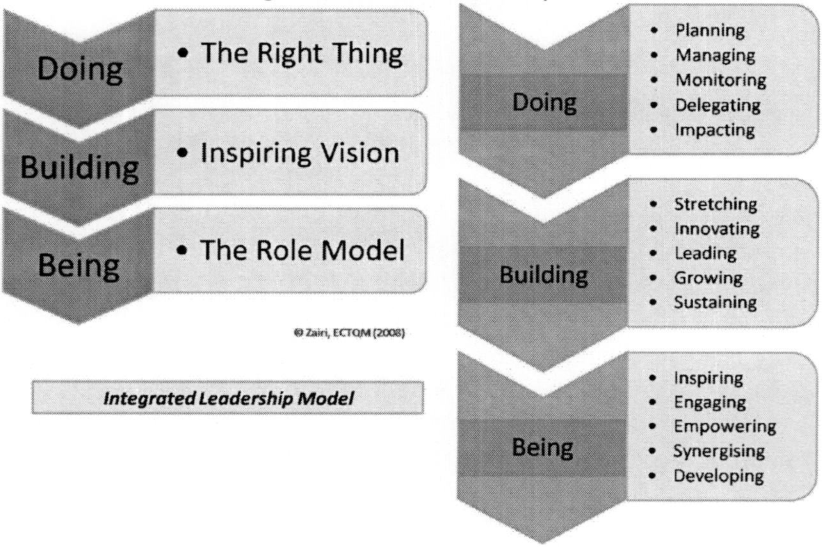

Fisher aptly sums up the essence of effective leadership by arguing thus that

"The main characteristics of effective leadership are intelligence, integrity or loyalty, mystique, humour, discipline, courage, self sufficiency and confidence."

James L. Fisher

Individual Leadership Capability

"A leader needs clear and challenging vision, a magic with words, the ability to motivate others, and the courage to stay on course and the persistence not to lose hope".

T.M. Hesburgh

"Self-security will be a hallmark of the leaders and exceptional organizations of the future. Self-security in an individual or a system brings a high ratio of coherence. Leaders or organizations with self-security can push power and authority downstream and develop centres of innovation and excellence at all levels of the organization".

The Peter F. Drucker Foundation

Trait theories have identified personal characteristics of successful leaders and the following have been viewed to be important:

- *Intelligence,* and a desire to solve complex problems or discover patterns in events that are prevalent,
- *Initiative*, the ability to perceive the need for action and to do something about it,
- *Self-assurance* and self confidence to believe in what they are doing, this is related to the individual's perception of their role in society and their aspirations to themselves,
- *The helicopter trait,* which is a descriptive term for the ability to understand a situation at different levels of detail.

Similarly, Martin (1993) established that effective leaders' in academic world were identifiable by five areas of expertise:

- *They are cultural representatives of their colleges and universities,*
- *As communicators they are continually striving for more efficient and more inclusive communication structure, networks and processes,*
- *They are skilled managers,*
- *They are planners/analysts,*
- *They are advocates of the institution and cultivate relationships with various groups and individuals on campus,*

Building on the same argument Pounder (2001) suggests the following as the key attributes of transformational leadership in higher education:

- *Inspirational motivation* – the leader acts as a model for subordinates, communicates a vision and uses symbols to focus efforts,
- *Integrity* – the leader "walks the talk", aligns deeds with words,
- *Innovation* – the leader is prepared to challenge existing constraints and processes by taking risks and experimenting. The leader encourages followers to take risks and experiments and treats mistakes as opportunities for learning rather than censure,
- *Impression management* – the leader is prepared to subordinate personal needs and desires to the general good. The leader is a "giving" person who is keen to celebrate subordinates achievements and whose personal warmth and caring to subordinates is not confined to their work lives,
- *Individual consideration* – the leader coaches and mentors, provides continuous feedback and links organizational members needs to the organization's mission,
- *Intellectual stimulation* – leader stimulates followers to rethink the old ways of doing things and to reassess their old values and beliefs.

Likewise, Rowley (1997) argues that most people are capable of some flexibility in the range of leadership styles that they are able to adopt. The style that a leader adopts is influenced by:

- *The leader's values and beliefs about their responsibilities to their subordinates and how work should be done,*
- *The leader's confidence and subordinates ability to tackle tasks effectively,*

- *The leader's tolerance of uncertainty – a more democratic management style involves handling unclear situations.*

Leaders thus must have emotional intelligence, which is really about:

- *Self awareness* – ability to recognize and understand the moods, emotions and drives as well as their effect on others,
- *Self regulation* – the ability to control or redirect disruptive impulses and moods,
- *Motivation* – a passion to work for reasons that go beyond money or status,
- *Empathy* – ability to understand the emotional make-up of others,
- *Social skill* – proficiency in managing relationships and building networks,

Thus emotional intelligence helps leaders to understand and connect well with others and move along with them.

Hoppe (2003) argues that identifying, nurturing and supporting potential leaders are critical components in maintaining a pipeline for continuity and infusion of new pools in academia. HEIs that prepare for the future will have an identification strategy and developmental plan that not only provides for the next generation of leaders but also ensures that they have the experience and skills necessary for success. Hope aptly sums up her feelings by quipping that;

"Selecting and nurturing academic leaders requires identifying effective leadership characteristics and providing experiences for potential candidates that both test and develop them"

Sherry L. Hoppe

Consequently, May (2008) suggests the following as leadership lessons for HEIs as:

- *It is the people skills that are most lacking but a simple and low level focus on these skills alone is not sufficient* to move people beyond what's familiar, comfortable and for which they are ostensibly rewarded,
- Many universities now and again organize so called mainstream and focused *leadership programmes, that in effect turn out to be more management than leadership,*
- *A focus on leadership means reminding people that they're capable of*. Helping them see what's possible if they actually achieve their research vision, their scholarly ambition, working together they can achieve so much,
- *Reminding people of the value of working together, then providing them with the skills to communicate with each other in language that others hear is essential.* What follows is development of skills to provide performance feedback, develop and implement processes that support them and imbed accountability, and skills to develop team,
- *Executive commitment is essential*. People must feel that they are not an experiment or the problem that needs to be fixed,
- *They must have their personal needs met*. They must be consulted and asked what they want to improve, they must be provided the time away for their research/teaching to spend on workshops and learning.

Southwell et al. (2005), argues that in development of academic leaders, the Australian higher education system and by extension other systems, tended to rely upon the "wisdom of experience" in relation to teaching and learning. Course coordinators are one such academic leader's who tend to be highly competent and qualified senior academics, who by virtue of their academic accomplishments, advance to the role of managing and leading a university course. However such course coordinators requires leadership skills that will enable them to create a vision of what course might be and then to foster a culture that supports and achieves that vision. Additionally, while they are vested with considerable academic, managerial and administrative responsibility, which is however accompanied by, limited line management or staffing authority. While the position is viewed as all-consuming and as having adverse impact on personal teaching and scholarly activities (Caroll & Wolverton, 2004), *yet very little support if any is given to prepare, support and recognize academics in this crucial academic leadership role.*

Academic Leadership and Constancy of Purpose

"Create constancy of purpose toward improvement of product and service, with the aim to become competitive and to stay in business, and to provide jobs."

Dr. W. Edwards Deming

Deming's famous "14 points" (ASQ, 2008) have been the foundation of quality since their inception. By design, point #1 is "*Constancy of Purpose*" which basically means maintaining a focus of the important long term vision- *NO MATTER WHAT*. Leaders establish constancy of purpose by anticipating and assessing the impact of future changes, nursing the culture of the organization needed to adopt the changes, and implementing the changes necessary to make the vision a reality.

Within a strong focus on the important long-term factors, many organizations waste huge amounts of resources shifting focus from one crisis to the next without ever making sustained progress. Leaders ensure the day-to-day issues don't result in a shirting of resources and attention from the organization's "critical few" priorities to the shifting priorities of the day. Without *constancy of purpose* the rate of improvement over the long term will be greatly diminished.

Constancy of purpose means that quality decisions are not situational. End of month quality is the same as beginning of month. It means that the long term benefit of the organization is not sacrificed to make short-term targets. It means having your eye on the competition, whether it is in your industry or coming from elsewhere, with plans to stay ahead. *Constancy of purpose* doesn't require the threat of a customer leaving to implement corrective actions based on root cause. It means that while your team may argue about how best to accomplish it, no one is confused about the commitment to deliver reliable quality. Constancy of purpose can only exist when leadership lives it, demonstrates it, and won't accept anything else.

Creating constancy of purpose

Belonging, power, freedom and fun are four essential components in creating constancy of purpose.

1) ***Belong*** *to the whole process of constancy of purpose. Belonging is a need as this stimulates staff to find meaningful ways and enhances believe in themselves to make valuable contributions,*
2) *Level of* ***power****. This gives direction and commitment to ideas,*
3) ***Freedom****. This gives autonomy to express ideas within defined parameters that are wide enough to be creative without losing sight of the purpose or objective.*
4) ***Fun at workplace****. People learn much more from others because the atmosphere created is one of exchange of ideas and experiences. Therefore communication is easier and conflicts are of the constructive type.*

Thus, since leadership and creativity often complement each other HEIs should ensures that its leaders constantly evolve themselves and needs to constantly have innovative ideas. HEIs leaders should also encourage creativity. Any creative idea finds acceptance if it is able to make significant contribution to a staff's life.

Deming's 14 points (Quality Register, 2008):

1. Constancy of purpose: Create constancy of purpose for continual improvement of products and service to society, allocating resources to provide for long range needs rather than only short term profitability, with a plan to become competitive, to stay in business, and to provide jobs
2. The new philosophy: Adopt the new philosophy. We are in a new economic age, created in Japan. We can no longer live with commonly accepted levels of delays, mistakes, defective materials and defective workmanship. Transformation of Western management style is necessary to halt the continued decline of business and industry.
3. Cease dependence on mass inspection: Eliminate the need for mass inspection as the way of life to achieve quality by building quality into the product in the first place. Require statistical evidence of built in quality in both manufacturing and purchasing functions.
4. End lowest tender contracts: End the practice of awarding business solely on the basis of price tag. Instead require meaningful measures of quality along with price. Reduce the number of suppliers for the same item by eliminating those that do not qualify with statistical and other evidence of quality. The aim is to minimize total cost, not merely initial cost, by minimizing variation. This may be achieved by moving toward a single supplier for any one item, on a long term relationship of loyalty and trust. Purchasing managers have a new job, and must learn it.
5. Improve every process: Improve constantly and forever every process for planning, production, and service. Search

continually for problems in order to improve every activity in the company, to improve quality and productivity, and thus to constantly decrease costs. Institute innovation and constant improvement of product, service, and process. It is management's job to work continually on the system (design, incoming materials, maintenance, improvement of machines, supervision, training, retraining).

6. Institute training on the job: Institute modern methods of training on the job for all, including management, to make better use of every employee. New skills are required to keep up with changes in materials, methods, product and service design, machinery, techniques, and service.
7. Institute leadership: Adopt and institute leadership aimed at helping people do a better job. The responsibility of managers and supervisors must be changed from sheer numbers to quality. Improvement of quality will automatically improve productivity. Management must ensure that immediate action is taken on reports of inherited defects, maintenance requirements, poor tools, fuzzy operational definitions, and all conditions detrimental to quality.
8. Drive out fear: Encourage effective two way communication and other means to drive out fear throughout the organization so that everybody may work effectively and more productively for the company.
9. Break down barriers: Break down barriers between departments and staff areas. People in different areas, such as Leasing, Maintenance, Administration, must work in teams to tackle problems that may be encountered with products or service.
10. Eliminate exhortations: Eliminate the use of slogans, posters and exhortations for the work force, demanding Zero Defects and new levels of productivity, without providing methods. Such exhortations only create adversarial relationships; the bulk of the causes of low quality and low productivity belong to the system, and thus lie beyond the power of the work force.

11. Eliminate arbitrary numerical targets: Eliminate work standards that prescribe quotas for the work force and numerical goals for people in management. Substitute aids and helpful leadership in order to achieve continual improvement of quality and productivity.
12. Permit pride of workmanship: Remove the barriers that rob hourly workers, and people in management, of their right to pride of workmanship. This implies, among other things, abolition of the annual merit rating (appraisal of performance) and of Management by Objective. Again, the responsibility of managers, supervisors, foremen must be changed from sheer numbers to quality.
13. Encourage education: Institute a vigorous program of education, and encourage self improvement for everyone. What an organization needs is not just good people; it needs people that are improving with education. Advances in competitive position will have their roots in knowledge.
14. Top management commitment and action: Clearly define top management's permanent commitment to ever improving quality and productivity, and their obligation to implement all of these principles. Indeed, it is not enough that top management commit themselves for life to quality and productivity. They must know what it is that they are committed to-that is, what they must do. Create a structure in top management that will push every day on the preceding 13 Points, and take action in order to accomplish the transformation. Support is not enough: action is required!

As illustrated in the figure 4 below, HEIs can only translate themselves into World class institutions by constantly adhering to excellence and quality leadership, which should indeed be the concern and focus of the 21st Century University.

Figure 10: Constancy of Purpose

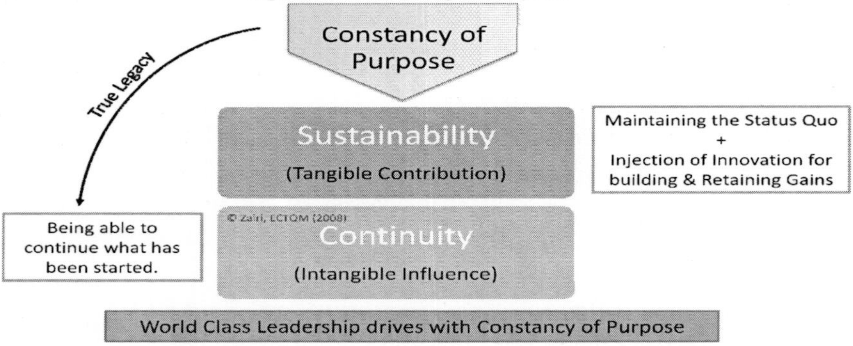

Collin Powell (Brainyquote, 2008) words aptly sums up the need for constancy of purpose and argues that *great leaders are almost always great simplifiers, who can cut through argument, debate and doubt, to offer a solution everybody can understand.* The result? Clarity of purpose, credibility of leadership, and integrity of organization, which is what modern university leaders should aspire to be.

Drivers Of Change For A New DNA

"Effective corporate renewal starts at the bottom, through informal efforts to solve business problems"

Tom Peters

The rate of organizational change has not slowed in recent years, and may even be increasing. The rapid and continual innovation in technology is driving changes to organizational systems and processes. Add to this the increased expectations of employees as they move more freely between organizations. And, of course, globalization has seen the tearing down of previous international market barriers. It is no wonder that relentless change has become a fact of organizational life. In spite of the importance and permanence of organizational change, most change initiatives fail to deliver the expected organizational benefits. This failure occurs for a number of reasons. You might recognize one or more of these in your organization (Businessperform, 2008).

- *absence of a change champion or one who is too junior in the organization*
- *poor executive sponsorship or senior management support*
- *poor project management skills*
- *hope rested on a one-dimensional solution*
- *political infighting and turf wars*
- *poorly defined organizational objectives*
- *change team diverted to other projects*

Failed organizational change initiatives leave in their wake cynical and burned out employees, making the next change objective even more difficult to accomplish. It should come as no surprise that the fear of managing change and its impacts is a leading cause of anxiety in managers.

No matter how well designed and planned your change programme is, not everyone will be singing its praises. Employees resist change for a wide variety of reasons, ranging from a straightforward intellectual disagreement over facts to deep-seated psychological prejudices. Some of these reasons for employee resistance may include (StrategyBusiness, 2008):

- *belief that the change initiative is a temporary fad*
- *belief that fellow employees or managers are incompetent*
- *loss of authority or control*
- *loss of status or social standing*
- *lack of faith in their ability to learn new skills*
- *feeling of change overload (too much too soon)*
- *lack of trust in or dislike of managers*
- *loss of job security*
- *loss of family or personal time*
- *feeling that the organization is not entitled to the extra effort*

If leaders identify and manage resistance to change poorly, they can very quickly strangle their change programme or, alternatively, slowly and unnoticeably starve it to death. It is important therefore that leaders' identifies the resisters of change and how are they're resisting. Change recipients who are dead against the change will either resist overtly, voicing their objections loudly and often, or covertly. Covert resisters operate from the underground, masking their defiance, but posing you a much more serious challenge (Businessperform, 2008).

With regard to recipients of change, four basic types of reaction to organizational change (Table 1) have been identified, namely:

Table 1: Reaction to Change

Enthusiasts	*These change recipients are intrinsically wedded to the change idea. They may agree dispassionately that the change will be of benefit to the organization, or they may stand to receive some personal gain from the change, such as a guarantee of job security, more status or a higher salary. Enthusiasts will use opportunities to broadcast approval for the change and will try to convince others of its merits. They will also model the new behavior early and will volunteer for membership of teams. These early adopters may also make good choices as trainers and coaches during the implementation process.*
Followers	*Followers range from those that are generally compliant, wishing to take the path of least resistance, to those that are initially reticent to adapt, but eventually do so once they accept the inevitability of the change. These change recipients will do what is required, but no more.*
Objectors	*Objectors will display their resistance to change whenever the opportunity arises. They may disrupt meetings, not attend training, take unapproved leave and refuse to carry out instructions. Objectors will continue to use superseded systems and processes when others are*

	taking up the new ways of doing things. They are not averse to arguing with managers and fellow workers and will try to convince others to continue with the old ways. In a unionized environment, resistance can take the form of strikes, lockouts, "work to rule", legal challenges and boycotts.
Underground	*Change recipients working for the underground have solid motivations for not making their resistance public. They may fear direct punishment, such as termination or fines, or more personal costs, such as ridicule or loss of status and authority. Managers who are against the change but need to be seen to be in support of it are prime candidates for promoting underground resistance. This style of resistance is, by its nature, always covert and can take many forms. Common among these are falsifying reports, inputting incorrect data, stealing, damaging infrastructure and equipment, using sarcasm, spreading rumors, excessive absences, shoddy work and "go slow".*

Understanding your organization and matching the initiative to your organization's real needs (instead of adopting the latest fad) is the first step in making your change program successful. Beyond that, recognize that bringing about *organizational change is fundamentally about changing people's behaviuor in certain desired ways*. As is apparent from the above list of reasons for failure, lack of technical expertise is not the main impediment to successful change. Leadership and management skills, such as visioning, prioritizing, planning, providing feedback and rewarding success, are key factors in any successful change initiative (Auxillium, 2008)

Coakley and Randall (2007), argues that academic leaders in HEIs must increasingly deal with demands from stakeholders such as students, parents and government at the same time as they are being held accountable for the curriculum and student learning environment. They suggest an adaptive leadership model that stimulates and guides implementation of effective changes within the academia. The components of such model proposed by Heifetz include:

a) *Brief description of situation – what is the issue at hand?*
b) *Identify change – What is it that requires to be changed? The challenge faced by the institution must be recognized,*
c) *Unbundle issues – what are the key issues that needs to be set apart? issues tend to be muddied or clogged up with opinions or rumour especially when dealing with stakeholders,*
d) *Frame the issues and focus on attention – What are the issues and have they been communicated effectively to all stakeholders to avoid resistance? Make stakeholders feel that they are an important part of the changes and must play an active role,*
e) *Secure ownership – Key stakeholders of the adaptive change must become leaders in the change initiative, which enable change to be both deep and long-term,*
f) *Manage stakeholder conflict and maintain stress – changes must be prudently managed to avoid conflict besides coping with stress arising from such changes,*
g) *Create a safe haven – create a space where people are able to discuss openly about their frustration without fear of a negative impact on their work – ventilation therapy.*

Perhaps it is fitting to remember that:

"*When we see the need for deep change, we usually see it as something that needs to take place in someone else. In our roles of authority, such as parent, teacher, or boss, we are particularly quick to direct others to change. Such directives often fail, and we respond to the resistance by increasing our efforts. The power struggle that follows seldom results in change or brings about excellence. One of the most important insights about the need to bring about deep change in others has to do with where deep change actually starts.*"

Robert E. Quinn

Creating a Distinctive Culture

"Culture does not change because we desire to change it. Culture changes when the organization is transformed; the culture reflects the realities of people working together every day."
Frances Hesselbein

A culture is defined by the beliefs, behaviours, and practices of a particular group. That is all of an organization's in-house jargon, shared values, and standards expressed in codes, rites, and myths relating to it. In the academic community, an academic culture embraces all attributes that relate to academic beliefs and behaviours and how these affects or positively impacts on students – the universities' finished products. If faculty and administrators know what an institution stands for they will likely be more willing to assume leadership roles. If leaders at the top of the institution demonstrate consistent values over a long period of time, others will share those values and will be motivated to pay the price of academic leadership. Inspiring others to share the vision is perhaps the most critical aspect in attracting and nurturing new leaders. Commitment to making a difference in the lives of others is the ultimate motivation (Auxillium, 2008).

Every organization has its own unique culture or value set. Most organizations don't consciously try to create a certain culture. The culture of the organization is typically created unconsciously, based on the values of the top management or the founders of an organization. Hewlett-Packard is a company that has, for a long time, been conscious of its culture (The HP Way) and has worked hard to maintain it over the years. Hewlett-Packard's corporate culture is based on 1) respect for others, 2) a sense of community, and 3) plain hard work. It has been developed and maintained through extensive training of managers and employees. HP's growth and success over the years has been due in large part to its culture (HP, 2008).

Another successful company that expends a lot of energy in maintaining its workplace culture is Southwest Airlines. Southwest is the only major airline in the U.S. that has been profitable in each of the last five years. It also has a good reputation as an employer. In an article written in the ACA (American Compensation Association) Journal, Winter 1995 issue, Herb Kelleher, Southwest's CEO, indicated how Southwest maintained its culture: "Well, first of all, it starts with hiring. We are zealous about hiring. We are looking for a particular type of person, regardless of which job category it is. We are looking for attitudes that are positive and for people who can lend themselves to causes. We want folks who have a good sense of humor and people who are interested in performing as a team and take joy in team results instead of individual accomplishments (SWA, 2008).

"*If you start with the type of person you want to hire, presumably you can build a work force that is prepared for the culture you desire...*

"*Another important thing is to spend a lot of time with your people and to communicate with them in a variety of ways. And a large part of it is demeanor. Sometimes we tend to lose sight of the fact that demeanor - the way you appear and the way you act - is a form of communication. We want our people to feel fulfilled and to be happy, and we want our management to radiate the demeanor that we are proud of our people, we are interested in them as individuals and we are interested in them outside the work force, including the good and bad things that happen to them as individuals.*"

In both of these examples, the top management of the companies were vigilant about maintaining their cultures. The behavior rules and boundaries are relatively clear and communicated often.

However, this is not typical. I believe most organizations operate with a diversity of cultures. This is especially true considering the increasing worldwide mobility of people and cultures and values.

The importance of corporate culture is growing as the result of several recent developments. Companies are encouraging employees to be more responsible and act and think like owners. In exchange for more flexible work schedules, employees are expected to always be "on-call." With the demise of more traditional communities (e.g. neighborhoods, etc.), companies are filling employees' need to belong to a community. At the same time companies are encouraging teamwork and the formation of teams. Other advantages of corporate culture are said to include:

- *Instructions are interpreted in a common way, so work is done to a similar standard and in a similar manner.*
- *Loyalty is increased, and replacing workers is an expense to be avoided.*
- *Motivation, and therefore productivity, is increased.*
- *Management control is increased*

Research into many businesses of all nationalities has shown a common pattern that successful businesses had developed a strong and positive group culture, which is about management as leadership and not just administration.

Building a Positive Corporate Culture

- **'Culture Carriers'** - these are key people, usually managers, who represent and spread the core values of the corporate culture.
- **Stability of the group** - it is more difficult for a culture to emerge if people are changing all the time.
- **Stories** - a group packages up its culture into stories which are frequently told and re-told, and which typify the values of the group e.g. 'the time we all stayed late on Xmas Eve to

get the last orders finished and then has an impromptu party at the local.'

- **Heroes -** individuals who typify to an extreme the values of the group.
- **Symbols -** these may be staff mottoes, the corporate mission statement or anything that symbolizes the core values.
- **Rites -** these are specific occasions, such as the annual office party, when the core values are publicly displayed. Formal award ceremonies are another example. These are especially important for enculturing new staff.
- **Rituals -** this means a standard pattern of behaviour at a specific occasion, such as the office party if things are always done in a particular pattern.
- **Courses -** attending in-house courses is an important way of team-building and communicating the core values.
- **Cultural Networks -** this means the informal contacts between employees where they reinforce core values, especially by passing them from older to younger group members (Auxillium, 2008)

Types of Corporate Culture

- **Adaptive Cultures.** These have as a core value the ability to adapt to change, especially in response to changing external circumstances.
- **Inert Culture.** This is a 'dead' culture totally unable to change.
- **Networked Organizations.** These are very sociable networks of small teams. They are highly creative. But loyalty is low.
- **Mercenary Organizations.** These are ruthless business machines dedicated to work and to success. But sociability is very low.

- **Fragmented Organizations.** These are really loose alliances of very independent workers, such as lawyers. Sociability and loyalty are both very low.
- **Communal Organizations.** These have high loyalty and high sociability. They act like one bog happy family. Recruiting new staff with similar values is important (Auxillium, 2008).

It is important to note here therefore that the type of culture prevailing in an organization will to a large extent determine the entity's vitality. Somme culture is harmful and academic leaders should thus strive to build and cultivate productive culture that allows the institutions to thrive amidst other challenges.
Therefore, organizational leaders shouldn't ignore corporate culture. Rather, it should be addressed in the organization's mission, vision, and goal statements, and emphasized in company sponsored training and company communication. The statements should include the following:

- *To be financially successful, etc. (employees want to belong to a successful organization)*
- *To be accepting of cultural (ethnic) diversity*
- *To encourage employees to "have a life" outside the company (provide sufficient paid time-off benefits and encourage employees to take the time)*

It is with this view in mind that Spendlove (2007) assert that academic credibility and experience of university life all of which are shaped by the prevailing culture are crucial for effective leadership in Higher education, as well as continued research alongside managerial roles. People skills, including the ability to communicate and negotiate with others were also felt to be important. He reminds HEIs leaders thus ....*leaders honour their core values, but are flexible in how they execute them. Perpetual optimism is a force of multiplier. Leaders who whine and blame engender those same behaviours among their colleagues.*

The New DNA – Creating A Leadership Brand

"Leadership should be more participative than directive, more enabling than performing"
Mary D. Poole

"Leadership should be born out of the understanding of the needs of those who would be affected by it."
Marian Anderson

Leadership must be a style and must *draw closer those that are being led to share the same vision and style as the leader*. In the words of Richard Branson – Virgin Empire, leadership should be about these things:

- **Motivated by something beyond money.** "Above all, you want to create something you are proud of.... That has always been my philosophy of business. I can honestly say that I have never gone into any business purely to make money. If that is the sole motive, then I believe you are better off doing nothing."
- **The importance of a good name.** "All you have in life is your reputation: you may be very rich, but if you lose your good name, then you'll never be happy. The thought will always lurk at the back of your mind that people don't trust you. I had never really focused on what a good name meant before, but that night in prison made me understand."
- **Big picture thinking & creative problem solving.** In his book, Branson tells the story of a Mike Oldfield concert that was to take place at Queen Elizabeth Hall. Oldfield, the featured artist, had decided he did not want to do it. This was a major promotional event, designed to bring visibility to Virgin Records' inaugural shining star. Tickets had been sold, the concert all set to go and Oldfield, that morning, had determined not to perform. Branson's creative problem

- **Dreaming impossible dreams.** Writes Branson, "My interest in life comes from setting myself huge, apparently unachievable challenges and trying to rise above them." Hence, in addition to successes in business, Branson became first to cross the Atlantic in a hot air balloon, the first across the Pacific, and the fastest to cross the Atlantic by boat. His life exhibits a "no limits" attitude that ever seeks to stretch the boundaries of what is achievable.
- **Success is not a formula, but it doesn't 'just happen.'** "*To be successful, you have to be out there, you have to hit the ground running, and if you have a good team around you and more than a fair share of luck, you might make something happen. But you certainly can't guarantee it just by following someone else's formula.*" A swashbuckling entrepreneur who lives life to the full, Branson has seized life by the throat and given it all he's got. And from here? To think he's only half begun!

SuperLeadership

There is need today for organizations to focus attention on Superleadership. Superleadership is leadership that inspires organizational success by showing followers how to lead themselves. SuperLeadership is a new form of leadership for the era of knowledge-based enterprises distinguished by flat organizational structures and employee empowerment. A super-leader is one who leads others to lead themselves through designing and implementing the system that allows and teaches employees to be self-leaders. Super-leaders help each of their followers to develop into an effective self-leader by providing them with the behavioural and cognitive skills necessary to exercise self-leadership. "Super-leaders establish values, model, encourage, reward, and in many other ways foster self-leadership in individuals, teams, and wider organizational cultures (Mainz & Sims, 1996).

...But why SuperLeadership?

"*The function of leadership is to produce more leaders, not more* followers." **Ralph Nader**

Employee self-leadership is the key to success in the new economy. With super-leadership, followers are treated – and become – self-leaders.

If superleaders are successful in providing strategic alignment and coaching people, they develop followers who are productive, work independently, and need only minimal attention from the superleaders, which should certainly be good to the academia too.

So then what is the perquisite for success?

- *Motivation to learn* – it's either the initial impetus to develop leadership skills or you need to make a driver,
- *Relevant and context* – leadership development has to be tailored to the academic. It must be practical, relevant and contextual,
- *A focus on leadership* is more compelling than a focus on management,

- *Engagement beyond one person is critical.* Support for leadership must be explicit, genuine and role-modelled at senior level,
- *Where leadership development starts at the top, it is more successful than one-on-one programmes* and has a more sustainable and deeper impact,
- *Where there is focus on leadership,* when there is engagement, better people practices follow.

The Importance of Values

"Put values first don't focus too much on the numbers. "Numbers aren't the vision; numbers are the products."

Jack Welch

"A leader is best when people barely know he exists, not so good when people obey and acclaim him, worse when they despise him....But of a good leader who talks little when his work is done, his aim fulfilled, they will say, "We did it ourselves."

Lao Tzu

Increasingly, companies around the world have adopted formal statements of corporate values, and senior executives now routinely identify ethical behavior, honesty, integrity, and social concerns as top issues on their companies' agendas.

In a recent research conducted by Van Lee, Fabish, and McGaw (2005) the trio found out that a large number of companies are making their values explicit. That's a change — quite a significant change — from corporate practices 10 years ago. The ramifications of this shift are just beginning to be understood.

At Xerox, CEO Anne Mulcahy says that corporate values "helped save Xerox during the worst crisis in our history," and that "living our values" has been one of Xerox's five performance objectives for the past several years. These values — which include customer satisfaction, quality and excellence, premium return on assets, use of technology for market leadership, valuing employees, and corporate citizenship — are "far from words on a piece of paper. They are accompanied by specific objectives and hard measures," adds Ms. Mulcahy.

If the new attention to values were simply a transitory reaction to the business scandals of recent years, or merely a public relations device to direct or deflect media and investor attention, it would be worth little note. But more companies are going well beyond simply displaying values statements: They are engaging in values-driven management improvement efforts. Among those efforts are training staff in values, appraising executives and staff on their adherence to values, and hiring organizational experts to help address how values affect corporate performance.
The research further established that:

- ***Ethical behavior is a core component of company activities.*** Of the 89 percent of companies that have a written corporate values statement, 90 percent specify ethical conduct as a principle. Further, 81 percent believe their management practices encourage ethical behavior among staff. Ethics-related language in formal statements not only sets corporate expectations for employee behavior; it also serves as a shield companies are using in an increasingly complex and global legal and regulatory environment.
- ***Most companies believe values influence two important strategic areas — relationships and reputation — but do not see the direct link to growth.*** Of the companies that value commitment to customers, 80 percent believe their principles reinforce such dedication. Substantial majorities

also categorize employee retention and recruitment and corporate reputation as both important to their business strategy and strongly affected by values. However, few think that these values directly affect earnings and revenue growth.

- ***Most companies are not measuring their "ROV."*** In a business environment increasingly dominated by attention to definable returns on specific investments, most senior executives are surprisingly lax in attempting to quantify a return on values (ROV). Fewer than half say they have the ability to measure a direct link to revenue and earnings growth.
- ***Top performers consciously connect values and operations.*** Companies that report superior financial results emphasize such values as commitment to employees, drive to succeed, and adaptability far more than their peers. They are also more successful in linking values to the way they run their companies: A significantly greater number report that their management practices are effective in fostering values that influence growth, and executives at these companies are more likely to believe that social and environmental responsibility have a positive effect on financial performance.
- ***Values practices vary significantly by region.*** Asian and European companies are more likely than North American firms to emphasize values related to the corporation's broader role in society, such as social and environmental responsibility. The manner in which companies reinforce values and align them with company strategies also varies by region.
- ***The CEO's tone really matters.*** Eighty-five percent of the respondents say their companies rely on explicit CEO support to reinforce values, and 77 percent say such support is one of the "most effective" practices for

Thus, the values included in most corporate value statements in America, Europe and Asia were:

- *Ethical behaviour/integrity,*
- *Commitment to customers,*
- *Commitment to employees,*
- *Teamwork and trust,*
- *Commitment to shareholders,*
- *Honesty/openness,*
- *Accountability,*
- *Social responsibility/corporate citizenship,*
- *Drive to success,*
- *Environmental responsibility,*
- *Initiative,*
- *Adaptability*

Similar values are expressed by Boeing (2008) in their Ethics Line: 1-888-970-7171, which states that *...in all our relationships we will demonstrate our steadfast commitment to:*

- ***Leadership*** - *We will be a world-class leader in every aspect of our business and in developing our team leadership skills at every level; in our management performance; in the way we design, build and support our products; and in our financial results.*
- ***Integrity*** - *We will always take the high road by practicing the highest ethical standards, and by honoring our commitments. We will take personal responsibility for our actions, and treat everyone fairly and with trust and respect.*
- ***Quality*** - *We will strive for continuous quality improvement in all that we do, so that we will rank among the world's*

premier industrial firms in customer, employee and community satisfaction.

- ***Customer Satisfaction*** *- Satisfied customers are essential to our success. We will achieve total customer satisfaction by understanding what the customer wants and delivering it flawlessly.*
- ***People Working Together*** *- We recognize our strength and our competitive advantage is -- and always will be -- people. We will continually learn, and share ideas and knowledge. We will encourage cooperative efforts at every level and across all activities in our company.*
- ***A Diverse and Involved Team*** *- We value the skills, strengths, and perspectives of our diverse team. We will foster a participatory workplace that enables people to get involved in making decisions about their work that advance our common business objectives.*
- ***Good Corporate Citizenship*** *- We will provide a safe workplace and protect the environment. We will promote the health and well-being of Boeing people and their families. We will work with our communities by volunteering and financially supporting education and other worthy causes.*
- ***Enhancing Shareholder Value*** *- Our business must produce a profit, and we must generate superior returns on the assets entrusted to us by our shareholders. We will ensure our success by satisfying our customers and increasing shareholder value.*

In his famous 25 lessons on leadership, Jack Welch (1000Ventures, 2008), sums up the golden virtues of leadership in the 21st century as:

- ***Lead managers muddle.*** Leaders inspire. Leaders are people who inspire with clear vision of how things can be done better.

- ***Manage less.*** "We are constantly amazed by how much people will do when they are not told what to do by management."
- ***Articulate your vision.*** "Leaders inspire people with clear visions of how things can be done better." The best leader does not provide a step-by-step instruction manual for workers.
- ***Simplify keeping things simple***. "Simple messages travel faster, simpler designs reach the market faster and the elimination of clutter allows faster decision making."
- ***Get less formal.*** "You must realize now how important it is to maintain the kind of corporate informality that encourages a training class to comfortably challenge the boss's pet ideas."
- ***Energize others***. Genuine leadership comes from the quality of your vision and your ability to spark others to extraordinary performance. Getting employees excited about their work is the key to being a great business leader.
- ***Face Reality Face reality***, then act decisively. Most mistakes that leaders make arise from not being willing to face reality and then acting on it.
- ***See change as an opportunity change***; is a big part of the reality in business.
- ***Get good ideas from everywhere***, new ideas are the lifeblood of business. "The operative assumption today is that someone, somewhere, has a better idea; and the operative compulsion is to find out who has that better idea, learn it, and put it into action - fast."
- ***Follow up follow up on everything***, follow-up is one key measure of success for a business.
- ***Get rid of Bureaucracy,*** the way to harness the power of your people is "to turn them loose, and get the management layers off their backs, the bureaucratic

shackles off their feet and the functional barriers out of their way."

- ***Eliminate boundaries,*** in order to make sure that people are free to reach for the impossible; you must remove anything that gets in their way. "Boundarylessness" describes an open organization free of bureaucracy and anything else that prevents the free flow of ideas, people, decisions, etc.
- ***Put values first don't focus too much on the numbers***. "Numbers aren't the vision; numbers are the products."
- ***Cultivate Leaders.*** Cultivate leaders who have the four E's of leadership: Energy, Energize, Edge, and Execution
- ***Create a learning culture,*** "the desire, and the ability, of an organization to continuously learn from any source, anywhere - and to rapidly convert this learning into action - is its ultimate competitive advantage."
- ***Involve everyone,*** business is all about capturing intellect from every person. The way to engender enthusiasm it to allow employees far more freedom and far more responsibility.
- ***Make everybody a team player;*** managers should learn to become team players. Take steps against those managers who wouldn't learn to become team players.
- ***Stretch targets and energize***. "We have found that by reaching for what appears to be the impossible, we often actually do the impossible; and even when we don't quite make it, we inevitably wind up doing much better than we would have done."
- ***Instil confidence,*** self-confident people are open to good ideas regardless of their source and are willing to share them.
- ***Have fun,*** fun must be a big element in your business strategy.
- ***Be number 1 or number 2,*** "when you're number four or five in a market, when number one sneezes, you get

- ***Live quality,*** - "we want to change the competitive landscape by being not just better than our competitors, but by taking quality to a whole new level."
- ***Constantly focus on innovation,*** "you have just got to constantly focus on innovation. And more competitors. You've got to constantly produce more for less through intellectual capital. Shun the incremental, and look for the quantum leap."
- ***Live speed,*** "speed is everything. It is the indispensable ingredient of competitiveness."
- ***Behave like a small company.*** Small companies have huge competitive advantages. They "are uncluttered, simple informal. They thrive on passion and ridicule bureaucracy. Small companies grow on good ideas - regardless of their source. They need everyone, involve everyone, and reward or remove people based on their contribution to winning. Small companies dream big dreams and set the bar high - increments and fractions don't interest them."

Leadership Lasting Legacy

"The final test of a leader is that he leaves behind him in other men the conviction and the will to carry on"

Walter Lippmann

"No organization is stronger than the quality of its leadership, or ever extends its constituency far beyond the degree to which its leadership is representative"

Edgar Powell

Scholars have long associated organizational effectiveness with its leadership and as argued by Pounders (2001) organizational effectiveness in HEIs is measured by:

- *Productivity – efficiency* – concerned with quantity or volume of what is produced and the cost of operation,
- *Cohesion* – extent of staff morale, interpersonal relationship, teamwork, and sense of belonging,
- *Information management communication* – ability of an organization to distribute timely and accurately information needed by its members to do the job,
- *Planning –goal setting* – ability to set goals and objectives and systematically plan for the future

Similarly, Ramsden (1998) contend that the future HEIs effectiveness will be about:

- *Encouragement and reward for learning and development*, - gains centre stage,
- *People at all levels working together* to enhance their creative capacities,
- *Failure seen, not as a sign of inferiority* but as an opportunity to learn,
- *An environment* in which groups and individuals feel a continued responsibility to learn and improve, and
- *Perspective that organizational and individual learning are linked,*

No wonder Collin Powell (Brainyquote, 2008) quips that:

"Organization charts and fancy titles count for next to nothing. In well-run organizations, titles are also pretty meaningless. But titles mean little in terms of real power, which is the capacity to influence and inspire".

HEI's thus needs to understand that their reputation is hinged on their effectiveness. HEI's leaders ought therefore to focus on organizational effectiveness and adapting their focus as their institutions changes; essentially shifting focus from control to commitment (Fig. 5). In the 21st Century HEIs leaders must accept that the tendency towards being "control freak" isn't any more the rule of the game and hence work towards securing the commitment of those they're leading.

Figure 11: Leadership shifts in HEI's

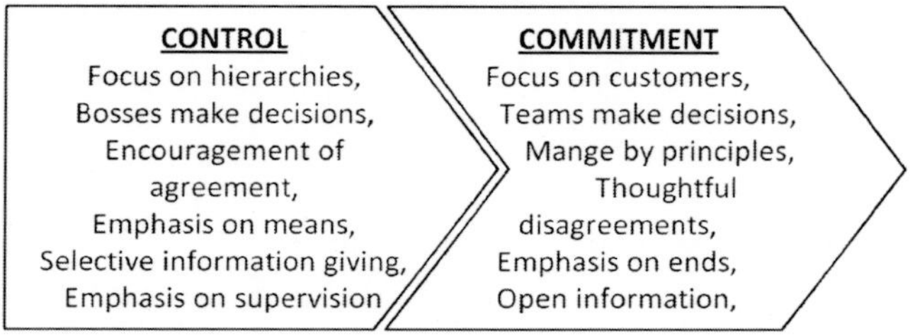

While pursuing this shift, leaders must serve as a bridge linking the past with the present and future. As argued by Seymour...

"Leaders are the ones who keep faith with the past, keep step with the present, and keep the promise to posterity."
Harold J. Seymour

Thus, the whole hallmark of excellent leadership must be about RESULTS. Leadership in HEIs if the 21st Century must be RESULTS - BASED LEADERSHIP, where:

- *Effective Leadership* = Leadership Attributes + Balanced Results
- *Effective Leadership* = Attributes × Results

Hence effective leaders must strive for excellence in both:
Kotelnikov (1000Ventures, 2008) sums up well the leadership legacy by arguing that it has to be about "COCA".

- ***Capability*** - *maximize organizational capabilities. Involve all and harness their potential,*
- ***Opportunities*** – *leaders must be at the forefront of identifying and exploiting opportunities that arise,*

- ***Commitment** – secure the commitment of everybody as you move along, its not about you alone as the leader its about everybody – organizational success impacts everyone, and*
- ***Action** – sound leadership practices must equally be matched by superior actions and that is the hallmark of excellent leadership!*

Figure 12: COCA Principle of achievement

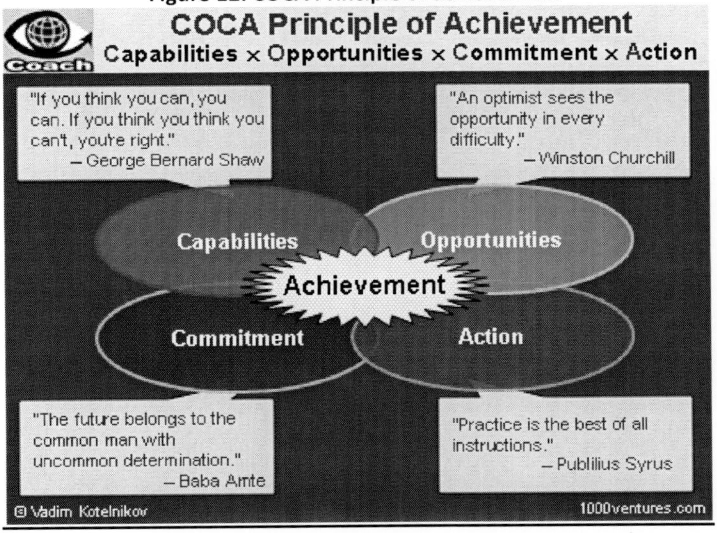

In conclusion, the quest for leadership excellence in HEIs should be summed up by these quotations:

"If I have seen farther than others, it is because I was standing on the shoulder of giants"

<u>Isaac Newton</u>

"A community is like a ship; everyone ought to be prepared to take the helm"

<u>Henrik Ibsen</u>

References

- 1000 Ventures (2008) - http://www.1000ventures.com - June
- ASQ (2008) http://www.asq.org - June
- Auxillium (2008) - http://www.auxillium.com/culture.shtml - June
- Boeing (2008) http://www.boeing.com - July
- BusinessPerform (2008) http://www.businessperform.com - June
- Carroll, J., and Wolverton, M. (2004), "Who becomes a Chair", *New Directions in Higher Education*, 126, 3-10.
- Coakley, L., and Randall, L.M. (2007), "Orchestrating change at the departmental level", Academic Leadership, Vol. 4(2), - Web page, www.academicleadership.org
- Hesburgh, T.M., "Academic leadership", *New Directions for Higher Educations*, Vol. 61 (1), pp.5-8.
- Hewlett Packard (2008) – www.hp.com – June
- Hoppe, S.L. (2003), "Identifying and nurturing potential academic leaders", *New Directions for Higher Education*, no. 124 (Winter).
- Lees, K., Christian, J., and Smith, D. (1994), "Leadership in schools and higher education: Improving organizational structures, school Community partnerships", Theoretical leadership frameworks, Northern Rocky Mountain Educational Research Association, Annual Meeting, October 6-8th
- Mainz, C.C., Sims, H.P. (1996), The Superleadership, Berrett-Koehler Publishers.
- Martin, J.L. (1993), "Academic deans: an analysis of effective academic leadership at research universities", Paper presented at the Annual Meeting of the American Educational Research Association, Atlanta, GA, April.
- May, D. (2008), "The challenges of leadership development in higher education sector", 10th April. - http://www.thepracticeofleadership.net

- Mumford, A. (1980), Making Experience Pay, McGraw-Hill, New York, NY.
- Pedler, M., Boydell, T., and Burgoyne, J. (1988), "Learning Company Project Report, Training Agency, Sheffield.
- Peters, T.J. and Waterman, R.H. (1982), In Search of Excellence, HarperCollins, London.
- Piasecka, A. (2000), "Not Leadership but leadership", *Industrial and Commercial Training*, Vol. 32 (7), pp.253-256.
- Pounder, J.S. (2001), "New leadership", and university organizational effectiveness: exploring the relationship, *Leadership and Organizational Development Journal*, Vol. 22(6), pp.281-290.,
- Powell, C. (2008) – www.brainyquote.com - June
- QualityRegister (2008), http://www.qualityregister.co.uk - June
- Rowley, J. (1997), "Academic leaders: made or born?", *Industrial and Commercial Training*, Vol. 29(3), pp.78-84.
- South West Airlines (2008) – www.southwest.com - June
- Southwell, D., Gannaway, D. Orrell, J., Chalmers, D and Abraham, C. (2005), "Strategies for effective dissemination of project outcomes", *The University of Queensland and Flinders University*.
- Spendlove, M. (2007), "Competencies for effective leadership in higher education", *International Journal of Education Management*, Vol. 21 (5), pp.407-417.
- StrategyBusiness (2008) - http://www.strategy-business.com - July
- Teelken, J.C., and Bosch, H.V.D. (2000), "Organizational leadership in Higher Education: Learning from experiences in Netherlands, Paper presented at the *European Conference on Educational Research, Edinburgh,* 20-23 September.
- Van Lee, R., Fabish, L., and McGraw, N., (2005), " The Value of Corporate Values", *Social Science Research Network (SSRN)* - http://www.papers.ssrn.com – July 2008.

Chapter 2
Creating an Effective and Conducive Academic Environment

Introduction

"To work in the world lovingly means that we are defining what we will be for, rather than reacting to what we are against"
Christina Baldwin

"Fact is, the work place to a great extent is "where we live." We need star accountants. Boffo saleswomen. Over-the-top creatives in marketing and new product development. And so on. But, since we're effectively talking about "where we live," good sense and good business and "good" engagement throughout the "supply chain," from vendor's vendor to customer's customer, we would benefit mightily—including on the P & L—if we insisted (!) on: "Pleasant." "Caring." "Engaged."
Tom Peters

"I think re-engineering or restructuring or downsizing or rightsizing or whatever you want to call it, it's basically firing, has gone way too far. Employees, as I've talked to them across the country, feel that they are not respected, they are not valued, and they are worried about their jobs. They simply feel that the company is no longer loyal to them. Why should they be loyal to the company, they ask me. Why should I go the extra mile? Why should I care?"
Robert Reich

"Our people are our greatest asset", it is often said. Sadly, in many cases the reality is the converse. In today's competitive business environment, organizations can no longer afford to waste the potential of their workforce. There are key factors in the employee's workplace environment that impact greatly on their level of motivation and performance. Find out what these factors are and how you can leverage them to create performance champions.

Defining the Academic Environment

Kirschner *et al.* (1997) have developed a model for studying academic environment and contend that the "academic environment" actually comprises three types of "environments":

- ***Study environment*** (where the students find a sufficient number of source materials and aids, and in which they are given a chance to construct an orientation basis of their own or with each other and determine their goals and activities they'll involve themselves in),
- ***Task environment*** (consists of the assignment or problem, the limiting conditions within which the student is expected to finish assignment or solve the problem, and aids which are available) and,
- ***Knowledge environment*** (is the sum total of all domain-independent knowledge that is available for the task and comprises three aspects: feedback, orientation and practice).

Entwustle and Tait (1990), contend that academic environments provided by departments in HEIs have direct effect on students' approaches to studying. Similarly, Ramsden (1979) asserts that students' perceptions of their departments, their teachers and learning task are shown to exert important influence on their overall learning and specifically, approaches to learning. Schor (2003) argues that maintenance of diligence, superlative organizational skills, ability to prioritize and flexibility to reprioritize, perseverance and a sense of humour are essential ingredients for maintaining an enabling academic environment.

At the University of Florida (2008), academic environment embraces amongst others: student's facilities and rights and responsibilities to usage of these facilities and beyond, Ethical behaviour and academic honesty and accountability, alcohol and drugs within the campuses, relationship with others and service to others. Thus, issues in academic environment may be said to include:

a) *Curriculum Development:-*
   - *Adequacy of instructional time,*
   - *Class sizes,*
   - *Class distraction,*
   - *Grades,*
   - *Monitoring of progression on a weekly basis,*
   - *Reinforced academic labs,*
   - *Co –curriculum activities interspersed with academic activities,*
   - *Pastoral care,*
   - *Adherence to individual students education plans,*
   - *Academic support,*

b) Staff development:-
   - *Staff recognition,*
   - *Workshops to improve skills,*
   - *Open door policy,*
   - *Staying current in respective fields,*
   - *Workshops on student development, - particularly for staff working with adolescents,*
   - *Enforcement of school rules,*
   - *Student recognition,*
   - *Provision of moral and spiritual guidance,*
   - *Provision for work ethics,*
   - *Staff interactions with students,*
   - *Bullying – Adopt-a-student programme/mentoring for first year students,*

c) Physical environment:-

- *Maintenance of aesthetics within the institution 's grounds,*
- *Removal of all forms of graffiti in the institution's buildings,*
- *Keeping classrooms and other buildings neat, clean and painted,*

d) *Administration:-*

- *Administrative goals and objectives articulated to staff on a regular basis,*
- *Staff evaluated annually,*
- *Staff committees established to provide input on administrative decision,*
- *Open door policy maintained by top administration,*
- *Long range plans executed,*
- *Holding staff in high regard,*

e) *Resource development:-*

- *Smart campuses,*
- *Active alumni activities,*

Thus, creating an amenable working environment in HEIs is crucial if the institutions are to develop and attain a world class institution status. Suggested hereunder is a model for growing a conducive academic environment that has been proposed for a 21st Century HEI, whose elements are subsequently explained hereunder:

Figure 13: Conducive Academic Environment

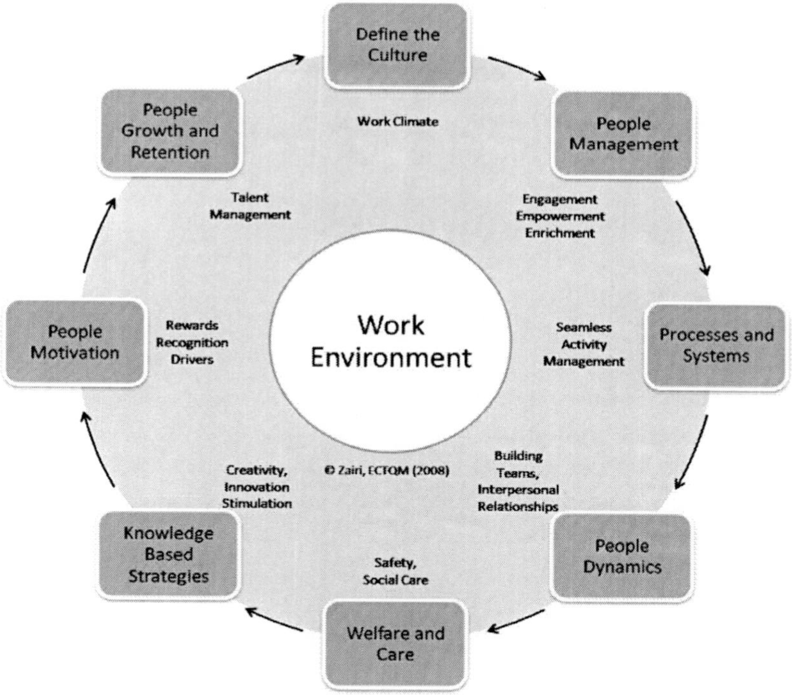

Define the Culture of a University

The corporate culture is all the attitudes, beliefs and values, which are a part of the business and the way in which they operate.

An organization's cultural norms are so all-pervasive that they are almost invisible, but if you would like to improve performance and profitability, norms are one of the first places to look. Ask yourself what employee beliefs or attitudes, including yours, relate to the question, "How are things done around here?" When you have the answers, you'll be on the track to understanding your own corporate culture and its relationship to organizational performance (Schein, 2008).

The successful manager cannot leave the development of a high-performance work culture to chance if the business is not to risk its very future. Fortunately, that needn't be the case. An alert manager can take the necessary steps to ensure that the quality of the work culture matches the quality of the organization's products or services. The quality of the work culture and the quality of employee performance go hand-in-hand. It is up to the manager to determine along which path they'll walk.

Influencing the culture

What creates and influences the culture? Schein (2008) and Humanresource (2008) argue that there are several major factors:

- **The manager's behaviour**. Studies indicate that the single greatest influence on the work culture is the manager. As Chrysler chairman Lee Iacocca says, "The speed of the boss is the speed of the team." Employees soon realize that the best way to get ahead in an organization, while staying out of trouble, is to pay attention not so much to what the manager says, but to what the manager does. Actions, in fact, do speak louder than words. The belief system of the manager, as indicated by the manager's behaviour, will usually be mirrored by a significant number of employees.
- **Employee selection**. Some of the major high-performance organizations, such as IBM, carefully select their employees to fit in with the existing corporate culture. They become "IBM-ers." Not everyone, of course, may want to work in such a uniform culture, but it does produce a highly productive organization, as well as very low employee turnover.
- **The nature of the business**. Some businesses have long-established cultures, either as individual organizations or as professions. For example, there are certain beliefs common to the newspaper business, whether you work for a small daily in rural Iowa or a large New York tabloid. The legal

profession has a common culture, no matter which aspect of the law you practice. So do long-distance truck drivers, nurses, or jockeys. Most professionals bring a set of cultural beliefs with them, regardless of where they work. The exception to this may be in new industries such as electronics, where neither the job roles nor the products even existed a few years ago. Firms in California's Silicon Valley, for example, literally had to build new corporate cultures since no models existed in their industry. According to consultant Robert Bly, this culture has developed into one of "high turnover, long work hours, intense enthusiasm for one's work, technology as king over marketing or the customer – and everyone's goal is to be an entrepreneur, not a vice-president." This can create excessive employee stress and tension, and drug use, alcoholism, and divorce are reported to be higher than normal in those industries.

- **The external culture**. An organization's internal culture can be strongly influenced by the culture of the community that surrounds it. Americans who set up businesses abroad soon learn that they must respect the local cultural beliefs if they expect to have a smoothly functioning organization.

Improving the culture

Since the nature and quality of the work culture seem to have a direct effect on organizational performance and profitability, managers understandably want to know how their work cultures can be improved. If this is an issue for you or your organization, here are some suggestions (DMReviews, 2008).

Establish a clear corporate mission. It is amazing how many organizations can't state in simple terms the reasons for their existence. Try it for yourself by completing the statement, "This organization exists for the purpose of..." If this proves difficult, you have discovered a good place to start improving your work culture. A clear and easily understood organizational mission statement makes it much easier for people within the organization to set priorities, make decisions, and determine values. It lets you know who you are as an organization. It helps everyone in the organization answer that most basic question, "What am I doing here?" An equally important component of the mission statement is that all of the organization's members be able to complete "The purpose of this organization is..." and arrive at much the same answer as does upper management. Many managers seem to assume that employees can do this, without ever really finding out.

Check it out for yourself: Have the member of your organization or work unit take a few minutes to complete the statement anonymously. Compare their statements with what you think is the purpose of your organization. The differences may astonish you.

It is imperative that managers clearly communicate to all members of the organization what the purpose of the organization really is. Without that understanding, employees do not feel that they are essential to the organization, its functions, or its future direction. They "just work there." The results can be mediocre job performance, absenteeism, low corporate loyalty, and high turnover. People only stay on a train as long as they have a clear idea of where it is going, and as long as its destination is the same as their own.

Keep the mission up front. Once an organization's purpose has been clearly established, the manager must ensure that it is continually kept in front of the organization's members. These should be words that the organization lives by, not words stored in the janitor's closet, and they need frequent reiteration. It isn't enough to remind employees at the annual company picnic or the yearly sales meeting; it must be done on an ongoing basis. It would be hard to maintain a religion in a culture where everyone comes to church on only one religious holiday.

Managers must reflect the desired culture. When an organization's mission and purpose have been made clear to all of its members, the manager must determine what behaviours are consistent with the desired culture and set an example of them. For example, if clear communication is important, then it is up to managers to recognize and reward it, as well as practice it themselves. If positive attitudes and beliefs are needed, then they must come from the top.

Employee learning must be ongoing. To generate a performance-oriented work culture, employees need to expand their skills and knowledge continually. They need to know what the organization expects in the way of quality products or service and how to achieve it. They need to be coached through new situations and helped to learn from any mistakes. Employees also need to be encouraged to try new ideas, methods, or approaches, so that organizational problems can be solved in innovative ways. Only in this way can managers develop a sufficiently supportive work culture to imaginatively solve the increasing number of problems brought on by an accelerated rate of change (Industrialrelations, 2008).

Managing and Growing Staff

"A good leader inspires others with confidence in him; a great leader inspires them with confidence in themselves"
Franklin D. Roosevelt

"A good leader can't get too far ahead of his followers"
Tacitus

"Forethought and prudence are the proper qualities of a leader"
Tom Landry

People strategy

Employers cannot deliver a full and competitive service if they do not have the right workforce or resources in place. A people strategy helps this. It recognises the benefits of having a committed, capable and skilled workforce that is focused on achieving the organization's objectives. It also presents a process through which employers can attain real service enhancements. The development and implementation of a people strategy ensures that the organizations' activities are aligned with reward and remunerations and workforce strategy (PMM, 2008).

Performance Improvement

A people strategy helps organizations to focus on the people management interventions that impact on the achievement of corporate objectives. It helps to develop an understanding of how different aspects of people management policies relate together, for example team-based working and sickness absence management. Research has shown that key people management interventions, such as recruitment and retention policies and internal communication, are closely linked to raising productivity and performance (Impactfactory, 2008).

People strategies need to be capable of development in order to adapt to changes, which influence workforce capacity and performance. For example, a strategic approach to "greening" your workforce can enhance employer branding as well as the council's reputation as community leader.

It is the quality of the employee's workplace environment that most impacts on their level of motivation and subsequent performance. How well they engage with the organization, especially with their immediate environment, influences to a great extent their error rate, level of innovation and collaboration with other employees, absenteeism and, ultimately, how long they stay in the job. Many studies have revealed that most employees leave their organization because of the relationship with their immediate supervisor or manager.

So, what are the workplace environment factors that need to be taken into consideration by any serious manager? Described below are the key factors and how each can be utilized by supervisors and managers to boost performance. An employee's workplace environment is a key determinant of their level of productivity. How well the workplace engages an employee impacts their level of motivation to perform. This then influences that employee's (Industrialrelations, 2008):

- *Error rate*
- *Level of innovation*
- *Collaboration with other employees*
- *Absenteeism and, ultimately, how long they stay in the job.*

The most important of these workplace environment factors that either lead to engagement or disengagement are shown in the following diagram. A close consideration of each of these factors is also very useful in ensuring that employees apply the skills they learn during training programs once they return to their workplace. Tending to the structural and interpersonal aspects of each of these factors enables employees to apply the required skills in a consistent and habitual way (Bedford, 2008).
The above factors are also important for getting the most out of your organizational change programs.

<u>Developing the right organisational attitude</u>

Effective performance management requires an ongoing dialogue with staff. A number of simultaneous actions are needed to help develop an organisational attitude where performance is managed well and really leads to service improvement (Schein, 2008).

a) It is important to make sure employees know the key organization objectives and priorities, what they should focus on and how they can contribute. Being given too many initiatives and plans tends to make employees feel overloaded.

b) Justify the benefits of making an effort to manage and improve performance, as employees need to know how it can help them deliver. You may wish to make these benefits service specific or more general such as ensuring resources are targeted where they are most needed, improving services and systems, better 'joining up' of activities across the council or helping develop employees to perform their roles more effectively.

c) Ensure that employees who perform well are rewarded and those who underperform are challenged. It is critical that councils back up what they say about performance by what they do. Employees are then more likely to feel that the way they are dealt with is fair and open and will also take the issue more seriously.

d) Involve employees in setting meaningful goals and performance measures for their work. This can be done informally between the employee and their immediate supervisor or as part of an organization's formal performance management process. The key here is that each employee is actively engaged in the goal-setting process and takes ownership of the final agreed goals and measures.

e) Act as advocates for employees, gathering and distributing the resources needed by them in order for them to be able to do a good job. Immediate supervisors and managers need to display the interpersonal skills required to engage employees and enhance their self-confidence. This includes providing positive encouragement for a job well done.

Developing Enabling Process & Systems

"Leadership is not so much about technique and methods as it is about opening the heart. Leadership is about inspiration—of oneself and of others. Great leadership is about human experiences, not processes.

Lance Secretan

Organizational system is made-up of five components, which generate these myriad of reactions within the organization (Industrialrelations, 2008):

- *Culture:* *The behavioral patterns (habits and conventions) generally adopted within the organization.*
- *Structure:* *The definition of jobs and the reporting hierarchy (organization chart), as well as the processes that combine people into teams as workflows across organizational boundaries.*
- *Internal economy:* *The budgeting, priority-setting, pricing (chargebacks), project-approval, and tracking processes that determine how resources flow through an organization and to its clients.*
- *Methods and tools:* *The procedures, methodologies, skills, and tools that people in an organization use.*
- *Metrics and rewards:* *The feedback loops that let people know how they are doing so they can adjust their behavior, and the incentives for improving performance*

It must be borne in mind by leaders that organizational system influences everyone's performance, and can be consciously designed for the better of the organization. By redesigning these five organizational systems' elements HEIs leaders can permanently modify the behaviour of an entire institution. Leaders must therefore plan to transform their institutions by focusing on all the five sub-systems. A leadership team must therefore develop a common vision of the end point, in assessing the gaps and analyzing their root causes, and in planning the right changes, in the right sequence, to attain their vision.

In a nutshell, sound process and systems management requires superior leadership – a human activity that comes from the heart and considers the hearts of others and a positive attitude rather than routine playing. More than anything else today, employees believe they are part of a system if the process has their heart. If there is one thing a leader can do to connect with followers at a human, or better still a spiritual level, it is to become engaged with them fully, to share experiences and emotions, and to set out clearly the processes of leadership (IDeA, 2008).

- **Role congruity** – Organizations have to work to ensure that the role that the employee is required to perform is consistent with their expectations on joining the organization and any subsequent training. The organization's role expectations are typically reflected in formal documents, such as Job Descriptions and Role Specifications. These expectations should be consistent with tasks allocated by the employee's immediate supervisor.
- **Defined processes** - Many errors, defects and customer complaints are the result of poor process management. Constrain the variability of how work is actually performed through documenting processes and communicating such expectations to employees. Verify on a regular or random basis that the work is actually performed in the way required. Along with goal setting, getting employees to help define and improve processes is a powerful opportunity for engagement.

Securing Hearts and Minds

"Leadership is much more an art, a belief, a condition of the heart, than a set of things to do. The visible signs of artful leadership are expressed, ultimately, in its practice".

Max DePree

"Good leaders make people feel that they're at the very heart of things, not at the periphery. Everyone feels that he or she makes a difference to the success of the organization. When that happens people feel centred and that gives their work meaning".

Warren Bennis

Regularly feed back to employees' information on how they are performing. This should consist of both positive feedback on what the employee is doing right as well as feedback on what requires improvement. The feedback needs to be as objective as possible and delivered with the appropriate interpersonal and conflict resolution skills. It can be a mix of both informal feedback and feedback delivered as part of a formal performance management cycle.

Playing fairly with others

People dynamics is all about playing fairly with other. Seven top ways of playing fairly with others at the work place have been suggested. They form the basis for effective work relationships. These are the actions that leaders should take to create a positive, empowering, motivational work environment for people (Humanrelations, 2008):

- ***Bring suggested solutions with the problems to the meeting*** *table. Some employees spend an inordinate amount of time identifying problems. Honestly? That's the easy part. Thoughtful solutions are the challenge that will earn respect and admiration from co-workers and bosses*

- ***Don't ever play the blame game****. You alienate co-workers, supervisors, and reporting staff. Yes, you may need to identify who was involved in a problem. You may even ask the Deming question: what about the work system caused the employee to fail? But, not my fault and publicly identifying and blaming others for failures will earn enemies. These enemies will, in turn, help you to fail. You do need allies at work.*
- ***Your verbal and nonverbal communication matters****. If you talk down to another employee, use sarcasm, or sound nasty, the other employee hears you. We are all radar machines that constantly scope out our environment. In one organization a high level manager said to me, "I know you don't think I should scream at my employees. But, sometimes, they make me so mad. When is it appropriate for me to scream at the employees?" Answer? Never, of course, if respect for people is a hallmark of your organization.*
- ***Never blind-side a coworker, boss, or reporting staff person****. If the first time a coworker hears about a problem is in a staff meeting or from an email sent to his supervisor, you have blind sided the coworker. Always discuss problems, first, with the people directly involved who "own" the work system. Also called lynching or ambushing your co-workers, you will never build effective work alliances unless your co-workers trust you. And, without alliances, you never accomplish the most important goals.*
- ***Keep your commitments****. In an organization, work is interconnected. If you fail to meet deadlines and commitments, you affect the work of other employees. Always keep commitments, and if you can't, make sure all affected employees know what happened. Provide a new due date and make every possible effort to honour the new deadline.*
- ***Share credit for accomplishments, ideas, and contributions****. How often do you accomplish a goal or complete a project with no help from others? If you are a manager, how many of the*

great ideas you promote were contributed by staff members? Take the time, and expend the energy, to thank, reward, recognize and specify contributions of the people who help you succeed. This is a no-fail approach to building effective work relationships.

- ***Help other employees find their greatness.*** *Every employee in your organization has talents, skills, and experience. If you can help fellow employees harness their best abilities, you benefit the organization immeasurably. The growth of individual employees benefits the whole. Compliment, recognize, praise, and notice contributions. You don't have to be a manager to help create a positive, motivating environment for employees. In this environment, employees do find and contribute their greatness.*

Despite playing fairly with others, there are instances leaders in organizations may have to deal with diffucult behaviours in the work place. Thus in dealing with difficult co-workers the following productive ways have been suggested (Essortment, 2008):

- **Start out by examining yourself**. Are you sure that the other person is really the problem and that you're not overreacting? Have you always experienced difficulty with the same type of person or actions? Does a pattern exist for you in your interaction with co-workers? Do you recognize that you have hot buttons that are easily pushed? (We all do, you know). Always start with self-examination to determine that the object of your attention really is a difficult person's actions.
- **Explore what you are experiencing with a trusted friend or colleague**. Brainstorm ways to address the situation. When you are the object of an attack, or your boss appears to support the dysfunctional actions of a coworker, it is often difficult to objectively assess your options. Anger, pain, humiliation, fear and concern about making the situation worse are legitimate emotions. Pay attention to the unspoken agreement you create

when you solicit another's assistance. You are committing to act unless you agree actions will only hurt the situation. Otherwise, you risk becoming a whiner or complainer in the eyes of your colleague.

- **Approach the person with whom you are having the problem for a private discussion**. Talk to them about what you are experiencing in "I" messages. (Using "I" messages is a communication approach that focuses on your experience of the situation rather than on attacking or accusing the other person.) You can also explain to your coworker the impact of their actions on you. Be pleasant and agreeable as you talk with the other person. They may not be aware of the impact of their words or actions on you. They may be learning about their impact on you for the first time. Or, they may have to consider and confront a pattern in their own interaction with people. Worst case? They may know their impact on you and deny it or try to explain it away. Unfortunately, some difficult people just don't care. During the discussion, attempt to reach agreement about positive and supportive actions going forward.
- **Follow up after the initial discussion**. Has the behaviour changed? Gotten better? Or worse? Determine whether a follow-up discussion is needed. Determine whether a follow-up discussion will have any impact. Decide if you want to continue to confront the difficult person by yourself. Become a peacemaker. (Decide how badly you want to make peace with the other person and how much you want your current job. Determine whether you have experienced a pattern of support from your boss.) If you answer, "yes," to these questions, hold another discussion. If not, escalate and move to the next idea.
- **You can confront your difficult co-worker's behaviour publicly**. Deal with the person with gentle humour or slight sarcasm. Or, make an exaggerated physical gesture – no, not that one – such as a salute or place your hand over your heart to indicate a serious wounding. You can also tell the difficult person that

you'd like them to consider important history in their decision making or similar words expressed positively, depending on the subject. Direct confrontation does work well for some people in some situations. I don't think it works to ask the person to stop doing what they're doing, publicly, but you can employ more positive confrontational tactics. Their success for you will depend on your ability to pull them off. Each of us is not spur-of-the-moment funny, but if you are, you can use the humour well with difficult co-workers.

- **If you have done what you can do and employed the first five recommended approaches with little or no success, it's time to involve others**. Note that you are escalating the situation. Prepare to talk with your boss. Take notes and address the issues, not as interpersonal problems, but as issues affecting your productivity, the work and your progress on projects. Tell your boss exactly what the difficult person does. Make a plan to address the issues. Perhaps involve your co-worker's boss. Recognize that a good boss is likely to bring your difficult coworker and his supervisor into a three or four-way discussion at this point. Expect to participate in follow-up over time.
- **Rally the other employees who might have an issue with the difficult person, too - carefully**. Sometimes, a group approach convinces the boss that the impact of the behaviour is wider and deeper than she had originally determined. Be careful with this approach, however. Know what works with your boss. You want to solve your problem, not make it look as if you are rabble-rousing and ganging up on another employee.
- **If these approaches fail to work, try to limit the difficult person's access to you**. Protect the needs of your business, but avoid working with the person when possible. Leave voluntary committees, Choose projects he or she does not impact. Don't hurt your own career or your business, but avoidance is an option.

- **Transfer to a new job within your organization**. Depending on the size of your company, you may never have to work with this difficult coworker again. Fleeing is definitely an option.
- **If all else fails, you can quit your job. What, flee, you ask? But, I wasn't the employee with the problem**. I was not the difficult coworker. All I tried to do was my job. You're right. But, what price, in terms of your happiness and success, are you willing to pay to stay? You need to decide whether the good in your current situation outweighs the bad or whether the bad outweighs the good.

In conflict management therefore, it is important to get to the bottom of the problem and seek ways and means of resolving any outstanding issues professionally and with integrity.

Building momentum for change

HEIs leaders must therefore actively work towards building support for change and in doing so they should (Capshaw & Koulopoulous, 1997):

- **Provide as much information as possible**, to as many employees as possible, about the business. Share financial information, customer feedback, employee satisfaction survey results, industry projections and challenges, and data from processes you measure. Assuming decisions about needed change are made based on relevant data, an informed workforce will understand and agree with the need for change. (They may not agree on the how and/or what, but you are miles ahead if you have agreement on the why and the whether.)
- **Create an urgency around the need to change**. Project, for your workforce, what will happen if you don't make the needed changes. Communicate this information honestly and use data whenever it is available. You do have compelling reasons for making the changes? Right?

- **Spend extra time and energy working with your front line supervisory staff and line managers** to ensure that they understand, can communicate about, and support the changes. Their action and communication are critical in molding the opinion of the rest of your workforce.
- **Align all organizational systems to support needed changes**. These include the performance management system, rewards and recognition, disciplinary approaches, compensation, promotions, and hiring. A consistency across all Human Resources systems will support faster change.
- **Align the informal structures and networks in your organization with the desired changes**. If you can tap into the informal communication and political network, you will increase change commitment. (As an example, eat lunch in the lunchroom and discuss the changes informally. Spend extra time communicating the positive aspects of the change to people you know are "key communicators" in your organization). Help employees feel as if they are involved in a change management process that is larger than themselves by taking these actions to effectively involve employees in change management.

Adopting a Caring Attitude

"The first step to leadership is servanthood"
John Maxwell

"The first responsibility of a leader is to define reality"
Max DePree

Employee welfare includes anything that is done for the comfort and improvement of employees and is provided over and above the wages. Welfare helps in keeping the morale and motivation of the employees high so as to retain the employees for longer duration. The welfare measures need not be in monetary terms only but in any kind/forms. Employee welfare includes monitoring of working conditions, creation of industrial harmony through infrastructure for health, industrial relations and insurance against disease, accident and unemployment for the workers and their families (Galacoral, 2008).

Why welfare?

At Bedford welfare is key to employee contentment (Bedford, 2008):

- *They provide better physical and mental health to workers and thus promote a healthy work environment*
- *Facilities like housing schemes, medical benefits, and education and recreation facilities for workers' families help in raising their standards of living. This makes workers to pay more attention towards work and thus increases their productivity.*
- *Employers get stable labour force by providing welfare facilities. Workers take active interest in their jobs and work with a feeling of involvement and participation.*
- *Employee welfare measures increase the productivity of organization and promote healthy industrial relations thereby maintaining industrial peace.*
- *The social evils prevalent among the labours such as substance abuse, etc are reduced to a greater extent by the welfare policies.*

Workplace incentives

Scholars have long established that to increase employee output and performance or team commitment employees require some incentives. Incentives are closely linked to the concepts of rewards and recognition. While the latter serve as after-the-fact "thank you's," incentives are carrots you can use to motivate employees to reach for a performance goal. Essentially leaders use incentives to excite its staff about their business objectives. However, when an organization wants to kick-start their level of enthusiasm or you require a truly exceptional effort, offering something beyond the ordinary can go a long way toward getting results. The following principles though need to be adhered to (Go2, 2008):

- **Describe rewards up front** - Giving employees a goal to strive for creates enthusiasm and can motivate them to work extra hard. Telling them up front what you're offering in return will help to create that extra spark when you need it most.
- **Money isn't the only option** - Incentives are most commonly associated with cash rewards. This *can* be effective in some environments, but should not be considered the only option. Depending on the resources you can afford, you might consider offering a trip, a day off, gift certificates, a trial promotion, a special plaque, or devoting organizational time toward something in the recipient's honour. Remember, not everyone is equally motivated by money, so it's important to know what your staff will respond to. Don't know? Ask them.
- **Rewards don't have to be large** - Scale your incentives to reflect the effort you require. It doesn't have to be big to be effective, but the size of the reward should mirror how much extra you're asking of your employees. If you need staff to go all out to meet your goals, make it worth their while. Let them know how important their dedication is to the organization by showing them what it's worth to you.
- **Make goals concrete and attainable** - Depending on what your needs are, you can structure team or individual goals for your staff. Outline a specific and measurable objective, whether it's to boost customer satisfaction, reduce waste, or increase sales by a certain amount over a specified time period. It's important to make the goals concrete, as you don't want any misunderstandings about whether goals

were met. Goals should be a stretch from regular outputs, but must also be reachable. Setting goals at unreasonably high levels will dampen employees' drive to achieve them. To have the desired effect, it's important to set your sights within reason.

- **Make recognition public** - The final step in using incentives is to publicly acknowledge those who have attained the goal. People want and need to be recognized. Turning the award into a celebratory event entrenches the value of their work for themselves and others.
- **One word of caution** - You don't want to create an environment where employees will always expect something extra just for doing their jobs. Use incentives on a limited basis when you really require staff to go the extra mile. These might be situations like getting through a busy time or overcoming a staffing shortage, or making the most of a seasonal sales campaign. Employees are likely to respond to incentives when they understand you're looking for more than the usual effort.

ITV Experience

In the case of ITV (2008), its employee incentive package involves:

- **Talent management** - We are committed to deal fairly with freelancers and creative talent – they are a crucial part of our business. Contracts with performers are usually negotiated through agents or lawyers under collective agreements with trade unions including Equity, the Musicians Union and the Writers Guild of Great Britain. We comply with child employment law and guidance from the Producers Rights Agency on child performers. We have also developed our own guidelines for casting teams to use when working with child performers. In 2006 we continued to update our comprehensive database of performance and skills information for the freelance community.

- **Work-life balance** - A flexible workplace is increasingly an important factor in attracting and retaining talent. Our Flexible Working Policy, introduced in 2003, will be amended in 2007 to accommodate changes in legislation for carers. Our existing policy allows anyone employed by ITV for six months or more and who cares for children under six years old to apply for a flexible working option.
- **Grievances and Whistleblowing** - While problems and concerns about work can often be resolved informally, our Grievance Policy allows employees to communicate their problems or concerns in a more formal way. During 2006, we worked with Public Concern at Work (www.pcaw.co.uk), a charity providing independent advice and promoting good practice on whistleblowing. Together we devised a new whistleblowing policy. PCAW now provides a confidential and independent helpline for our people to contact if they have a concern about wrongdoing or a serious risk that could damage the public, our workforce or our reputation. Our audit committee receives regular reports on the effectiveness of the new policy. During 2006 no significant issues were raised.
- **Redundancy** - During 2006, we made 92 voluntary and compulsory redundancies. These were managed in line with our Redundancy Policy, which requires a period of consultation during which support is provided to help employees to find alternative employment within ITV. Where this is not possible, employees receive a redundancy payment in line with their entitlement.

INFOCOMM Development Authority of Singapore (IDA)

IDA (2008) argues strongly that organizations should understand and respect everyone's need to balance personal/family and work commitments. An employee with work-life balance will be a motivated and committed contributor. As such, employers should offer a wide range of employee well-being and pro-family policies and programmes to create a more conducive and employee friendly work environment so as to motivate its employees to give their best. IDA programmes include:

- **Well-being Programmes and Activities -** To encourage employees to lead a healthy life-style, our recreational club, regularly organizes fun-filled activities like inter-statutory games, sports carnival, exercise classes, health talks, "eat with your family" day and a Staff Appreciation cum Celebration event are vital. These activities help employees to unwind and offer opportunities for interaction and bonding amidst a culture that encourages diverse views, creative thinking, learning and sharing. Flexi-fit time is offered to employees to have the flexibility to take time-off to exercise during office hours where possible. Facilities for stress management and promotion of healthy well-being are also provided and are a clear priority to IDA.
- **Pro-family Policies and Practices -** Leave benefits such as marriage, maternity, paternity, child-care, adoption and compassionate leave also serve to meet employees' needs for a balanced work and family life are provided. Unpaid leave is also available to employees who may need to take an extended period off to take care of their family or for further education.
- **Flexible Work Arrangement** - Another notable family-friendly work practice is the availability of flexible work arrangements. Married female employees may apply for part-time employment if they are unable to commit full time due to child-care and family commitments. Telecommuting work arrangement is also available whereby employees may choose to work from home in the event of child-care emergencies and/or other unforeseen circumstances.

- **Employee Support Schemes** - A suite of employee support schemes and services should be provided for employees to enjoy both a fulfilling job and an enriched family and personal life. Some of the benefits under this scheme include marriage and newborn gifts, subsidy for mobile and broadband usage and flexi-benefits reimbursement for child-care and children's educational expenses. In addition, corporate passes for the zoo, Bird Park and science centre as well as holiday bungalows are offered for the use of employees and their families. Family-life education and health promotion talks and workshops are organized regularly for couples and families.

Developing Knowledge-Based Strategies

"Leadership and learning are indispensable to each other"

John F. Kennedy

"Good leaders develop through a never-ending process of self-study, education, training, and experience".

Manual on military leadership

Capshaw and Koulopoulos (1999) contend that knowledge management has captured the attention of executives throughout the global corporate arena. Those who are succeeding have observed firsthand that knowledge management is much more than an amalgamation of technologies. In contrast, the one thing that frequently distinguishes knowledge management projects among other strategic initiatives is the passion, fearlessness and confidence of the knowledge leader.

They argue that while knowledge leadership is not new, managing the knowledge of a process is a requirement in any enterprise, even an enterprise of only one person. Consider the transient nature of today's workforce, along with the challenges of connecting and mobilizing geographically distributed teams who are engaged in technical modern work, and you have an appreciation for the immense demand for greater sophistication in the way knowledge is managed. Whatever knowledge is, wherever it resides or however it is managed, few would disagree that knowledge is an essential part of our individual and organizational ability to innovate, compete and succeed. Given that, few would doubt that the roles and responsibilities of knowledge leaders are an essential ingredient of competition in the next millennium.

Knowledge Leader

Knowledge leaders are undeniably a new breed of manager. They do not fall neatly into a compartment on an organization chart. You will find them on the high pinnacles of the command and control organization as often as you will find them in the nooks occupied by highly specialized teams. Creating a niche for the knowledge leader requires both an understanding and an acceptance of this looseness in affiliation and title. It also requires that the individual tasked with knowledge management responsibilities be intensely focused on the promotion of knowledge management practices and solutions. The operative question here is not, "Do I need knowledge leadership?" but rather, "What kind of leadership do I need?" By learning about the types of knowledge leaders that are in enterprises today, you can begin to define which of these roles best suits you and your organization. A multi-client study conducted by The Delphi Group revealed that, in practice, knowledge leadership spans a broad domain of positions and types of individuals. Regardless of the differences in title or organizational placement, knowledge leaders exhibit similar qualifications. The most notable have hybrid business/information technology experience, at least ten years (and often much more) of line-of-business experience, an entrepreneurial attitude and a relatively high level of interest in career definition and development. They also exhibit acumen in corporate communication throughout the formal hierarchy reflected in most organization charts, as well as in the informal networking that occurs in communities of practice or the "corporate underground." It is through all these channels that knowledge leaders introduce methods and systems to match knowledge seekers with knowledge providers (Kirschner et al., 1997).

Why Knowledge leaders?

Why do organizations need knowledge leaders? Simply put, to bridge the natural hurdles to sharing knowledge within the large enterprise. This is the very essence of knowledge management. Organizations of all sizes and vertical expertise have come full circle to realize that communication of best practices, not application of technology, is at the heart of knowledge management's ability to meet business goals and user needs. This is typically fostered through fluid communication channels in an open culture. Unfortunately, neither comes naturally to a large organization. Leadership is needed to foster the climate, the practices and the incentives for knowledge sharing.

To prove the point, knowledge leaders highlighted in the study repeatedly cite skills in knowledge collection, organization, categorization and communication, rather than advanced skills in specific information technologies, as critical to their success. Although it is virtually impossible for an organization to leverage its collective knowledge in the absence of technology today, knowledge leaders must first possess (or quickly equip themselves with) the skills needed to traverse an organization's network through effective face-to-face communication, as well as through electronic means.

Types of Knowledge Leaders

Many organizations have taken the step of appointing a highly visible figure, the chief knowledge officer (CKO), to leverage the collective mind of an enterprise. This approach is the subject of many knowledge leadership discussions. Although there are a number of organizations with a CKO in place, this phenomenon is only one of several approaches in practice today to instil knowledge leadership. Many organizations have embraced knowledge leaders, but they have such titles as knowledge analyst, knowledge manager and knowledge steward. These individuals function very differently than the CKO and often express strong opinions against a central point of knowledge ownership (Capshaw and Koulopoulos, 1999):

The **knowledge analyst** is responsible for collecting, organizing and disseminating knowledge, usually on demand. Knowledge analysts provide knowledge leadership by becoming walking repositories of best practices a library of how knowledge is shared and should be shared across the organization. The liability, of course, is that knowledge analysts can easily take all of the best practices with them if they leave the organization. There is also a risk that these individuals become so valuable to the immediate constituency that they are not able to move laterally to other parts of the organization where their skills are equally needed.

The **knowledge manager** is responsible for coordinating the efforts of engineers, architects and analysts. The knowledge manager is most often required in large organizations where the large number of discrete knowledge-sharing processes risk fragmentation and isolation. The knowledge manager provides coordination across processes within a business unit. The risk in having knowledge managers is that fiefdoms (albeit large ones) may form around the success of each manager's domain. Regardless of this pitfall, the knowledge manager may successfully fill the niche of knowledge leader in an organization that realizes the lack of coordination in each of its business units is a primary deterrent to the sharing of knowledge among employees.

However, this single business unit approach can present its own problems in the form of fragmentation of knowledge. In these cases, the organization often relies on a central, command- and-control knowledge leader to provide continuity across multiple, discontinuous groups of knowledge workers.

The **chief knowledge officer** is responsible for enterprise-wide coordination of all knowledge leadership. The CKO typically reports to or is chartered by the CEO. Although it would seem reasonable that the CKO be part of IT (perhaps reporting to the CIO), this is not often the case. The CKO is not tasked with ownership of the technology infrastructure but rather the methods, practices and content comprising knowledge management solutions. At present, this role is almost always a solo performer with little, if any, staff and no immediate line-of-business responsibility. The CKO role requires advanced knowledge of the collective repositories, skills and expertise that can, if properly matched to the needs of the organization, increase responsiveness to customers (internal and external) and suppliers, which ultimately provides competitive distinction.

Putting a CKO in place is a potential point of sub-optimization. You may end up with someone whose vision of knowledge management dilutes the effectiveness of managing knowledge in each of the particular business units, projects or teams. Instead, these groups need to find the best way to manage knowledge within their area. By its nature, knowledge management is driven by lines of business (LOBs) and people at the extremities of the organization. Therefore, the best you can hope to do is coordinate the knowledge management process, but not truly control it. Because of this, a single knowledge leader, across all lines of business, is tough for LOB managers to support.

The **knowledge steward** is responsible for providing minimal, but ongoing, support to knowledge users in the form of expertise in the tools, practices and methods of knowledge management. The steward is in the most precarious and most opportunistic of positions. Usually, he or she is an individual who has fallen into the role of helping others to better understand and leverage the power of new technologies and practices in managing knowledge. The term "steward" best resonated in the interviews with the study participants; it conveys responsibility and a willingness to guide others, yet it is also non-intrusive and the near antithesis of ownership.

What is Your Institution's Need?

Knowledge leaders are educators of best practices and stewards of the frameworks that facilitate knowledge creation and sharing. But they are not owners. Knowledge leadership builds the bridges. Organizational leadership builds the culture. It is the knowledge workers themselves who build the reasons to use knowledge management.

CKO, knowledge manager, architect or steward how does an organization identify the optimal style of knowledge leadership for its needs? Your vice president of customer care or manager of systems and applications may be your unsung knowledge leader. It may be there is no one. Look at the state of your organization's knowledge sharing, the level of sponsorship for knowledge leadership and the receptivity of its culture today. Then act accordingly. For instance, it would be a mistake to put a CKO into an organization that has little executive interest in knowledge management and where LOB managers exhibit a fundamental mistrust of one other. A CKO cannot make up for a pathology of poor communication and mistrust.

There is little doubt that knowledge leadership is an essential ingredient of competition in the next millennium. Begin now to nurture these roles in your organization. Chances are, whatever their title, you already have knowledge leaders at work who, with a bit of sponsorship, would be ready, able and very willing to step into the role.

In the words of Brecher it must be remembered that:
"There are many elements to a campaign. Leadership is number one. Everything else is number two".
Bernd Brecher

Competing With Talent Motivation and Retention

"Management means helping people to get the best out of themselves, not organizing things."
Lauren Appley

Walking your talk is a great way to motivate yourself. No one likes to live a lie. Be honest with yourself, and you will find the motivation to do what you advise others to do."
Vince Poscente

Twyla Dell (Essortment, 2008) writes of motivating employees, "The heart of motivation is to give people what they really want most from work. The more you are able to provide what they want, the more you should expect what you really want, namely: productivity, quality, and service." (An Honest Day's Work (1988). Thus, motivating staff and creating a favourable environment pays off in many practical ways:

- ***Reduces turnover****. Employees who like their jobs stay in it longer.*
- ***Saves time and money****. Lower turnover means the business spends less time and money hiring and training new employees. There is also frequently less loss and fewer accidents.*
- ***Raises productivity and performance standards****. When a business develops experienced employees who have been with the organization for an extended time, things get done faster and better.*

- ***Reduces absenteeism and tardiness.*** *Motivated workers come to work on time and they come in when scheduled.*
- ***Reduces problems.*** *Motivated employees solve many of their own problems without your having to get involved.*
- ***Creates a more pleasant work environment.*** *Motivated employees like their jobs and look forward to coming to work.*

Motivation is the inner drive that makes people want to reach both personal and professional goals. Motivation comes from inside a person, which is why managers can't give it to their employees. Instead, they can show employees how their jobs fulfill their own needs, interests, values, and personal goals. Every employee has special needs, interests, values, and personal goals. Identifying these things will help managers understand what employees want and need from their jobs, which will help them create an environment conducive to motivation. But they must be willing to spend the time to talk with their employees and learn more about them in order to identify their needs, interests, values, and goals (Industrialrelations, 2008).

Money is not a sufficient motivator in encouraging the superior workplace performance required in today's competitive business environment. Managers and supervisors will need to be comfortable with working with the whole gamut of workplace factors that influence employee motivation. Skills required include the ability to engage employees in mutual goal setting clarify role expectations and provide regular performance back. Time and energy will also need to be given to providing relevant performance incentives, managing processes, providing adequate resources and workplace coaching. Last but not least, to drive their organizations to peak performance managers and supervisors must put out front the human face of their organization. Paramount here is the human-to-human interaction through providing individualized support and encouragement to each and every employee.

<u>Some ways to help improve employee motivation include</u>

Motivation experts (Motivationstrategies, 2008), contend that improving employee motivation should include:

- *Recognizing employee efforts.*
- *Appreciating employee commitment to the job.*
- *Inviting employees to be a part of the decision-making.*
- *Providing training opportunities.*
- *Following through on promises.*

One pitfall that many managers fall into is that they think employees are motivated by only one thing: money. According to many surveys, employees are more interested in things such as appreciation, participating in decisions, feeling a part of a team, having promotion opportunities, working in pleasant surroundings, and working for a manager to whom they can feel loyal.

Motivation strategies may be either positive or negative (Essortment, 2008). Positive motivation encourages good performance. Examples of positive motivation include verbal praise, cash bonuses, and time off. Negative motivation discourages poor performance. Examples of negative motivation include reprimands, formal discipline, and the loss of employee privileges.

Most management experts (Essortment, 2008) say that while both positive and negative motivation can help managers get the desired performance results from employees in the short-term, positive motivation provides more than just performance results. For example, managers who use positive motivation (Motivationstrategies, 2008):

- *Keep the workplace positive and improve employee morale.*

- *Help promote teamwork rather than competition between employees.*
- *Experience lower turnover.*
- *Improve employee loyalty to the business.*

Praise, competition, and recognition can be effective motivators, as long as they are used correctly.

When managers sincerely compliment an employee, they:

- *Improve morale: A kind word can put anyone in a good mood.*
- *Shape behavior: Praising good efforts and performance makes employees more likely to repeat that behavior.*
- *Encourage commitment: Employees want to work where they are liked and appreciated.*

HEIs leaders must therefore remember that **"Behaviour that is rewarded is behavior that is repeated"**

Many managers believe that competition is a good motivator. It can be, but it can also be dangerous and discouraging. Managers who pit employees against each other often do more harm than good. Some employees don't do well in competitions because they aren't equal in experience, knowledge, or skill level. Other employees might not like the stress involved in competition. This hurts teamwork. A more effective technique is to put employees in competition with themselves or to put a team of employees in competition with another department or another business (Go2, 2008).

Employee motivation is highest during the first few days or weeks on the job. That's when employees are most concerned about doing things right, pleasing his or her manager, and showing they are

willing to go the extra mile. That's also the best time for managers to use strategies to keep that motivation level high.
Motivation begins with recruitment/selection and continues throughout the employee's career with a business (DMReview, 2008).

- **Recruitment/Selection:** Learn something about the needs, interests, values, and goals of job applicants. Explain what the job will involve. Take applicants to the work area so they can see the surroundings in which they'll work.
- **Orientation:** Make employees feel good about their decision to work for the company.
- **Training:** Good training tells employees that the manager and the business care enough to give them the instruction and direction they need to succeed.
- **Coaching:** Managers need to coach on an ongoing, informal basis. They should lead their employees as the coach of a sports team does. Praise costs nothing and takes only a few seconds to say. It also helps employees feel good about their managers, their jobs, and themselves.
- **Performance Reviews:** Regular performance appraisals help keep motivation levels high. During formal reviews, managers should begin by explaining what employees do well and correctly. As they point out problems, they should also suggest ways the employee can improve and solicit plans from the employee. Managers should be sure to show that they want to help employees improve. They should also discuss long-term career goals and plan ways for employees to learn more on the job.

Some useful additional motivation tips (Motivationstrategies, 2008) include:

- *Explain the skills employees must have to do their jobs. Review their job descriptions in detail with them.*

- *Get to know employees and use motivation techniques appropriate to each person.*
- *Help employees want to become motivated.*
- *Open lines of communication between management and employees.*
- *Whenever possible, allow employees to participate in decisions affecting them.*
- *Give employees credit when due.*
- *Be willing to accept responsibility themselves when problems arise.*
- *Give employees authority to perform their tasks.*
- *Respect employees' abilities. Let employees do what they're trained to do, even if the manager could do it faster or better.*

Towards motivating staff, HEIs must learn how to act strategically by:

- *Fashioning the right workplace environment for effective skills transfer*
- *Developing powerful stakeholder partnerships*
- *Identifying your organization's key workplace performance enhancers and inhibitors*
- *Adopting a structured approach to needs analysis, program development and implementation*
- *Focusing on high impact activities before, during and after training*

Employee Recognition

Although you may not be aware of it, most of your employees aren't as loyal as you think (Humanresource, 2008). The fact is, a large percentage of them are either actively seeking "better" employment or would leave immediately if another position popped up. With such a lack of committed employees, how can your business thrive?

The answer is not necessarily to replace your staff, but to motivate your current employees in ways that'll create a sense of loyalty and respect throughout your workplace. A great way to do this is to create employee recognition programs. These programs will make each employee feel valued for a job well done.
Recognizing employees for individual and group accomplishments shows them that manager's notice and care about them. Recognition can include praise for a job well done, but there are other occasions when it's appropriate to recognize employees. These might include (Industrialrelations, 2008):

- *Birthdays*
- *Service anniversaries*
- *Completion of a difficult task*
- *Having a good attitude*
- *Saving time or money*

The Right Way to Implement Employee Recognition

Most employees have an annual or biannual review. And while these reviews can be used to create positive reinforcement, they are not enough to keep the energy flowing year round. To be effective, employee recognition must be given often to applaud your staff members for their hard work and success.

I am more afraid of an army of 100 sheep led by a lion than an army of 100 lions led by a sheep.

Talleyrand

Growing Human Capital

"Leaders don't force people to follow—they invite them on a journey"

Charles S. Lauer

"Leadership has a harder job to do than just choose sides. It must bring sides together"
Jesse Jackson

Growing people entails a purposeful focus towards improving people's capabilities and work environment through (Bedford, 2008):

- ***Mentoring/coaching*** - *Make available to employees' skilled and respected people to help them perform better in their current role and to assist them develop further into a future role. Mentors and coaches may be internal to an organization or external. Either way, they will need to possess the necessary facilitation skills to assist employees apply existing sills and develop new skills.*
- ***Employ cross-functional teams, tools, techniques and structures*** *to incorporate diverse perspectives into the relocation and redeployment process.*
- ***Conduct broad-based needs assessment*** *to create a win-win solution for the company and employees affected by relocation.*
- ***Develop targeted selling points and incentive packages*** *to inspire employees to relocate to the new facility.*
- ***Proactively address employees' issues and concerns*** *through early and consistent communications of relocation/redeployment packages and support services.*
- *Employ integrated change and transition management tactics during relocation to maintain employee satisfaction and corporate productivity,*
- ***Maintain productivity*** *during corporate reorganization and transition.*
- ***Improve employee satisfaction*** *during and after the move.*
- ***Improve employee performance*** *and retention.*

- ***Reduce costs**. Cutting costs enables the university to conserve and apply more of its resources towards people development.*

Employee Retention

Recruiting the right employees and keeping the right employees matters, especially now. A recent Society for Human Resource Management (SHRM, 2008) press release revealed the answer to the question of what people plan to do when the job market rebounds. The majority of the Human Resource (HR) professionals and managers surveyed agreed that turnover will rise significantly once the job market improves. Both groups felt that the job market will improve within the next year, according to the latest Job Recovery Survey.

The survey is produced by SHRM and CareerJournal.com, the free, executive career site of *The Wall Street Journal*, two of my personal favourite sites. The survey results include responses from 451 HR professionals and 300 managerial or executive employees.
"We're surprised by the percentage of executive employees who say they plan to jump ship once hiring rebounds," says Tony Lee, editor in chief/general manager of CareerJournal.com. "And with 56 percent of HR professionals agreeing that turnover will rise, we're interested to see what types of retention efforts those companies launch to keep their best employees on board."
Employees cited the following three top reasons they would begin searching for a new job:

- *53 percent seek better compensation and benefits.*
- *35 percent cited dissatisfaction with potential career development.*
- *32 percent said they were ready for a new experience.*

HR professionals were asked which programs or policies they use currently to help retain employees. The following three are the most common programs employers are using to retain employees:

- *62 percent provide tuition reimbursement.*
- *60 percent offer competitive vacation and holiday benefits.*
- *59 percent offer competitive salaries.*

Most HR professionals surveyed (71 percent), in large organizations (those with more than 500 employees), thought it would be extremely likely or somewhat likely to experience an increase in voluntary turnover once the job market improves. Forty-one percent from small organizations (1-99 employees) said it was extremely likely or somewhat likely that turnover would increase. Fifty-three percent of respondents from medium organizations (between 100 and 499) thought the same.

Creating a Harmonious Work Environment

As HEIs leaders Endeavour to grow their people, they must be conscious of potentially harmful practices that may stand in the way of growing its people, namely (Impactfactory, 2008):

- **Gesticulating.** *Waving your arms around and talking bollocks.* ***(I know people who'd get an honours degree in this, and not necessarily just people at work)***
- **Blamestorming.***Sitting around in a group, discussing why a deadline was missed, or a project failed, and exactly who was responsible.*
- **Seagull Manager.** *A manager who flies in, makes a lot of noise, craps on everything and then leaves.*
- **Assmosis.** *The process by which people seem to absorb success and advancement - by sucking up to the boss rather than working hard.*
- **Cube Farm.** *An office filled with partitions or cubicles.*
- **Stress Puppy.** *A person who seems to thrive on being stressed out and whining all the time.*
- **Adminisphere.** *The rarefied organisational layers that start just above the rank and file. Decisions that fall from the "adminisphere" are often profoundly inappropriate or irrelevant*

to the problems they were designed to solve. This is often affiliated with the dreaded "administrivia" - needless paperwork and processes. ***(These are encountered daily, usually the higher in the "adminisphere" the decision comes from the less sense it makes)***

HEIs, need to create a training and development support process that will ensure that the employee training they do works. To make training and development more effective the following ten suggestions and approaches will make HEIs training more effective and transferable; their application will result in measurable differences to the universities performance (DMReview, 2008; Industrialrelations, 2008; Humanresource, 2008):

- **Make sure the need is a training and development opportunity.** Do thorough needs and skills analysis to determine the real need for employee training and development. Make sure the opportunity you are pursuing or the problem you are solving is a training issue. If the employee is failing in some aspect of her job, determine whether you have provided the employee with the time and tools needed to perform the job. Does the employee clearly understand what is expected from him/her on the job? Ask yourself whether the employee has the temperament and talent necessary for her current position; consider whether the job is a good skill, ability, and interest fit?
- **Create a context for the employee training and development.** Provide information for the employee about why the new skills, skill enhancement, or information is necessary. Make certain the employee understands the link between the training and his job. You can enhance the impact of the training even further if the employee sees the link between the training and his ability to contribute to the accomplishment of the organization's business plan and goals. It's also important to provide rewards and recognition as a result of successful completion and application of the training. (People like completion certificates,

for instance. One company I know lists employee names and completed training sessions in the company newsletter). This contextual information will help create an attitude of motivation as the employee attends the training. It will assist the employee to want to look for relevant information to apply after the session.

- **Provide training and development that is really relevant to the skill you want the employee to attain** or the information he needs to expand his work horizons. You may need to design an employee training session internally if nothing from training providers exactly meets your needs. Or, seek out providers who are willing to customize their offerings to match your specific needs. It is ineffective to ask an employee to attend a training session on general communication when his immediate need is to learn how to provide feedback in a way that minimizes defensive behaviour. The employee will regard the training session as mostly a waste of time or too basic; his complaints will invalidate potential learning. Whenever possible, connect the employee training to the employee's job and work objectives. If you work in an organization that invests in a self-development component in the appraisal process, make sure the connection to the plan is clear.
- **Favour employee training and development that has measurable objectives and specified outcomes** that will transfer back to the job. Design or obtain employee training that has clearly stated objectives with measurable outcomes. Ascertain that the content leads the employee to attaining the skill or information promised in the objectives. With this information in hand, the employee knows exactly what he can expect from the training session and is less likely to be disappointed. He will also have ways to apply the training to the accomplishment of real workplace objectives
- **Provide information for the employee about exactly what the training session will involve**, prior to the training. Explain what is expected of the employee at the training session. This will

help reduce the person's normal anxiety about trying something new. If she knows what to expect, she can focus on the learning and training transfer rather than her potential discomfort with the unknown. (When I offer a team building session, as an example, people invariably ask me if they will have to touch each other or "do group hugs." They don't, but this really drives home the point for me about letting people know what to expect prior to attending the session.)

- Make clear to the employee that the **training is her responsibility and she needs to take the employee training seriously**. She is expected to apply herself to the employee training and development process before, during, and after the session. This includes completing pre-training assignments, actively participating in the session, and applying new ideas and skills upon returning to work.
- Make sure that internal or external training providers **supply pre-training assignments**. Reading or thought-provoking exercises in advance of the session promote thoughtful consideration of the training content. Exercises or self-assessments, provided and scored in advance of the session, save precious training time for interaction and new information. These ideas will engage the employee in thinking about the subject of the session prior to the training day. This supplies important paybacks in terms of his interest, commitment, and involvement.
- **Train supervisors and managers either first or simultaneously so they know and understand the skills** and information provided in the training session. This will allow the supervisor to: model the appropriate behaviour and learning, provide an environment in which the employee can apply the training, and create the clear expectation that she expects to see different behaviour or thinking as a result of the training. An executive, who has participated in the same training as the rest of the organization, is a powerful role model when he is observed applying the training.

- **Train managers and supervisors in their role in the training process.** The average supervisor has rarely experienced effective training during his career. Even rarer is the supervisor who has worked in an environment that maximized transfer of training to the actual workplace. Thus it is a mistake to believe that supervisors automatically know what must happen for effective training to take place.
- **You can coach supervisors about their role.** Provide a handy tip sheet that explains in detail the organization's expectations of the supervisor in support of effective training. At one General Motors location, the education and training staff provided a three-hour class called, *The Organization and the Training Process*. The session was most effective in communicating roles and responsibilities to supervisory staff.
- **Ask supervisors to meet with employees prior to the training session** to accomplish all I have recommended in this article. Discuss with the individual what he hopes to learn in the session. Discuss any concerns he may have about applying the training in the work environment. Determine if key learning points are important for the organization in return for the investment of his time in the training. Identify any obstacles the employee may expect to experience as he transfers the training to the workplace.

Importantly, in growing and retaining people, HEIs leaders must always remember that:

"A boss creates fear, a leader confidence. A boss fixes blame, a leader corrects mistakes. A boss knows all, a leader asks questions. A boss makes work drudgery, a leader makes it interesting. A boss is interested in himself or herself; a leader is interested in the group"

Russell H. Ewing

References

- Beady, C.H., and Beady, M.O. (1993), "A systematic approach to creating an effective academic environment for African – American students: Lessons from a Private School", *Occasional Paper No- 7*, Cleveland State University, Cleveland, Ohio.
- Capshaw, S., and Koulopoulos, T.M. (1999), "Knowledge Leadership", *D.M. Review Magazine*, May.
- DMReview.Com (2008) - http://www.dmreview.com – June.
- Entwistle, N., Tait, H. (1990), "Approaches to learning, evaluation of teaching, and preferences for contrasting academic environments", *Higher Education*, Vol. 19 No.2, pp.169-94.
- Essortment (2008) - http://www.essortment.com – July.
- Gala Coral (2008) - http://www.galacoral.co.uk – June.
- Go2 (2008) - http://www.go2hr.ca – June.
- Humanresource (2008) - http: //humanresources.about.com – June. Bedford County Council (2008) - http://www.bedford.gov.uk – June.
- Impact Factory (2008) - http://www.impactfactory.com, June.
- Improvement & Development Agency (IDeA) (2008) - http://www.idea.gov.uk – July.
- Industrialrelations (2008) - http://industrialrelations.naukrihub.com – June.
- Infocomm Development Authority (2008) - http://www.ida.gov – June.
- ITV (2008) - http://www.itvplc.com – June.
- Kirschner, P.A., Van Vilsteren, P.P.M., Hummel, H.G.K., & Wigman, M.C.S. (1997). A study environment for acquiring academic and professional competence. *Studies in Higher Education,* 22(2), 151-171.
- Motivationstrategies (2008) – www.motivationstrategies.com - June
- PMM Plc (2008) - http://www.p-mm.co.uk – June.

- Ramsden, P. (1979), "Student learning and perceptions of the academic environment", Higher Education, Vol. 8 No.4, pp.411-27.
- Schein, E.H. (2008), "Organizational culture & leadership", - www.roysmithtraining.co.uk – June.
- Society for Human Resource Management (SHRM), (2008) – www.shrm.org – June.
- University of Florida (2008) - http://www.dso.ufl.edu – June.

Chapter 3
Driving Excellence in Academia

Introduction

"Traditionally, there is a great synergy between standards organisations and open-source projects. Standards organisations are slow-moving and produce stable standards with broad buy-in. The risk with standards is that they are academic and not practical. Open-source organisations take emerging standards and ensure that they are practical. They are acting rapidly, and can provide the input standards organisations need to make practically useful standards, rather than only academically correct standards"

Per Kroll

"In the opening years of the new century, our colleges and universities have reached a watershed between the failing end of a once golden era and an economic, structural, and technological transformation lying just over the campus horizon. As a consequence, they must rethink what they do, for whom they do it, and how they can do it more effectively, more efficiently, and with greater concern for the welfare of what will be a larger and demographically different body of undergraduates"

Mel Elfin

Driving Academic Excellence

Higher education has profoundly changed in the past two decades, and those involved in the academic enterprise have yet to grapple with the implications of these changes. The world around us is changing, and becoming smaller. Education and communication are changing and becoming more global. Students of the 21st century universities are at the vanguard of these changes, and in countries around the world, researchers and educators are realizing that the current models of education are is not compatible to the future challenges. In countries as diverse as the United States, Australia, Japan, the United Kingdom, and all across Europe, attention is slowly beginning to turn to how to take advantage of the new skills and abilities common to today's learners, and how to maximize their potential by changing the structure and operations of the universities.

Globalization and rapid technological advancements are having dramatic effects on the ways we communicate and conduct business as well as in our personal lives. Hence universities play a major role in increasing students' understanding of the world around them. Recruiting and developing global employees is a priority for companies competing in today's international marketplace. Mergers, alliance structures, and joint ventures across national boundaries have created the demand for multinational teams of employees and managers capable of working with corporations and executives from different countries and cultures. The fast pace of change in international business requires that university graduates have relevant education and training in preparation for the increasingly competitive local and global marketplace.

To be an 'excellent university' is a decent and honourable thing, but no 'excellent' university these days can feel entirely comfortable, since universities are not now judged solely on their local or even national contribution, but their international standing. The competition to be ranked among the world's top universities is increasing, with much jostling for position on international league tables. As international competition for students and academics increases, this question of being world class is very much on the front burner for university leaders. Many people talk about 'world class' universities, but what the term means is often left hovering in the air, undefined. Based on the literature survey, four factors are found fundamental to attain a world class university status (Nanus,1992):

First, it must show a commitment to breadth and excellence in all fields of human inquiry, not simply in a particular niche. Uniform excellence across all fields is an ideal that no university achieves in practice, but it is a fine ambition. One senses that universal, high ambition in great universities, coupled with real excellence in most fields, most of the time.

Second, world class universities engage in cutting-edge research whilst at the same time teaching the next generation, their students. Teaching and research are intrinsically bound together, with top researchers inspiring and mentoring their students. In turn, students themselves inspire and challenge their teachers. Much of the talk about world class universities centres around the production of exciting discoveries and universities' contribution to the economy and to human enrichment through the development of cultural knowledge. But every bit as important as these is the role of universities as educators. World class universities produce students who will go on to be leaders in all walks of life.

Third, great universities must allow their researchers the freedom to experiment, succeed, and sometimes fail. They must be able to make grand mistakes as well as grand discoveries. It is often through making those mistakes that the grand discoveries are made. This implies a degree of inefficiency, but it is a necessary inefficiency and a corollary of greatness. A university operating with a completely utilitarian mindset will forego the opportunities that a more open-ended system allows.

Fourth, world-class universities have permeable boundaries. This means encouraging interdisciplinary research and teaching; it means working with the private sector, for example, fostering and encouraging partnerships with industry; and it means encouraging international collaboration. World class universities look outward, and think beyond conventional boundaries today, we educate students more and more of whom will go on to live and work in a range of cultures. We must equip them for this life, partly by what we teach them, partly by what other experiences we offer them, who they meet as students and the composition of the study body.

Excellent universities play a central role in addressing the challenges of the 21st Century. They are crucial for the development of knowledge-based economies and for thriving civil societies. Their roles in leadership training and in educating growing proportions of the population in the skills needed for complex, modern societies are essential. They provide research and analysis for addressing problems and opportunities in both the private and public sectors. In the cross currents of globalization, they are one of the most important points of contact between the national and the international environments. Their global networks establish a platform for cooperation among nations and their citizens. The existence of viable institutions of higher education is a requirement of any modern democratic society.

Yet, higher education faces significant challenges throughout the world. Enrollment growth has created gigantic institutions unable to serve individual students well and has led to bureaucratically complex academic systems. This expansion, plus a changing view of the role of higher education, has led to financial problems everywhere. Research, always an important role of higher education, continually grows more expensive. Such trends as the rapidly growing number of private institutions of higher education and the interlinking of academic institutions and systems across borders influence the development of higher education. Understanding these major issues and finding ways to effectively address them in different national settings require cross cultural analysis and international attention.

Therefore, to become an excellent university a HEI must understand the context of change if they are to develop constructive ways for contemporary institutions to cope with the realities of the 21st century. The collaborative work of scholars in both industrialized nations and in developing countries that focuses on common problems is a promising approach precisely because higher education institutions are by their nature international and links among academic institutions worldwide are essential.

Seymour (1997) described higher education institutions as adaptive organisations that are "... survival driven, reactive in nature" (p. 7). Historically they have been resistant to change and take comfort in the ways things have always been. Seymour suggested that adaptive organisations function successfully as long as the environment was stable. When the environment becomes dynamic, "... status-quo thinking remains predominant to the point of ignoring or minimizing serious questions or concerns" (p. 7). Thus, he suggested, was the situation higher education found itself in the 1980s and 1990s.

Seymour (1997) suggested the emergent organisational learning paradigm answered the challenges to the adaptive organisation and aligned with quality principles and practice. He advocates, excellent organisation are learning organisation that has change embedded in its culture and is anticipatory not reactive. It focuses on clear goals, key processes to achieving better results, management by fact, and "... cycles of planning, execution, and evaluation" (p. 7).

Basic educational programme and courses have become commodities worldwide. More specifically, developing countries have a competitive advantage in low-cost manufacturing and services, with excellent staff available at one-fifth of the cost of a developed country staff at the same level. To be competitive, universities must provide high value by being immediate, innovative, integrative, conceptual and multidisciplinary. Higher education programme require creative, flexible and interactive components to meet the continuously changing demands of global corporations. To remain viable, programme must meet the expectations of participants and employers in designing learning transferable to tomorrow's highly competitive international business environments.

Figure 14: The Academic Excellence Model

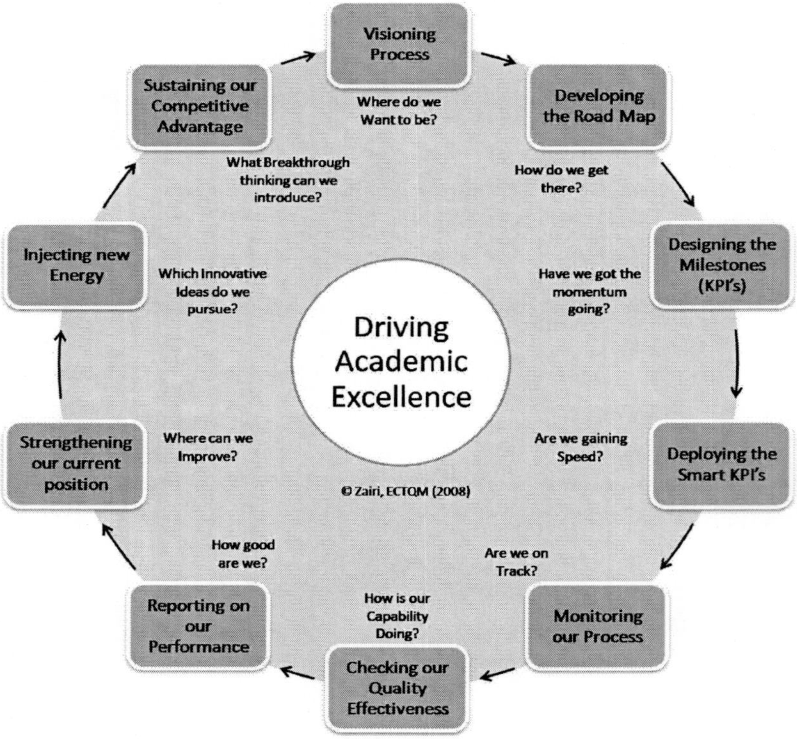

The Academic Excellence Model below is built on the dedicated, creative and synergistic efforts of different stakeholders in all different activities working in mutually supportive roles. A major realigning of activities into an integrative rather than centralised management and control structure reinforces these supportive behaviours. The model suggests a step by step approach for designing organisational structure and direction of leadership within the university that will motivate individual units to learn collectively and collaboratively to support and integrate different components of the institute to provide a truly unique and excellent international business education programme.

Visioning Process

"Leaders establish the vision for the future and set the strategy for getting there; they cause change. They motivate and inspire others to go in the right direction and they, along with everyone else, sacrifice to get there. ~ share this Vision saying

John Kotter

"Vision without action is merely a dream. Action without vision just passes the time. Vision with action can change the world. ~ share this Vision saying"

Joel A. Barker

Vision is a simple statement or understanding of what the firm will be in the future. This vision is forward looking and identifies the desired long-term status. Hence, Nanus (1992) define vision as , '...A vision articulates a view of a realistic, credible, attractive future for the organisation, a condition that is better in some important ways than what now exists. While discussion about vision, it is critical to understand the difference between vision, mission and purpose of an organisation. Mission is a declaration of what a firm is and stands for – reflecting its values and purpose. The mission statement identifies core concepts, e.g. purpose, values and beliefs, standards of behaviour, or corporate-level aims. These core values can provide the guides for effective decision making within the organisation Vision and mission reinforce and support strategy; conversely, strategy provides a coherent plan for realizing the vision and mission. Top executives provide the context for strategy formulation and implementation through modelling the vision and mission. Vision and mission statements provide direction but not strategies in and of themselves. They convey organisational identity and purpose to stakeholders. Vision and mission are powerful tools, but they must be realized through carefully crafted and executed strategy. Vision and mission therefore reinforce and support strategy; conversely, strategy provides a coherent plan for realizing vision and mission. While, purpose explains the long-term objectives of the organisation.

Effective leaders communicate the values of the organisation to their employees by translating the vision and mission into day-to-day activities. To do this effectively, leaders talk with customers, identify the organisation's critical success factors, and share this information about the things the organisation absolutely must do well in order to attract and retain customers. Creating alignment is essentially policy deployment, the step-by-step process of translating the organisation's vision and mission into strategies supported by goals and objectives that in turn become work activities for the employees. Effective leaders ensure that the organisation's vision, mission and strategies, goals and daily activities remain focused on these critical factors so that they can achieve and sustain competitive advantage (see figure-2 below). They derive vision very carefully from a focused strategy which is anchored in specific goals and objectives. Without this focus, the organisation will not be as effective at creating and maintaining a customer focus.

Hence the reasons for developing vision are-

- competing for business and resources, most organisations will benefit from a vision that articulates where they wish to be
- stimulating development of mission and objectives
- exploring new strategic opportunities

- extrapolating the current picture unlikely to be sufficient for strategy development
- taking as a challenge for management

Figure 15: Relationship between vision and SCA
Adapted from Lynch ,2008

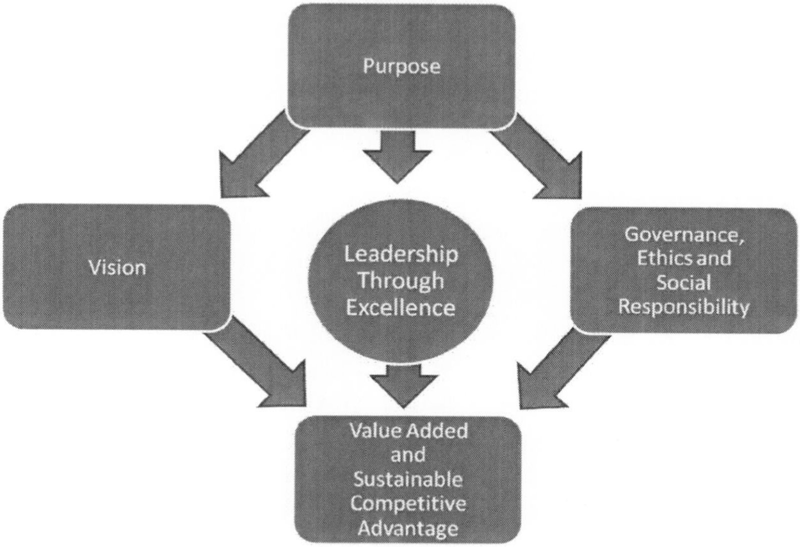

To emphasis on the impact of vision in an organisation Burmeister, (2003) quotes, "The three fundamental characteristics of leadership are commonly held to be; vision, inspiration, and followers, but these are also generally regarded as residing on the periphery of management". Yukl (1998) attempts to clarify the leader's role by explaining that developing a compelling vision is difficult at best, and does not lend itself well to the management process. He claims that managers typically employ verbose mission statements replete with quantitative objectives and detailed action steps outlining the types of activities to be performed, whereas leaders use a dynamic vision stating not only what is to be pursued but why it is worthwhile and exciting. However, this is not a compelling argument, as it implies that managers are unable to communicate why a course of action is worthwhile and exciting, and also that leaders are not concerned with setting measurable objectives and mapping out plans for their achievement.

Maccoby (2000) offers a useful perspective, by highlighting the difference between strategic leaders and operational leaders. He argues that the role of a strategic leader is to envision the company's future and to invest the resources necessary to create it, while the role of the operational leader is to implement the vision. This is perhaps a more useful categorisation, rather than attempting to draw definitive distinctions between the role of the leader and that of the manager in the context of organisational vision.

Vision attributes

Although many different attributes for a vision have been postulated, seven commonly shared attributes have been identified by Baum et al: brevity, clarity, future orientation, stability, challenge, abstractness and desirability or ability to inspire.(1998) Kantabutra (2003), in an attempt to develop a vision theory, asserted that the seven vision attributes interact to affect overall organisational performance initially through the attributes' effects on organisational members. A brief vision alone will not significantly affect overall performance because it may not be clear to employees as to what needs to be done (e.g. Conrad, 1990), or it may not challenge the employees to do their best (Collins and Porras, 1994). A clear vision alone will not create significant positive effects on employee satisfaction because it may be too long, making it difficult for a leader to communicate it frequently (e.g.Yukl, 1998). However, clarity has been identified as a significant vision attribute (Kantabutra, 2003).

A vision may be too concrete and not abstract, thus making it difficult for the leader to form an effective group (Messick and Mackie, 1989) to carry out the vision. Moreover, abstractness reflects stability in the vision because it implies no drastic change over time (e.g. Gabarro, 1987). An unstable vision can suggest to employees a lack of managerial integrity and commitment to the vision (Kouzes and Posner, 1987; Parikh and Neubauer, 1993), negatively affecting their satisfaction. A brief, clear, abstract, challenging, and stable vision will not draw employee commitment in working toward the vision unless it is inspiring or desirable (Morden, 1997). In addition, when a vision is not inspiring or desirable, it is difficult to develop a shared vision , critical to enhancing overall organisational performance. An inspiring vision that is only clear, brief, abstract, challenging, and stable will have no power to attract emotional commitment from followers because it does not offer a view of a better future (Nanus, 1992). Without a better future picture, employees cannot be drawn from where they presently are to work towards the vision (Senge, 1990).

Baum et al. (1998) investigated relationships between vision content and attributes, and organisational performance in new ventures. They found that vision attributes of brevity, clarity, future orientation, stability, challenge, abstractness, desirability or ability to inspire; and content of venture growth imagery impacted venture growth positively, both directly and indirectly, via vision communication. For example, in excellent organisations all the activities such as branding be founded on a clear vision; a single brand idea embodied in a trademark. For example, Mercedes Benz is synonymous to “the ultimate luxurious driving pleasure” while Apple, now known as Macintosh, is renowned as “innovation for the creative person” (Parikh and Neubauer, 1993).

Organisations spend a lot of time developing vision and mission statements. Do they work? Vision is the articulated powerful and preferred "future state" image of where the organisation wants to be. The visioning process is most effective when derived from inspiration rather than manipulation. Employees become hypocritical and cynical about these statements when they feel manipulated and left out, but committed to making it work when they are inspired by being part of the process. Successful visioning ignites continuous development and learning in organisations. Some of the benefits of a successful vision are listed below (Tichy and Devanna, 1986)-

<u>The Benefits</u>

- *Unites employees around a common dream*
- *Links the work of different departments*
- *Creates a framework for decision making*
- *Establishes the underpinning for planning*
- *Examines the present business state*
- *Identifies inconsistencies in business*

An organisation's start up energy and commitment is naturally high. Workplace morale and enthusiasm subside when the first blush of newness is over. Organisations must recognize these typical rhythms and be ready, from time to time, to actively focus on attitudinal and behavioural renewal. The visioning process is an ideal and central strategy for facilitating organisational renewal. Harvard Business professor Rosa Beth Moss Kanter mentioned that the very strategies and ideas that make an organisation successful today can cause it to fail tomorrow. Renewal is a natural part of the larger business cycle. Visioning can significantly influence the performance of the organisation if dedicated attention is paid to the arduous and lengthy process.

<u>Dedication must include (</u>Pace and Faules, 1989)

- Creating alignment between individual and organisational values, mission and vision
- Having staff from all levels and a diversity of departments (as well as representative stakeholders) actively participate and give feedback about the process
- Acknowledging that visioning is emotional and will evoke conflict

- Ensuring that an effective process is in place to facilitate conflict

<u>Questions to aid Visioning</u>:

- *How do we get to the preferred future state?*
- *How will we know we've arrived?*
- *What will help us? What will delay us?*
- *What strategies and programmes are needed?*
- *What's working (we should keep doing)?*
- *What's not working (we should stop doing)?*
- *How will we check our progress?*
- *How will we conduct the implementation?*
- *What are the implementation phases?*
- *What have we learned up until now?*

The need for Visioning Processes is intricately related to organisational change. Does change create the need for visioning or is it the other way around? This is probably a "chicken or egg" question. One thing we know for sure...change is going to be around forever! When individuals or groups embrace a vision they have more energy and spirit to get the job done. The vision becomes a credo by which to perform exceptionally. It can breathe new life into a tired workplace and help remind people why they do what they do (especially on those days when they feel they've "fallen off the wagon"). Below is shown some characteristics of excellent institutions that have a well defined and well communicated vision (Conger and Kanungo, 1987):

Characteristics of Successful Organisations with a clear vision

- Having an integrated system that is consistently achieving the right things. The organisation is managed as an integrated system that is achieving a level of performance that is pleasing all stakeholders. Having an inspiring mission and vision. The organisation has a clear, effective, and widely understood mission and vision.

- Demonstrating effective values and behaviours. Leadership, from top to bottom, demonstrates desired values and reinforces the right behaviours.
- Nurturing effective environments and relationships. Leaders create environments and facilitate relationships that enable effective and efficient work.
- This incorporates inclusiveness, openness, the right tools, empowerment, sharing of information, knowledge management, people development, and satisfaction at all levels.
- Effective communications are happening all the time.
- Activities are measured, and results are used for constant improvement, decision-making, and goal setting.

Many organisations have acknowledged the importance and power of supporting workplace spirituality. Visioning is part of that larger process. Participating in visioning and living the vision statement helps release the spirit of both the individual and the organisation.

Thus , HEI's should have a clear vision derived trough a systematic process with a clear focus on what they want to be and what they want to achieve in order to be an excellent university. This vision is also needs to be well communicated to all levels of staff, so that it is blended in all the activities of the university in order to achieve excellence. As aptly summed up by Newton, the usefulness of vision to achieve something phenomenal-

"If I have seen further, it is by standing upon the shoulders of giants."

Sir Isaac Newton

Developing the Roadmap

"Academic disciplines are subject to being overtaken by attacks of "knowingness"-- a state of mind and soul that prevents shudders of awe and makes one immune to enthusiasm"

Richard Rorty

"All you need is the plan, the road map, and the courage to press on to your destination."

Earl Nightingale

Development of roadmap for Excellence in academia is a guide to what can be improved, how and when to improve in all the functional areas of an institution. It is a bold, proactive move to create a long-term solution for the challenges and opportunities that lie ahead for HEIs. The strategic intent for the clear roadmap is to ensure that the individuals, departments, and all the relevant stakeholders within the institution work together to reach its common goals. To attain academic excellence, an institution needs to change on a fundamental cultural level, rather than on a school/ departmental/ divisional or a programme level. The transformation roadmap is the strategy and initial action plan for transforming a HEI to world Class University. The Drive to excellence will create a long-term solution for the challenges and opportunities that lie ahead of a HEI in the 21st century environment. Roadmap development is a cultural shift in how the whole institute views its business—the business of serving students, citizens, community, government, businesses and other stakeholders.

The goal of the development of roadmap is to meet the growing and changing needs of the organisation through:

Quality of Service: Both internally within organisation and externally with different stakeholders, the focus should be on quality of service delivered within a culture of continuous improvement.

Innovation in Service Delivery: Continue the tradition of the organisation, eg., creative, out-of-the-box thinking, making innovation ongoing , part of the fabric of bigger institute etc..

Reducing Cost: The goal should not simply to cut costs. The goal should be to take advantage of scale, technology, and innovation to manage budgets and resources for maximum effectiveness.

The development of roadmap can be divided into three phases

Figure 16: Steps for roadmap development
(Source: State of Minnesota's Drive to Excellence Report,2005)

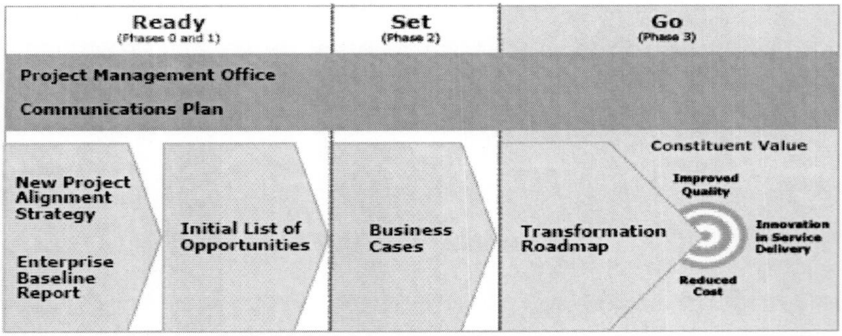

Ready: Data gathering—surveys, interviews, and idea generation to identify areas for improvement. The purpose of the Ready phase is to define the "as-is" state for both technology and business processes in the university. Key activities in this phase can be project initiation and organisation, including building blended teams of departments and lecturers, inventorying IT assets, surveying agencies about both technology and process, building an enterprise tool to store the data etc.

To get started, a university should identify areas of improvement, assess those opportunities, and then develop initial business cases for implementation of specific projects. This can be called as "The Transformation Roadmap," In this phase HEIs should-

1) Collect currently available baseline information on the relevant areas
2) Assess existing business functions and its environment

Set: Research into the ideas and data to identify valid opportunities for improvement. The opportunities can be organized into broad categories, eg., "Business Transformation Areas (BTA)," which then can be developed into initial business cases by the teams.

Once the BTAs are identified by the teams and approved by the Steering Committee, the focus should be shifted to validation and prioritization. Within each BTA, individual business cases should be developed, including a description, an explanation of expected benefits, a cost and resource estimate, and a risk assessment. In order to do that, they should-

3) Analyze improvement opportunities
4) Plan initial implementation

Go: This is the final stage where managers design the sequencing of the business cases, identifying interdependencies, and developing governance, policy, and structural recommendations. All of that information can then be formed into the final well designed roadmap.

Designing the Milestones (KPI's)

"KPIs are at the core of any performance management initiative and are fundamental to the alignment of business activity with enterprise goals and initiatives,"

David Hatch

KPIs are set of quantifiable measures that a company or industry uses to gauge or compare performance in terms of meeting their strategic and operational goals. KPIs vary between companies and industries, depending on their priorities or performance criteria. Also referred to as "key success indicators (KSI)". A company must establish its strategic and operational goals and then choose the KPIs which best reflect those goals. For example, if a software company's goal is to have the fastest growth in its industry, its main performance indicator may be the measure of revenue growth year-on-year. A company's KPIs will be stated in its annual report. Also, KPIs will often be industry-wide standards, like "same store sales", in the retail sector. Measuring your organisation's success depends on identifying and prioritising the metrics that really matter. Using the wrong metrics can give you an incomplete or irrelevant snapshot of your business. Worse still, the wrong key performance indicators (KPIs) can create false confidence about your company's direction.

There is unprecedented interest in performance indicators in education and, increasingly, in higher education. The reasons for this interest are multiple, but chief among them is that higher education has emerged as a priority public issue for governments at the state and national levels. Even if economic development is not part of the nomenclature associated with a state's higher education system, college and university education is increasingly "recognized as a strategic, human resource investment which should contribute to building a knowledgeable, creative, innovative and advanced labour force—capable of succeeding in global competition and generating economic growth". Interest in performance indicators, particularly as they relate to accountability in higher education, is often accompanied by a lack of understanding of what they are and how they can be used. While being a part of higher education's lexicon, they often articulate divergent views relating not only to their utility but also the rationale for such indicators.

Many view them as an intrusion on institutional autonomy and an external threat—used by the government in the allocation of resources. They are also seen by some as providing superficial information, lacking perspective and substance, and as dangerously misleading.

So, what are performance indicators? They are defined and used in many ways, as evidenced not only by a review of the literature but also by how they are being utilized and applied in a variety of higher education and policy environments. A basic definition is as follows: Performance indicators are data, usually quantitative in form, that provide a measure of some aspect of an individual's or organisation's performance against which changes in performance or the performance of others can be compared.80 Performance Indicators (PIs) are quantifiable measurements, agreed to beforehand, that reflect the critical success factors of an organisation. They will differ depending on the organisation.

For example:

- *A business may have as one of its Performance Indicators the percentage of its income that comes from return customers.*
- *A college or university may focus its Performance Indicators on graduation rates of its students.*
- *A Customer Service Department, in line with overall company Performance Indicators, may have as one of its PIs the percentage of customer calls answered in the first minute.*
- *Performance Indicators for a social service organisation might be number of clients assisted during the year.*
- *Whatever Performance Indicators are selected, they must reflect the organisation's and/or state's goals, be key to its success, and be quantifiable (measurable).*
- *Some examples of performance indicators for higher education include:*

- *Numbers of degrees awarded,*
- *Average time to completion of degrees,*
- *Graduates' performance on external and licensure exams,*
- *Faculty success in attracting competitive research grants, and*
- *Faculty reputations with peers.*

Increasingly, higher education performance indicators also include measures like:

- *the employability of graduates,*
- *student loan default rates,*
- *student and public satisfaction as measured by surveys,*
- *cost per student or programme, and*
- *revenue generated from research licenses and patents.*

As Borden and Bottrill point out, “the term performance indicators may seem straightforward, but even a brief examination of the literature reveals that many shades of meaning have been attached to this concept.”81 But while there may be some differences in categorization and the language of performance indicators utilized by higher education, there is also a surprising degree of similarity. While the following is not intended to be comprehensive, it does provide an outline of the ten indicators that are most often considered in reports and analysis of the issue.

- **Participation/Access**. The participation/access indicator is meant to provide a measure of the total number of students served during a reporting period—hence an emphasis on head counts and registrations. In the case of head counts, this is a straight count of bodies served. In the case of registrations, this is a count of students served within programme areas. Full-time Equivalents (FTEs) present a different dilemma. There are a number of quite different formulas for calculating full-time equivalents. In general, though, all the formulations attempt to represent total instructional load (including part-time with full-time students) in terms of the load represented by a full-time

- **Completion/Retention**. Completion/retention is an indicator that can be potentially damaging to institutions that are actively engaged with learners who are not residential or full-time. Despite all reasonable explanations concerning students' expectations, personal circumstances, and the invaluable services rendered to such students, there is a strong sociopolitical view that degree-granting institutions are effective and efficient only to the extent that they graduate students at the degree level in some optimal period of time.
- **Transfer Student Performance**. The transfer student performance indicator pertains to how well institutions prepare students to transfer to programmes at the universities. Usually, this implies that such students originate from formally designated transfer programmes at the colleges and that the students move immediately from college to university.
- **Financial Indicators**. Financial indicators provide the state and its institutions of higher education with a tool for examining their financial position relative to benchmarks or baseline data, national averages, other comparable institutions and from one financial year to the next. As with any performance indicators, it is important that, for any organisation or institution, no single figure is considered in isolation from any others. It is more often a particular combination of indicators viewed together that will

indicate those financial areas where the organisation may have strengths or Weaknesses.

- **Space Utilization**. The space utilization indicator is meant to be a measure of how effectively conventional institutions use their costly physical plants. Often the absence of this type of substantial overhead cost is used as an argument that society must look more toward distance education as a cost-effective way of addressing the ever-growing demand for higher education.
- **Student Satisfaction**. Data for student satisfaction are typically collected by survey methodology. The survey is usually (but not necessarily) conducted on graduating students.
- **Employment Indicator**. The employment indicator is also determined through surveys. In the case of on-campus students, the issue generally is whether they have found employment after graduating, whether the employment they find is related to their university work, and how well their university education serves them in the world of work.
- **Employer Satisfaction**. Employer satisfaction as an indicator reflects a focus directed at the colleges and universities. Typically it reflects formal and informal feedback from employers of alumni and students.
- **Research Indicators**. Research indicators have not proven to be an issue at this point in time within some states, yet it is an important PI when considered within the context of transparency and information dissemination. This is particularly pertinent when there is a major state commitment to research. For institutions that have a lesser research mandate but have the usual teaching and service roles, the question often arises as to how they should be measured. Because such institutions—often referred to as regional or comprehensive institutions of higher education—are primarily undergraduate teaching institutions with limited programmes and small faculty complements, expectations regarding research intensity must necessarily be scaled down appropriately. How this is decided

and what benchmarks are reasonable are important, but as yet unresolved, questions. It should be understood, however, that at regional or comprehensive colleges and universities having "research" or "scholarship" as part of their mission statement, there is a commitment to research and development that advances the state of understanding and practice within their programmes of study as well as in the advancement of application in their fields of expertise. It can be argued that their specialized contributions should count as a measure of their institutional performance.

- **Community Service and Economic Impact**. Community service has traditionally been considered part of the mandate of higher education. However, describing community service, let alone measuring it, has proven to be difficult in practice. The compromise in some states has been to determine and report the economic impact of an institution or system on its local community or state level. The methodology is based on determining the amount of local expenditures that can be attributed to higher education. The greatest portion of this expenditure is derived from the operating revenues of the university.

Deploying the Smart KPIs

"A university anywhere can aim no higher than to be as British as possible for the sake of the undergraduates, as German as possible for the sake of the public at large-- and as confused as possible for the preservation of the whole uneasy balance"

Clark Kerr

"A university floats on paper and rewards the creation of more words on paper"

Robin W. Winks

Internationally, higher education systems have come under increasing public and governmental scrutiny with respect to what they do, how well they do it, and at what cost. In some instances, a formalized accountability exercise has been implemented, usually based on the notion of "performance indicators." In some cases, where HEIs are in the public sector, attempts have been made to formulate a theoretical basis from which to derive performance indicators. For example, in the UK performance indicators are defined operationally and are arrived at through some political process involving negotiations between government agencies and higher education. As a result, sets of performance measures may differ somewhat from country to country as well as from institution to institution. In general, though, performance indicators are developed for application to conventional campus-based institutions.

Conversely, in the United States, higher education is being pressed for greater accountability and improved attention to student learning or student outcomes and quality. Legislators in many states have moved towards "performance incentive funding," as appropriations are based, at least in part, on whether universities and colleges are accomplishing stated goals. Key Performance Indicators (KPIs) are intended to help an organisation—including a state and its higher education enterprise—define and measure progress toward a set of actual or perceived organisational goals. Once an organisation has analyzed its vision, mission, defined its goals, and identified all its stakeholders, it needs a way to measure progress toward those goals. Performance Indicators are those measurements. A public concerned with the balance between costs and benefits of higher education demands more information on institutional operations and outcomes. In particular, the various stakeholders are calling for a demonstration of the extent to which higher education is meeting state and institutional goals and objectives. A plethora of "useful" measures and other efforts have flooded the literature of higher education. Ultimately, it is the responsibility of each country and its colleges and universities to define and describe their own goals, to place them in the context of peer group comparisons, and to demonstrate to the public the position it holds in higher education.

While in the international context the concepts of accountability and quality assessment higher education constitute the primary focus, in most discussions regarding performance indicators in general, the primary focus of attention has been cost efficiency and undergraduate education, with less attention on graduate education and research. There is an apparent desire in some quarters for graduate education to be more responsive to a free-market economy, for the production of Ph.D.'s in certain subject areas to be somehow streamlined, and for private/public partnerships to be encouraged.

How performance indicators are used

A useful (albeit less than definitive) characterization of performance indicators is according to their primary use. For example, Kaufman argues that performance indicators should be linked to specific processes or activities because such a link is essential to determine whether a process or method is performed correctly. The relevance of this view to conventional classroom instruction is arguable—as evidenced by the prolonged debate over how to improve teaching and reengineer university curricula.

An alternative view of performance indicators is to use them to guide institutional resource allocation and institutional planning. Typically, performance indicators at this level condense detailed operational data into simpler, summative measures that derive much value-added information because of their more direct relationship to a specific organisational context. A third view of performance indicators is their role in addressing issues of political accountability and funding priorities. Dochy, Segers, and Wijnen characterize performance indicators in this context as a "public sector surrogate for the information generated elsewhere by the market system". Inherent in this concept of performance indicators as accountability measures is a sense of expectation of what educational institutions are supposed to do, how they do it, and how efficiently and effectively they function. However, institutions providing collegiate education have consistently had to contend with ill-defined, often inconsistent expectations that vary according to the audience to be addressed. Even within the walls of the academy, there is considerable ambiguity about the role of universities in our modern world. This state of affairs is complicated because of the various stakeholders served by higher education (with their differing expectations) and the fact that most colleges and universities are funded to varying degrees with public money (which implies another complicated set of expectations).

Without a national policy framework within which the indicators are to be collected and used, their utility is questionable and they are usually simplistic and convenient measures that may bear no relationship to the performance of colleges and universities, particularly as they may relate to individual expectations and/or stated goals. Clearly it is important that the performance indicators used should be subject to informed interpretation and judgment. Even to the extent that expectations can be clarified and agreed on, there is still the considerable challenge of formulating an appropriate measurement and obtaining the requisite data. In many instances, some sub-optimal or proxy measure must suffice. Often there is just plain disagreement about what expectations are reasonable and how best to measure any given expectation. When governments, policy-making bodies, the institutions themselves, and sometimes miscellaneous other agencies are involved, formulating performance indicators and obtaining measures for them becomes a political process. As a result, there are not necessarily absolutes with regard to the formulation and measurement of performance indicators in the public accountability context. That said, at least so far as conventional universities are concerned, there does seem to be a surprising commonality in practice.

This session's knowledge work addresses only performance indicators for two reasons. One is that each level of interest—i.e., national, regional, system, or institutional, as described here—requires its own detailed treatment of performance indicators because of their context-dependent nature and the fact that they can vary greatly according to the general purpose they are meant to serve. The other reason is that institutions of higher education have had to respond to pressures of "political accountability and funding priorities," and the process whereby the indicators can be arrived at and the specific form they have taken have both been shaped by these pressures. As we see from an examination of the KPIs in the HEIs of UK, the pressures of "political accountability and funding priorities" have led to an emphasis on measuring input and—to a lesser degree—outcome, not process.

Performance indicators and related measures are only a necessary first stage in assessing institutional performance. There remains the issue of deciding what meaning and implications should be attached to the numerical values. This takes the discussion into the realm of "benchmarking" (in the sense of performance standards). Benchmarking presents generic problems for higher education: with what do HEIs compare a given measure and how much of a difference is significant?

Reason for interest in performance indicators

Interest in performance indicators for higher education has been growing, not only in the United Kingdom but also in many other countries. This interest has been driven by a number of pressures, such as:

- *to add to the information that prospective local and international students, their parents, school counsellors, and others can use in guiding their choice of institution for enrolment*

- *to compare characteristics and performance across institutions in order to inform future developments in the delivery of education services;*
- *to provide greater transparency in the way the higher education sector operates;*
- *to illustrate the diversity of higher education institutions;*
- *to contribute to public accountability of funds; and*
- *to assist the future development of higher education policies.*

Ideally, the indicators would share the virtues below. It is highly unlikely, however, that individual indicators will meet each of these requirements, and those involved in the development of a state's accountability system will need to consider where compromises are necessary-

- *The indicators should be sufficiently provocative and relevant to encourage*
- *The commitment of resources to monitoring and action. They should therefore*
- *Correspond with widely shared state and institutional values and priorities.*
- *They should be capable of definition that is meaningful across state and*
- *System differences, without excessive caveats, and must be applicable in*
- *Mission-differentiated systems or institutions.*
- *They should measure state-level qualities rather than institutional-level qualities; however, they should be sufficiently relevant at the institutional level as well.*
- *They should be easy for all constituencies to interpret.*
- *They should be detailed enough to detect small developments over time.*

They also must be stable over time to allow continuity of measurement. The above reflect lessons drawn from international and national experiences in order to improve quantitative reporting on the performance of higher education.

Criteria for performance indicators

In practice it can be difficult to devise a performance indicator that fulfils all of these. Many PIs are likely to score less well in one or two criteria. Less-than-perfect indicators can, however, represent a valid starting place if refinements are carried out when more insight into the area is gained. What is crucial, however, is that the indicator is developed in the context of clearly identified users and use, and is thus fit for the purpose. There are a number of general characteristics of performance indicators that can help to ensure that proposed indicators will be useful and effective (Ittner and Larcker, 1998),.

- **Cost Effective** - Another important criterion is to balance the cost of collecting information with its usefulness. Where possible, an indicator should be based on information already available and linked to existing data collection activities. Managers are likely to have already assessed the costs and benefits of using the PIs for managing their services, so such indicators should inherently be cost effective. When a new indicator is needed, it should be designed to minimize the burden of assembling the information on an organisation and its employees. This will almost inevitably involve some degree of trade-off between the costs of collection and analysis of information, and the ideal PI. Obsolete indicators should be discarded to keep the costs of data collection to a minimum.
- **Clearly Defined** - A PI should have a clear and intelligible definition in order to ensure consistent collection and fair comparison. Vague descriptions can lead to misinterpretation and confusion. Care should be taken to avoid making the definition too complex, so that people

have difficulty in collecting the information. Definitions that are too restrictive or too broad may also create problems. Overly narrow definitions may make it difficult for some of the data providers to deliver the information, while overly broad definitions could allow for a number of different ways of counting what is being measured, thus making comparison difficult. Some of the data used to calculate a PI might already be defined and collected by other agencies. Using an existing definition can be helpful in ensuring consistency. Care should also be taken to avoid a definition that is close to, but different from, an existing definition, which could duplicate the effort involved in data collection and lead to confusion.

- **Timely -** The KPI should be based on data that are available within a reasonable time-scale. This timescale will depend on the use made of the data. Some data are collected on a weekly or even daily basis, as they are needed in the operational management of the service, whereas others are available once a year for more strategic and long-term purposes. Organisations need to be aware of the risk of basing decisions on data that are out of date and no longer accurate.
- **Unambiguous -** It should be clear whether an increase in an indicator value represents an improvement or deterioration in service. A change in an indicator should be clearly and unambiguously interpretable, and indicators should be designed and measured so that improvement in the indicator is possible only through an improvement in the service. Setting a target can often be helpful in reducing ambiguity.
- **Relevant -** Indicators should be relevant to the organisation; for example, performance indicators should relate to the strategic goals and objectives of the organisation or of a specific service area. Such an approach will also limit the risk of setting up PIs just because data are available, rather

than to meet a need in the organisation. Indicators also should ideally be relevant to the people providing the data. The danger is that if an indicator is not seen as relevant, they will not bother to collect the information accurately. Relevance to the user of the KPI is also important, but it may not be possible for a single indicator to be relevant to all users due to the differences in perspectives and interests. One possibility is to conduct a stakeholder analysis and accordingly target the performance information on the various groups and their respective needs.

- **Easy to Understand and Use** - It is important that indicators are described in terms that the user of the information will understand, even if the definition itself has to use technical terminology. Indicators focused on the public should avoid management jargon or abstract concepts, for example using "full-time equivalent staff numbers" in a comparison where "staff numbers" would be more understandable.
- **Allowing for innovation** - The definition of an indicator ought not to deter organisations from developing innovative processes or coming up with alternative methods, systems, or procedures to improve service delivery. KPIs should ideally be constructed to allow and encourage such innovation to take place. Indicators that focus on outcome and user satisfaction are more likely to do this than indicators that are tied into existing processes.
- **Comparable** - Indicators should ideally be comparable on a consistent basis both between organisations and over time. The first ideal can be difficult to achieve due to differences in data standards, collection methods etc., and will depend on well-thought-out, agreed-upon definitions. The second ideal, comparison over time, is often easier to achieve, as many aspects of a service will not change, or will change only slowly. But in this case as well, the way data are measured and collected within an organisation may change

even if the service itself does not. An essential aspect of the comparability of performance indicators is the inclusion of the context within which the comparison is taking place. External or internal circumstances can differ to such a degree that comparison is invalid. If indicators are not directly comparable, one possible solution could be to standardise data. For example, numerical ratios can be used to level out demographic differences between areas (for example, spending per person over). However, to create such ratios demands good and detailed information for the denominator. An alternative may be to disaggregate data, to separate the components that can be compared from those that would distort results. Decomposing data in this way may increase the number of indicators, but could be necessary to obtain usable comparative data.

- **Statistically valid** - Indicators should be statistically valid. Performance indicators based on a small number of cases are likely to show substantial annual fluctuations. In these instances, it should be considered whether a performance indicator is the right method for gauging performance development or whether a larger sample size is possible.
- **Verifiable** - The indicator also needs to be collected and calculated in a way that enables the information and data to be verified. The indicator should allow aggregation and desegregation of the data so recalculation can take place, and, if appropriate, a description should be available of the statistical techniques and sampling methods used. The indicator should be based on robust data collection systems, and it should be possible for managers to verify the accuracy of the information and the consistency of the methods used. This stresses the importance of good internal quality controls in different levels of the organisation. External reviews, for example in the form of external audits and inspections, should ideally complement these internal control processes. Evidence, preferably

documentary evidence, must be available for all indicators so that they can be verified. Documentary evidence can also add weight to a qualitative (yes/no) indicator for which there may be little other evidence.

- **Attributable** - Service managers should be able to influence the performance measured by the indicator (that is, it should either be totally within their control or at least open to significant influence). If this is not the case, the incentives for making an effort to improve performance will diminish, and the performance indicators may be regarded as unfair and discourage staff and managers. Crosscutting issues can present particular problems, where managers must accept joint responsibility for performance.
- **Responsive** - A performance indicator should be responsive to change. An indicator where changes in performance are likely to be too small to register will be of limited use. This can be the case particularly with qualitative (yes/no) indicators, as progress towards achieving a "yes" is not captured. This problem can sometimes be overcome by using a number of "yes/no" indicators together to give a picture of progress, or by converting a yes/no indicator to a numerical one by asking what proportion of the processes meet the "yes" criterion. Able to avoid perverse incentives. When constructing a performance indicator, it is important to consider what behaviour an indicator ought to encourage. Indicators that might encourage counter-productive activity should be avoided if possible. Examples are PIs that encourage staff or managers to shift problems over to other organisations or areas not being measured or to allocate disproportionate resources to activities because they are being measured. KPIs should not be open to easy manipulation, and use of several counterbalancing indicators will sometimes be necessary to discourage such behaviour.

In summary, Key Performance Indicators can provide a measure of the common features of higher education institutions as well as their diversity. They also can reveal a number of aspects of the student experience at higher education institutions and assess the performance of institutions in several areas that are relevant to the core purposes of higher education institutions. Other indicators, particularly those related to the financial performance of institutions, attempt to gauge the resources available to them. HEIs that intend to attain academic excellence should set clearly defined and comparable KPIs, so that they can check against their performance in order to improve their status in all different categories.

Monitoring Process:

"Figures are only useful if we know how to use them; they are no use on their own"?

Deming

In order for performance measurement to contribute effectively to the management of organisations it is necessary to provide feedback loops from measures to actions (Kaplan and Norton, 1992). This leads to the recognition that there are different types of performance measure, especially for long term business improvement initiatives. The need for managers to undertake improvement programme such as total quality management, six sigma, or lean production is now well established. These programmes promise outputs like better product quality and low production costs. However, the programme is complex and the process for achieving the likely outputs involves many variables. Since output measures can be too highly aggregated to be actionable (Ittner and Larcker, 1998), it is important to identify the in-process measures that, if delivered, will ensure that the output is delivered. Very simply, what gets measured gets done. Effective organisations recognize that if they cannot measure, they cannot manage. They know that if they do not have sufficient information about a process, product, or service, they cannot control it. And if a process cannot be controlled, the organisation is at the mercy of chance. So, effective organisations choose their measures wisely and then use the information they provide to make decisions.

Why is an effective performance measurement system necessary?
One of the chief goals of a performance measurement system is to provide leaders with a multi-dimensional and qualitative view of their organisation. A measurement system is a critical element in the strategic planning process because it allows an organisation to measure progress toward goals and objectives. Performance measures are decision tools that enable leaders to link their strategy with day-to-day operations. Effective organisations measure the performance of areas that the organisation values the most. Measurement systems allow effective organisations to (Neely, 1998):

- Determine that a gap exists between desired and actual performance.
- Determine the root cause of the gap.
- Determine the necessary corrective action to eliminate root cause of the gap.
- Determine whether or not the corrective actions eliminated the root cause and closed the gap between the actual and desired performance.

Quality Assurance Mechanisms in Transnational Education

Most countries are not able to monitor the quality of educational offerings exported to other institutions across their borders (Lenn, 1998). It was recorded that 51% of transnational education programme offered by Australian universities did not have any adequate quality monitoring mechanisms (David, Olson, and Bohm, 2000). Governments in countries such as Israel and India had criticized British universities for granting franchises to low-quality education providers in developing countries (Lenn, 1998). Whenever a reputable institution delivers education outside its own national borders, the quality of its programme has to be maintained. It is therefore necessary to establish quality assurance mechanisms in order to maintain a high standard of delivery of transnational programme by both the providing and receiving countries.

Lee (1997) also discussed the different models of linkages and highlighted the characteristics of active and passive linkages. She generally described the active roles played by the active partner which included on-site supervision to ensure quality and sufficient provision of resources by colleges. Altbach and Philip (1999) remarked that in some twinning arrangements, local academic staff members were used to deliver and read materials provided by the overseas universities. Passive partners allow college lecturers to set and mark assignments and examination scripts (Lee, 1997c). There was little direct supervision or involvement by faculty from the "home" university and the whole operation was similar to McDonald's approach of franchising the "brand name" to a franchisee (Altbach and Philip, 1999). Since there is an existence of both active and passive linkages, definitely there would be variation in quality assurance mechanisms of transnational programme. So far, only three tertiary institutions, the British Open University, Saint-Louis University (St. Louis, Missouri), and Monash University (Australia) had undergone a process of quality assurance outside their own national contexts (Lenn, 1998). Many transnational providers are not subjected to any internal quality assurance mechanisms on external quality assurance regimes as they do not belong to any official higher education system of any particular country (ESIB, 2003). The European Student Handbook onTransnational Education (2003) had raised a number of quality assurance questions which needed to be solved to ensure a good delivery of transnational education. World class institutes are above these complexities. Before making any alliance with an international university, they make sure the delivery, learning outcomes, student competencies, academic qualifications, assessments and other KPIs are set at the same level of the home country institute.

Regulation and Quality Assurance Mechanisms Adopted by Exporting Countries

Complaints from the importing countries on quality problems had driven the British to establish guidelines for greater scrutiny of transnational education (Lenn, 1998). The Higher Education Quality Council of the United Kingdom (HEQC---now incorporated into the new Quality Assurance Agency), which audited the quality assurance policies and practices of British universities and colleges, also undertook a separate audit on the collaborative institutions of United Kingdom institutions located in the United Kingdom and overseas (Lenn, 1998). After visiting 20 overseas partners of United Kingdom institutions in Greece, Hong Kong, Malaysia, Singapore, and Spain, HEQC published a Code of Practice for Overseas Collaborative Provision in Higher Education (HEQC, 1996). In the United States, the regional institutional accrediting bodies adopted a "Principles of Good Practice in Overseas International Education Programmes for Non-US Nationals" to scrutinize the higher education established in overseas (Lenn, 1988). The transnational accrediting activity is becoming more structured with the accreditor directly accrediting an American programme when it travels abroad. Nonetheless, the HEIs those are aspired to attain or sustain world class status, should not be restricting themselves according to the criteria set by accrediting agencies. They should have their preset KPIs with strict guidelines so that they make sure they maintain similar if not identical programme across the globe. Otherwise, they are bound to lose credibility in the long run if they intend to gain short term by compromising the standard.

Regulation and Quality Assurance Mechanisms Adopted by Importing Countries

In the majority of the importing countries of HEIs, very few established comprehensive quality assurance practices related to transnational education are developed and implemented in receiving countries. In Hong Kong, an ordinance called Non-local Higher and Professional Education Ordinance, which required transnational providers to register the courses they offered in Hong Kong, came into force in December 1997 (French, 1999). The main purpose of having the registration process is to ensure that standards of transnational courses delivered in Hong Kong are maintained at levels comparable with courses conducted in the countries where overseas institutions are situated (French, 1999). Similarly, most of the countries, such as central and eastern European countries have also adopted very strict measures towards the operation of transnational education. Transnational providers are required to submit an application when establishing higher institutions in Slovak Republic. In a case where the application is rejected, the founder is required to dissolve the branch campus of the foreign university (Hrabinska, 2000).

For example, in Malaysia, the development of transnational education is carefully steered and monitored by the government to meet the national education needs and economic development needs. To have a better management and monitoring of the education system, the government had tabled 5 legislations to position Malaysia as a regional higher education hub. Out of the 5 legislations, 3 legislations have affected the establishment, management and development of private colleges, while the other two are related to universities and university colleges2 and national higher education fund. One of the legislations is the National Council on Higher Education Bill which was tabled in 1996 to plan, formulate, and determine policies and strategies for the development of both public and private higher institutions in Malaysia (Malaysia 1996). The setting up of this council has been able to coordinate and oversee both the public and private higher institutions. The government would like the private colleges to complement and supplement the efforts of the public universities by setting up colleges in the less developed regions of the country and providing more advanced technical education and facilities (Lee, 1997). Hence the exporting institutions need to maintain a different set of KPIs in order to operate in the international market. Again, The world class universities check those very carefully and develop their strategy in such a way that they do not have to compromise the standard of the programme.

Hence, world class universities should develop a strategy to take advantage of adopting an approach which is clear in understanding the purpose of measures and the removal of measures that do not contribute to required outputs. If input or process measures are seen that are not linked to, and therefore do not contribute to, an output then clearly their use is redundant, and they should be removed. Conversely, measures of inputs and outputs, which are clearly related, and are cross checked by "process" measures, provide managers with the instrumentation necessary to pilot their operations professionally towards their desired destination.

Checking Quality Effectiveness

Studying current performance levels, trends over time and comparison data for the key measures and indicators allows an organisation to see what is working and what is not. Excellent universities design audits to appraise the activities, practices, records, or policies of the organisation in a well structured manner; they determine whether a company has the ability to meet or exceed a standard. Audits provide many benefits; including allowing the organisation to see what is really taking place. This insight can enable the organisation to take action before potential problems become serious issues. Information provided by the audit can point to where action is necessary in order to contain the problem. Audits enable organisations to see which processes, policies, procedures, and practices are effective and which are not.

What do excellent organisations audit?

A variety of circumstances can initiate an audit. Audit programmes may be part of meeting customer contract requirements or government regulations. Audits do not have to have an outside instigator; it is not unusual to see a company utilize internal auditing systems to verify its own performance to key metrics. Audits may also examine aspects of equipment, software, documentation, and procedures. Audits of systems such as material handling or accounts receivable can reveal poor practices that need to be improved. Supplier quality and record-keeping practices can also be checked. Internal and supplier audits allow a company the opportunity to verify conformance to specifications and procedures. Since audits identify opportunities for improvement, companies may perform a product or service integrity audit to verify that the process is performing in an optimal fashion (McBurnie and Pollock, 2000). Using audits to identify process problems reduces opportunities for nonconformities. Whatever the reason, audits provide companies with information concerning their performance, the performance of their product or service, and areas for improvement. Audits help organisations determine the answers to a variety of questions including (Raudsepp,1987),:

- *Have value-driven improvements been made?*
- *Have costs of quality been reduced?*
- *Have lead times been reduced?*
- *How do the measures of performance measure up?*
- *Is the company achieving its objectives?*
- *Are the correct procedures being followed?*
- *Are new and more efficient methods of performance documented and used where applicable?*
- *Are records being properly retained and used to solve production problems?*

- *Are preventive maintenance schedules being followed?*

What do excellent HEIs do with the information when an audit is completed?

Whether the audit is internal or external, the recommendations of the auditors are critical to the excellent universities seeking to improve. It is leadership's response to these results that matters. When discrepancies between the actual and desired performance are uncovered, it is up to leadership to examine the gap and create and implement a plan of action to deal with the gap. However, leaders of excellent universities follow very focused strategy to deal with any type of distinct deviations.

Typical auditing programmes of an excellent organisation include a planning phase, the actual audit, reports recommending improvement, and follow-up action plans.

Figure 17: PDCA Cycle

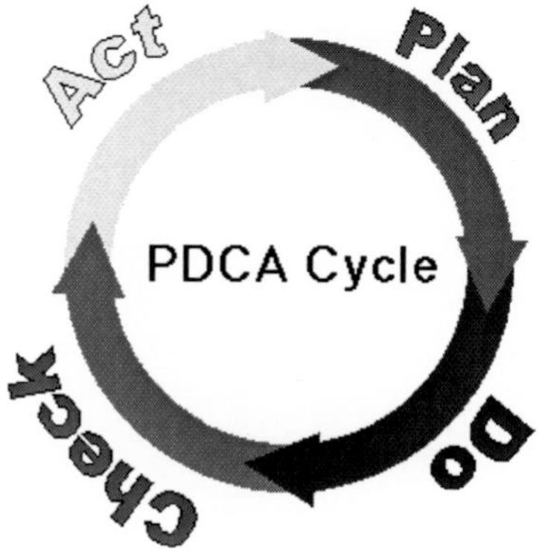

Source: Bold from Deming p.132, Plain from BPC p.52

1. Plan: To begin, those planning the audit need to identify its purpose or objective. A statement of purpose clarifies the focus of the audit. Following this, planners will need to identify the who, what, where, when, why, and how related to the audit.

- *-Who is to be audited?*

- *-Who is to perform the audit?*
- *-What does this audit how to accomplish?*
- *-What are the performance measures?*
- *-Where the audit will be conducted?*
- *-When will the audit be conducted?*
- *-Why is the audit being conducted?*
- *-Is the audit to judge conformance to standards?*
- *-What are the critical standards?*
- *-How will the audit be conducted?*

Those about to be audited should be informed by an individual in a position of authority. Clear statements of the reasons behind the audit (why), the performance measures (what), and the procedures (how) should be given to those being audited.

2. *Do*: Using the information clarified in the planning phase, the audit is conducted. Often an introductory meeting is held by the participants to discuss the scope, objectives, schedule, and paperwork considerations. After the opening meeting, examiners begin the process of reviewing the process, product, or system under study. Auditors may require access to information concerning quality systems, equipment operation procedures, preventive maintenance records, inspection histories, or planning documents. Auditors may conduct interviews with those involved in the process of providing a product or service. Any and all information related to the area under study is critical for the success of the audit. During the review process, auditors document their findings. These findings are presented in a general summary at a closing meeting of the participants. Within a short period of time, perhaps 10 to 20 days, the auditors will prepare a written report that documents their findings, conclusions, and recommendations.

3. *Check/Study*: Audits provide information about the participant's strengths, weaknesses, and areas for improvement. Upon receipt, the auditor's report is read by the participants in the audit. During this phase of the audit cycle, they respond to the report and develop an action plan based on the recommendations of the auditors. This action plan should specify the actions, assign responsibilities, and provide a time frame required to deal with the issues raised by the audit.

4. *Act*: Once adopted, the action plan becomes the focus of the improvement activities related to the audited area. Auditors and company administrators should follow up at predetermined intervals to evaluate the status of the continuous improvement action plan. This ensures that the recommendations and conclusions reached by the auditors, and supported by an action plan, assist the company in reaching its continuous improvement goals.

In short, leaders of excellent organisation take the recommendations of the auditors seriously knowing that improvements are critical to the organisation's future success. Where the audit has revealed discrepancies between the actual and desired performance, leadership will want to examine the gap and determine and implement a plan of action to deal with the gap. This systematic auditing reveals where improvements can be made. Creating responses to these needs for improvement will make the organisation much stronger for the future. Leaders of excellent universities recognize that in the short term, they will be incurring many costs to set the current situation right, but long term profits and competitiveness will improve. As Sallis (2002) suggested that the use of self-assessment is the first diagnostic step toward achieving excellence. Using a self-assessment model allows an organisation to discover and document its strengths and weakness and to decide how best to make improvements. It is from this point that the organisation can develop action plans for continuing development. Hence universities aspiring to be world class need to remember that:

Quality principles and practices can be applied to any system…. But their real value accrues only when they are applied within an environment that is actively building a methodology for learning—a goal, a process, a measure, and a cycle for planning, executing, and evaluation. Only within that paradigm can our colleges and universities begin the work of charting their own futures.

Seymour

Reporting On Performance

"My strong point, if I have a strong point, is performance. I always do more than I say. I always produce more than I promise."

Richard Milhouse Nixon

Leaders use measures of performance to ensure alignment between the organisation's mission, strategy, values, and behaviour. Measures of performance enable effective organisations to define the meaning of success numerically. Effective performance measurement systems are used for understanding, aligning, and improving performance at all levels and in all parts of the organisation. In order to know how they are doing in key areas that affect their customers' value perceptions, organisations must select and track indicators of their performance efforts.

Documentation describes how work must be accomplished. Structured correctly, documentation will apply to a variety of situations, not just specific products. Documents serve as guides and ensure that work is performed consistently. Sound documentation can be used to determine and correct the causes of poor quality. Documentation defines existing work methods and provides a foundation for improvement. A high-quality documentation control system will contain records that are easily identified and used in the decision-making process

(Raudsepp,1987). Once the data and information have been gathered, a report summarizing the significant strengths and weaknesses of the area under study is created. In this report, the gap between the existing and the desired levels of performance is documented.

A good report will focus on patterns of standards violations and elements missing from a strong system. Items, services and processes that do not meet established requirements will be identified, according to the importance of the problem and the affected work. The information related to quality problems should be tracked and the resultant issues should be prioritized based on the company's established prioritization system. The prioritization process in the report should be based upon various factors including environmental and safety considerations, repetitive nature of the issue, programmematic concerns, fiscal concerns, and regulatory implications etc. After prioritization, the issues should be tracked and managed through resolution in accordance with the company's Corrective Action/Issue Management system.

Identifying Quality Problems

While reporting the performance quality problems may be identified by internal organisation sources (e.g., workers, customers, suppliers) or by an external source (customer/regulator). Once identified, quality problems must be evaluated to determine significance and documented. The method for determining the significance of a problem and the process for handling problems must be documented in the QAP (Pfeffer, 1994),. An effective organisation is one in which the quality problems are identified through its own internal resources doing introspective assessments and mentioning it in the report. An effective organisation also promotes a no-fault environment in which personnel have the mandate, freedom and responsibility to, and are expected to, identify potential quality problems and recommend improvements without fear of reprisal in the report.

Other information that could indicate conditions adverse to quality should be reviewed and evaluated may be generated by internal or external organisations, and, the reviews/evaluations should include conditions. In classifying conditions adverse to quality, the review should consider repetition of specific conditions adverse to quality, as well as the relationship or similarity between different conditions, in a manner and at a frequency that ensures that significant quality trends are identified and evaluated for appropriate correction. Conditions adverse to quality should be reviewed to determine the existence of trends. The significance of identified trends should be evaluated to determine whether further action is necessary. Problems, regardless of significance, should be identified, documented, and processed in accordance with a graded approach. This includes minor quality problems that may not follow the more formal processes for quality problem documentation and disposition.

Identify the causes of problems and include prevention of recurrence as part of corrective action planning

The report on performance should define the necessity and process to perform Root Cause Analysis (RCA) for conditions adverse to quality. An excellent university will requires RCA to be performed and documented for significant conditions adverse to quality. The report should define the criteria for when RCAs are required. For those instances where a formal root cause process is specified as required, but, it is determined to not be appropriate or practical, documented justification is required (Pascale and Athos, 1981),.

The causes of quality problems are typically included in the circumstances immediately preceding the problem and are often obvious anomalies. It is important for compensatory measures and remedial actions to be implemented to prevent further propagation of the problem. However, remedial action alone does not prevent recurrence of the problem. In this regard, the Root Cause Analysis

(RCA) process is key to identifying the "true" or "underlying" cause(s) of problems, which aids in identifying appropriate corrective actions that can prevent recurrence, and ensure continuous improvement (ibid).

Hence the world class universities will have a predetermined structure of a systematic report to be done based on the self-assessment/ auditing so that the management can understand the information and take effective decisions based on the well written report.

Strengthening On Current Position

"Excellent firms don't believe in excellence - only in constant improvement and constant change.

Tom Peters

Many processes develop over time, with little concern for whether or not it is the most effective manner in which to provide a product or service. When customer complaints arise or financial results aren't as expected, seek out wasteful processes and improve them. The processes providing the products and services will need to be improved with the aim of preventing defects and increasing productivity by reducing process cycle times and eliminating waste. The key to refining processes is concentrating on the process from the customer's point-of-view and identifying and eliminating non-value added activities. Eliminating non-value added activities clarifies the process and allows it to focus on meeting the needs, requirements, and expectations of the customer.

An excellent organisation will follow four primary steps for strengthening their current position through improvement: Prevention and Detection, Identification and Control, Correction, and Improvement. Management is responsible for leadership and commitment to quality achievement and improvement within a framework of public, worker, and environmental safety.

Management retains the primary responsibility and accountability for the scope and implementation of the of the improvement project. However, every individual in the organisation is responsible for achieving quality in his or her activities. Senior management should require and cultivate the achievement and improvement of quality at all levels of the organisation and ensure that the process of improvement is understood and implemented. This document provides an interpretation of what is needed for an effective Quality Improvement Process. The model and description below portrays a generic process for managing continuous improvement.

The Ramp of Improvement

This is a schematic representation of the use of the PDCA cycle in the improvement process. As each full PDCA cycle comes to completion, a new and slightly more complex project can be undertaken. This rolling over feature is integral to the continual improvement process, which catapults the institution to the path of excellence. More complex tasks and projects are then initiated and scaled up.

Figure 18: The Ramp of Improvement

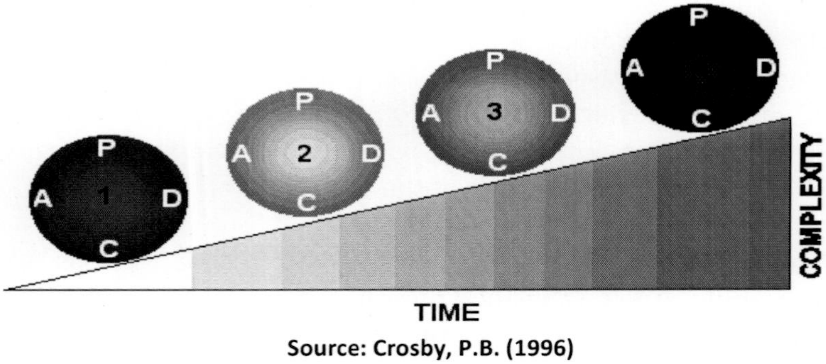

Source: Crosby, P.B. (1996)

Kaizen philosophy - continuous incremental improvement

The Kaizen method of continuous incremental improvements is an originally Japanese management concept for incremental (gradual, continuous) change (improvement) that can also be applied in the HEIs. K. is actually a way of life philosophy, assuming that every aspect of our life deserves to be constantly improved. The Kaizen philosophy lies behind many Japanese management concepts such as Total Quality Control, Quality Control circles, small group activities, labour relations. Key elements of Kaizen are quality, effort, involvement of all employees, willingness to change, and communication(Crosby, 1996).

Japanese companies distinguish between innovation (radical) and Kaizen (continuous). K. means literally: change (kai) to become good (zen). The foundation of the Kaizen method consists of 5 founding elements:

1. *Teamwork,*
2. *Personal discipline,*
3. *Improved morale*
,4. *Quality circles, and*
5. *Suggestions for improvement.*

Thus, by embedding and creating an amenable environment under, which Kaizen philosophy is applied, HEIs will rapidly reap the benefits of quality improvement. Kaizen's foundation and emphasis is really on three core factors (Kanji and Asher, 1993):

- Elimination of waste (muda) and inefficiency
- The Kaizen five-S framework for good housekeeping

1. *Seiri - tidiness*
2. *Seiton - orderliness*
3. *Seiso - cleanliness*
4. *Seiketsu - standardized clean-up*
5. *Shitsuke – discipline - standardization.*

When to apply the Kaizen philosophy?

Although it is difficult to give generic advice it is clear that it fits well in incremental change situations that require long-term change and in collective cultures. More individual cultures that are more focused on short-term success are often more conducive to concepts such as Business Process Reengineering.

When Kaizen is compared to BPR is it clear the K. philosophy is more people-oriented, easier to implement, requires long-term discipline. BPR on the other hand is harder, technology-oriented, enables radical change but requires major change management skills.

Kaizen is a daily activity, the purpose of which goes beyond simple productivity improvement. It is also a process that, when done correctly, humanizes the workplace, eliminates overly hard work ("muri"), and teaches people how to perform experiments on their work using the scientific method and how to learn to spot and eliminate waste in business processes.

To be most effective kaizen must operate with three [citation needed] principles in place (Lorsch, 1986):

- *Consider the process and the results (not results-only) so that actions to achieve effects are surfaced;*
- *Systemic thinking of the whole process and not just that immediately in view (i.e. big picture, not solely the narrow view) in order to avoid creating problems elsewhere in the process; and*
- *A learning, non-judgmental, non-blaming (because blaming is wasteful) approach and intent will allow the re-examination of the assumptions that resulted in the current process.*

People at all levels of an organisation can participate in kaizen, from the CEO down, as well as external stakeholders when applicable. The format for kaizen can be individual, suggestion system, small group, or large group. At Toyota, it is usually a local improvement within a workstation or local area and involves a small group in improving their own work environment and productivity. This group is often guided through the kaizen process by a line supervisor; sometimes this is the line supervisor's key role. While kaizen (at Toyota) usually delivers small improvements, the culture of continual aligned small improvements and standardization yields large results in the form of compound productivity improvement. Hence the English usage of "kaizen" can be: "continuous improvement" or "continual improvement."

This philosophy differs from the "command-and-control" improvement programmes of the mid-twentieth century. Kaizen methodology includes making changes and monitoring results, then adjusting. Large-scale pre-planning and extensive project scheduling are replaced by smaller experiments, which can be rapidly adapted as new improvements are suggested.

The Toyota Production System is known for kaizen, where all line personnel are expected to stop their moving production line in case of any abnormality and, along with their supervisor, suggest an improvement to resolve the abnormality, which may initiate a kaizen (Sallis,1993),.

The cycle of kaizen activity can be defined as:

- *Standardize an operation*
- *Measure the standardized operation (find cycle time and amount of in-process inventory)*
- *Gauge measurements against requirements*
- *Innovate to meet requirements and increase productivity*
- *Standardize the new, improved operations*
- *Continue cycle ad infinitum.*

Therfore HEIs that have a continuous improvement culture improve their performance by learning from their own experience and that of others and by sharing the information more broadly. These organisations regularly identify sources of information that are relevant to their work or operations. They analyze these information sources for both good work practices and adverse work practices. They take appropriate action in response to the value of these improvement opportunities. The Lessons Learned and Best Practice processes establish opportunities for performance improvements within the quality programme and product lines.

Lessons learned and best practice opportunities can be identified from a number of internal and external sources. They will be incorporated into the assessment plan and can provide substantial value to the organisation in improving overall performance. All areas of an organisation can benefit from lessons learned and best practices (both strengths and areas for improvement) by emphasizing improvement and learning as a routine part of their ongoing organisational work processes and project activities. Excellent HEIs also identify customers and deliverables (products or services), gather data about past and current performance, set performance goals for improvement, and collect data to measure success in meeting goals which make them more customer centric and aspire to exceed customers expectation through the continuous improvement process. As suggested by ***Kim Collins***-

Strive for continuous improvement, instead of perfection"

Injecting New Strategic Thinking

"We need innovation in education and dedication to the task before us"

Alan Autry

"Innovation distinguishes between a leader and a follower"

Steve Jobs

Innovation can be viewed as "the development and implementation of new ideas by people who over time engage in transactions with others within an institutional order" (VanDenVen, 1986, p. 590). It involves the generation of new processes and products and the implementation of these ideas in order to develop competitive advantage for the enterprise. Tushman and Nadler (1986) suggest that innovation can be incremental, synthetic or discontinuous. The first type involves gradual changes to products or processes; the second involves the combining of existing ideas in new ways while the third involves the creation of radically new ideas. Innovation is also strongly linked to risk taking (Norris, 1981). Innovation, therefore, involves not only new ideas and their development, but also change and risk.

An important element in innovation is creativity (Raudsepp, 1987), which requires information to be processed so the result is new, original and meaningful (Badaway, 1985, p. 29). Burgelman (1984) suggested that an enterprise seek to develop "internal corporate venturing" for this purpose, which may be achievable by empowering middle management (Kanter, 1982), or by forming "innovation management task forces" that can motivate employees and implement strategies (Foster and Pryor, 1986). Creative organisations frequently have a climate in which the line between work and play is blurred (Sonnenberg, 1991). Senior management within such enterprises are supportive of subordinate staff and encourage autonomy and risk taking (Pearson, 1988). Such initiatives may be increasingly important within industries where product and process technologies have reached the limits of further development. Under such conditions investment in human resources through training and skill development can become a source of competitive advantage (Pfeffer, 1994).

According to Quinn (1980; 1985), successful innovation requires a market orientation, an internal management style (structure and culture) that fosters innovation and a "non-linear" planning process that is flexible and permits all functional areas to contribute to the process (Takeuchi and Nonaka, 1986). Indeed, culture seems to be a critical variable in the innovation process (Baran et al., 1986;). Gresov (1984) suggests that culture and organisational structure are linked and that there is an inverse relationship between the homogeneity of an organisation's culture and innovation within that organisation. Of critical importance is the need to develop a balance between chaos and control (Quinn, 1985). To achieve innovation, the planning process (strategy formulation) needs to be "non-linear" or "holistic" (VanDenVen, 1986). This is consistent with Takeuchi and Porter's (1986) suggestion that marketing strategy must coordinate and link all aspects of an enterprise's activities. An innovative approach to product development that is gaining acceptance is turning customers into innovation partners. With this approach, the customer is given a technological tool kit for designing his or her own products and making product innovations. This approach is implemented using the following steps (McIntyre, 1982):

- *develop a tool kit for customers that is easy to use*
- *increase the flexibility of your own production processes*
- *carefully select the first customers to use your took kit*
- *continually improve your tool kit*
- *adapt your business practices to suit the innovation partnership approach.*

Bharadwaj et al. (1993) noted the importance of the complexity of assets and the number of co-specialized assets. The more complex the assets needed to market a service, the more sustainable an innovation will be as a source of competitive advantage. This is also true for services in which the number of co-specialized assets is high. Competitors will find it difficult to emulate an innovation if the process is complex.

Case study: Ryan Air

Ryanair was founded in 1985 as a small Irish-based competitor to

Aer Lingus, the Irish national airline, and British Airways on the lucrative Dublin-London route. Initially, the new company adopted a full-service business model similar to those of the two national carriers, but that strategy took Ryanair nowhere. In the early 1990s, under the leadership of Michael O'Leary, Ryanair transformed its prospects after it decided to re-invent itself by replicating the SWA model in the British Isles, later extending it to Europe. Now proud to be seen as "the Southwest Airlines of Europe", Ryanair currently outperforms its US role model in terms of growth and profitability, and looks set to overtake "the world's favorite airline", British Airways, in terms of annual numbers carried within the next two to three years.

Competitive advantage based on a privileged market position usually tends to reflect significant first-mover advantages in market-specific investments, skills and infrastructure (aircraft, location-routes, landing rights, etc. in the case of the airlines), which follower companies will find more expensive to replicate. For example, as competitors now rush to follow Ryanair into the same competitive space within the European airline industry, its CEO gives them little hope for success. As Michael O'Leary sees it, there are "huge barriers to entry now, and none of these new airlines is going to find a price point below Ryanair".

Sustaining Competitive Advantage

"As they approach the new millennium, organisations are striving to realize new levels of competitiveness, productivity and customer service through the use of leading-edge information technologies"
Lawrence Weinbach

Sustainable competitive advantage concept suggests that "market success" (measured by growth in market share and profits) is the outcome of delivering a successful combination of "distinctive competencies" that gain and sustain a competitive edge over rivals within international education markets. The idea that competitive advantage can be derived from internal skills, resources or assets (distinctive competencies) is widely referred to as the "resource-based view" of the firm (Collis and Montgomery, 1995).

Organisational culture has been defined as "the dominant values espoused by an organisation" (Deal and Kennedy, 1982), "the philosophy that guides an organisation's policy toward employees and customers" (Pascale and Athos, 1981), or "the basic assumptions and beliefs that are shared by members of an organisation" (Schein, 1985), although numerous other definitions exist (Smircich, 1983). Peters and Waterman (1982) argued that organisations with strong cultures or commonly shared values obtain superior performance. However, the ability of culture to be a source of competitiveness seems to be contingent upon the extent to which an organisation's culture "fits" the prevailing conditions within its external environment (Schein, 1984).

Managing culture for sustainable competitive advantage requires careful attention to be paid to the language and behaviour used within the enterprise, as well as to its values and beliefs (Fiol, 1991). The symbols used to define an organisation's structure and the behaviour of its members can also play a decisive role in defining its culture (Barley, 1983). Johnson (1992) describes corporate culture as a "web" of interrelated elements. The importance of organisational culture to sustainable competitive advantage has been outlined by Barney (1986), who noted that, while culture needs to be firmly based within the organisation, it should also be flexible to encourage innovation. Gronroos (1990) highlighted the need for service enterprises to develop customer oriented service cultures in which the organisation chart is inverted and customer and front line staff becomes the primary focus. The ability of culture to provide a source of competitive advantage is also linked to its ability to generate strategically valuable innovation through organisational learning (Williams, 1992). An enterprise needs to develop strong core values that emphasize innovation and flexibility if it is to develop sustained superior financial performance (Barney, 1986). Indeed:"Specific corporate culture or climate is important for innovation. The enterprises that seemed most successful in the realm of innovation were those with a relatively high degree of internal competition to achieve and a willingness to experiment with and reward innovation (Baran et al., 1986, p. 23)."

However, in order to gain sustainable competitive advantage, and for firms to be really effective, the advantage must be (VanDenVen, 1986):

- *difficult to mimic*
- *unique*
- *sustainable*
- *superior to the competition*
- *applicable to multiple situations*

Examples of company characteristics that could constitute a sustainable competitive advantage include:

- *superior product quality*
- *extensive distribution contracts*
- *accumulated brand equity and positive company reputation*
- *low cost production techniques*
- *patents and copyrights*
- *government protected monopoly*
- *superior employees and management team*

In addition, Porter and Fuller (1986) have noted that organisations can also achieve sustainable competitive advantage through expanding to foreign markets, building and maintaining high brand image, through coalition, integration or strategic alliance, organisational expertise, ICT.

Figure 19: Sustainable Competitive Advantage

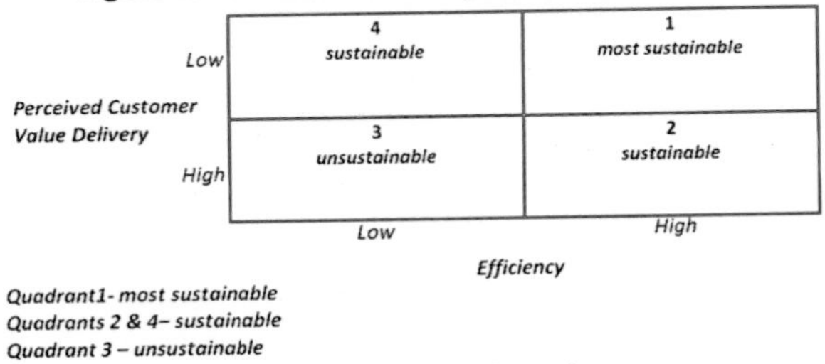

Porter and Fuller (1986)

The list of potential sustainable competitive advantage characteristics is very long. However there are some commentators that claim that in a fast changing competitive world, none of these advantages can be sustained in the long run. They claim that the only truly sustainable competitive advantage is to build an organisation that is so alert and so agile that it will always be able to find an advantage, no matter what changes occur. Hence the HEIs should come out with breakthrough ideas and thinking to add value to their organisation in order to attain and sustain their position as excellent organisations. The model above shows that in order to have most sustainable competitive advantage, HEIs need High perceived customer value delivery and High efficiency (i.e. quadrant 1).

Corporate Examples of sustainable competitive advantage:

As one of the world's largest and most profitable companies for decades, General Electric (GE) supports its platform for innovation and market leadership with an organic growth rate target of 8 percent per year. Growth and productivity initiatives have built GE to a scale achieved by only a handful of other companies. Its 2007 revenue of $178 billion, up 14 percent over 2006 with a 9 percent organic growth rate, makes it the world's sixth largest corporation. "Our companywide initiatives focused on organic growth, services, global expansion, and ecomaginations are delivering positive results," says CEO Jeffrey Immelt. "We achieved our twelfth straight quarter of organic revenue growth of two to three times global GDP" ("GE Reports Record Fourth-Quarter and Full-Year Results for 2007," press release, Jan. 18, 2008).

Procter & Gamble (P&G), the world's largest consumer products company, with 2007 revenue of $76 billion, built a strong foundation for consistent growth, which now averages 5 percent to 7 percent per year. Its new model for growth, called Connect and Develop, seeks to acquire half of its innovations from small to midsize entrepreneurial companies and university and government labs. P&G leverages its strength by using new ideas to grow core businesses and by developing higher margin and more asset-efficient businesses where it can achieve global leadership.

Both companies' approach to growth and scale includes:

- *Development of leaders who can provide required focus on growth and management competence*
- *A solid plan that is developed, adhered to, and "played" hard every day*
- *A view of the growth process as a marathon, not a sprint*
- *Use of an innovation pipeline*
- *A balanced portfolio approach to existing/new businesses and geographic markets*

Leaders of today's largest and greatest growth companies work vigorously to achieve dominance in their fields. They are vigilant about managing operations as efficiently as possible, but they also know that long-term success almost always requires continued top-line growth and increasing economies of scale, as cost-cutting and operational improvements have finite benefits.

References

- Barney, J. (1991), "Firm resources and sustained competitive advantage", Journal of Management, Vol. 17 No.1, pp.99-120.
- Baum, J.R., Locke, E.A., and Kirkpatrick, S.A. (1998) 'A Longitudinal Study of the Relation of Vision and Vision Communication to Venture Growth in Entrepreneurial Firms', Journal of Applied Psychology, 83: 43-54.
- Collins, J.C., and Porras, J.I. (1994) Built to Last: Successful Habits of Visionary Companies, London, Century.
- Collis, D.J, Montgomery, C.A (1995), "Competing on resources: strategy in the 1990s", Harvard Business Review, Vol. 73 No.4, pp.118-28.
- Conger, J.A., and Kanungo, R.N. (1987), 'Toward a Behavioral Theory of Charismatic Leadership in Organizational Settings', Academy of Management Review, 12: 637-647.
- Conrad, C. (1990) Strategic Organizational Communication: An Integrated Perspective, Orlando: Harcourt Brace Jovanovich College Publishers.
- Crosby, P.B. (1996), "Thinking about excellence", Journal for Quality and Participation, Vol. 19 No.6, pp.70.
- Deal, T.E, Kennedy, A.A (1982), Corporate Culture: The Rites and Rituals of Corporate Life, Addison-Wesley, Reading, MA,.
- Fiol, C.M. (1991), "Managing culture as a competitive resource: an identity-based view of sustainable competitive advantage", Journal of Management, Vol. 17 No.1, pp.191-211.
- Foster, W.K., Pryor, A.K (1986), "The strategic management of innovation", The Journal of Business Strategy, Vol. 7 No.1, pp.38-42.
- Gabarro, J.J. (1987) The Dynamics of Taking Charge
- Ittner, C.D., Larcker, D.F. (1998), "Innovations in performance measurement: trends and research implications", Journal of Management Accounting Research, Vol. 10 pp.205-38.

- Johnson, G (1992), "Managing strategic change: strategy, culture and action", Long Range Planning, Vol. 25 No.1, pp.28-36.
- Kanji, G. and Asher, G. (1993), "Total quality management process: a systematic approach", Journal of Total Quality Management, Vol. 4, (Suppl.)
- Kantabutra, S. (2003) 'An Empirical Examination of Relationships Between Customer and Staff Satisfaction in Retail Apparel Stores in Sydney, Australia' Unpublished Doctoral Dissertation,
- Kanter, R.M (1982), "The middle manager as innovators", Harvard Business Review, Vol. 60 No.4, pp.374-86.
- Kaplan, R.S., Norton, D.P. (1992), "The balanced scorecard – measures that drive performance", Harvard Business Review, Vol. 70 pp.71-9.
- Kouzes, J.M., and Posner, B.Z. (1987) The Leadership Challenge: How to Get Extraordinary Things Done in Organizations, San Francisco: Jossey-Bass.
- Maccoby, 2000 M. Maccoby, Narcissistic leaders: The incredible pros, the inevitable cons, Harvard Business Review (2000, January–February), pp. 69–77.
- McIntyre, S.H (1982), "Obstacles to corporate innovation", Business Horizons, pp.23-8.
- Morden, T. (1997) 'Leadership as Vision', Management Decision, 35(9): 668-676. Macquarie Graduate School of Management, Macquarie University, Sydney.
- Nanus, B. (1992) Visionary Leadership: Creating a Compelling Sense of Direction for Your Organization, San Francisco, CA: Jossey-Bass.
- Neely, A. (1998) Three modes of measurement: theory and practice International Journal of Business Performance Management Volume 1, Number 1 / 1998
- Norris, W.C (1981), "Developing corporate policies for innovation: a program of action", Long Range Planning, Vol. 14 No.4, pp.34-42.

- Pace, R.W., and Faules, D.F. (1989) Organizational Communication, New Jersey: Prentice Hall.
- Parikh, J., and Neubauer, F. (1993) 'Corporate Visioning', in D. E. Hussey (Ed), International Review of Strategic Management, Wiley: Chichester, pp. 105-116.
- Pascale, R.T., Athos, A.G (1981), The Art of Japanese Management, Simon & Schuster,, New York, NY.
- Pearson, A.E (1988), "Tough-minded ways to get innovative", Harvard Business Review, pp.99-106.
- Peters, T, Waterman, R.H (1982), In Search of Excellence: Lessons from America's Best-run Companies, Harper and Row, New York, NY,
- Pfeffer, J (1994), "Competitive advantage through people", California Management Review, pp.9-28.
- Porter, M.E., Fuller, M.B. (1986), "Coalitions and global strategy", in Porter, M.E (Eds),Competition in Global Industries, Harvard Business School Press, Boston, MA, pp.315-43.
- Raudsepp, E (1987), "Establishing a creative climate", Training and Development Journal, pp.50-3.
- Schein, E.H. (1984), "Coming to a new awareness of organizational culture", Sloan Management Review, pp.3-16.
- Senge, P.M. (1990) The Fifth Discipline: The Art and Practice of the Learning Organization, New York: Currency Doubleday.
- Seymour, D. (1995). The AQC Baldrige report. Lessons learned by nine colleges and universities undertaking self-study with the Malcolm Baldrige National Quality Award Criteria. Washington, DC: American Association for Higher Education. Retrieved April 30, 2005, from http://www.aahe.org/Archives/menu.html
- Sonnenberg, F.K (1991), "Strategies for creativity", The Journal of Business Strategy, pp.50-3.
- Tichy, N.M., Devanna, M.A. (1986), The Transformational Leader
- Tushman, M., Nadler, D (1986), "Organizing for innovation", California Management Review, Vol. 28 No.3, pp.74-92.

- VanDenVen, A (1986), "Central problems in the management of innovation", Management Science, Vol. 32 No.5, pp.590-607.
- Williams, J.R (1992), "How sustainable is your competitive advantage?", California Management Review, Vol. 34 No.2, pp.29-51.
- Yukl, G. (1998), Leadership in Organizations, Prentice-Hall, Upper Saddle River, NJ,

Chapter 4
Assessing Academic Excellence

Introduction

"Hold yourself responsible for a higher standard than anybody expects of you. Never excuse yourself"
Henry Ward Beecher

"... we never do anything well, unless we love it for its own sake"
Wollstonecraft, Mary

"It is by no means enough that an officer be capable...He should be a gentleman of liberal education, refined, manners, punctilious courtesy, and the nicest sense of personal honor... No meritorious act of a subordinate should escape his attention, even if the reward be only one word of approval. Conversely, he should not be blind to a single fault in any subordinate"
John Paul Jones

"Education is not the filling of a pail, but the lighting of a fire"
W. B. Yeats

Assessing Academic Excellence

"Academic excellence" in its broadest sense, encompasses activities and outcomes in all areas of academic work. And it includes teaching, research, administration and service to the university and broader community. The quest for quality has become a critical concern for organisations in both industrial and service sectors, especially in view of the profound impact of quality on overall performance (Loh *et al.*, 1997). In the context of the higher education sector, quality is, in fact, increasingly recognized as a fundamental underpinning for institutional innovation and continuous improvement (Piper, 1993). In the new external environment characterized by greater accountability, resource constraints and growing competition, universities urgently need to have visible mechanisms for quality assurance in all spheres of their activities.

The actual definition of quality is as elusive as the terms used to define it operationally or philosophically—as it was different for each of its earliest proponents. Murgatroyd and Morgan (1993) attempted to capture the definition of quality by looking at three basic definitions: quality assurance as determined by standards and evaluation; contract conformance as determined by a specified, negotiated standard for a contract; and customer-driven quality as determined by meeting or exceeding the expectations of customers. Murgatroyd and Morgan believe that today's quality revolution "... places emphasis on customer-driven quality supported by contract conformance and quality assurance" (p. 51). Fundamentally, then, it does not have to be one or the other, but a balance of all three depending on the organisation, the environment both external and internal, and the theory or model upon which it organizes its mission, vision, leadership and planning.

It is acknowledged that there are competing definitions and usages of the term quality, within higher education (Mizikaci, 2006).In the context of this workshop, however, the focus is on quality in terms of quality assurance and quality enhancement. The term quality assurance refers to the policies, processes and actions through which quality is maintained and developed (McKimm, 2003). It is concerned with addressing the issue of product or service non-conformance, it involves ensuring fitness for purpose (Lomas, 2004). This is the concept which is also underpinned in the UK Quality Assurance Agency (QAA), the quality assessment body for educational institutions, subject review methodology (Ottewill and Macfarlane, 2002). The process in this context can be conceptualised as two related sub-activities, one concerned with management for quality and the other with quality management (Hodgkinson and Brown, 2003). The generic term, quality management, is often used to describe both the goals of an organisation and the processes whereby an organisation might achieve those goals. It is useful to distinguish between these two meanings by using the term, management for quality, for the processes whereby the quality of a product or service is achieved and, quality management, for the quality of the processes per se. The distinction between the two meanings is similar to the difference between, doing the right job (management for quality) and, doing the job right (quality management).

The quality of the management processes (quality management), is dependent upon an understanding of how people learn, how they interact, and how they sustain, develop, or even destroy, a culture. However, although understanding is the basis, it is also necessary for well articulated methods of evaluation of the management processes involved. These methods are often referred to as quality audits or annual monitoring and review. They usually consist of audit trails that map the degree of coherence of the system, the links between different components, and the closure of feedback loops in the system (Colling, and Harvey, 1995).

Institutions of higher education talked about quality for many years before the business community determined that it was important (Burke & Minassians, 2003). "Unfortunately, the academic community never determined with any precision the objectives of undergraduate education nor developed systematic methods for assessing campus achievements". Resources and reputation have been the determining factors in institutional excellence in higher education for the last 20-25 years. That is to say that institutional excellence has been about "... the quantity of campus resources, the quality of admitted students, and the reputation of faculty research… and nothing about the quality or the quantity of the services provided to students, states, and society…" (ibid, p. 7)

Daniel Seymour (1997) provided another view of the history of quality in higher education. He cited the intersection of decreasing confidence in higher education beginning in the mid 1980s and the increasing application of quality principles in industry as espoused by W. Edwards Deming, Joseph Juran, and Philip Crosby as the pivotal beginning. The perceived lack of unresponsiveness from higher education to the complaints of parents, students and legislatures was matched by a "high riding" quality movement in corporate America (13,p. 5). Inevitably the question arose about the application of quality principles to higher education.

Assessment is a centerpiece of a total quality management (TQM) strategy. This aspect of quality pursuit is the lever for any quality initiative to be credible, acceptable and effective. Indeed the ultimate success of any quality strategy rests critically on the power of its assessment system in terms of key criteria such as appropriateness, usefulness, validity and reliability (Porter and Tanner, 1996). More importantly, a formal assessment plan is a foundation towards a constantly adaptive and entrepreneurial university. A university which takes quality assessment seriously emerges as a self-critical community of students, academic staff, support staff and administrators each contributing to and striving for continuous improvement and innovation (Cullen et al., 2003).

Within the overall context of quality assurance and control, the specific purpose of the Higher Education Institute's (HEI) self-assessment initiative is to improve the academic enterprise with three key objectives:

- *to develop processes and structures for the attainment of desired quality.*
- *to appraise the current state of quality;*

- *to benchmark quality performance indicators to be achieved; and*

It follows therefore that in the 21st Century HEIs should be about academic excellence and higher on their agenda. There should be robust approaches that are both inward and outward looking, focusing on the micro and macro aspects of the university processes and programmes and as well as maintaining a competitive edge in the international academic arena. The Suggested model (Fig. below) if adopted should propel institutions towards that desired level.

Figure 20: A Model for Assessment in Academic Excellence

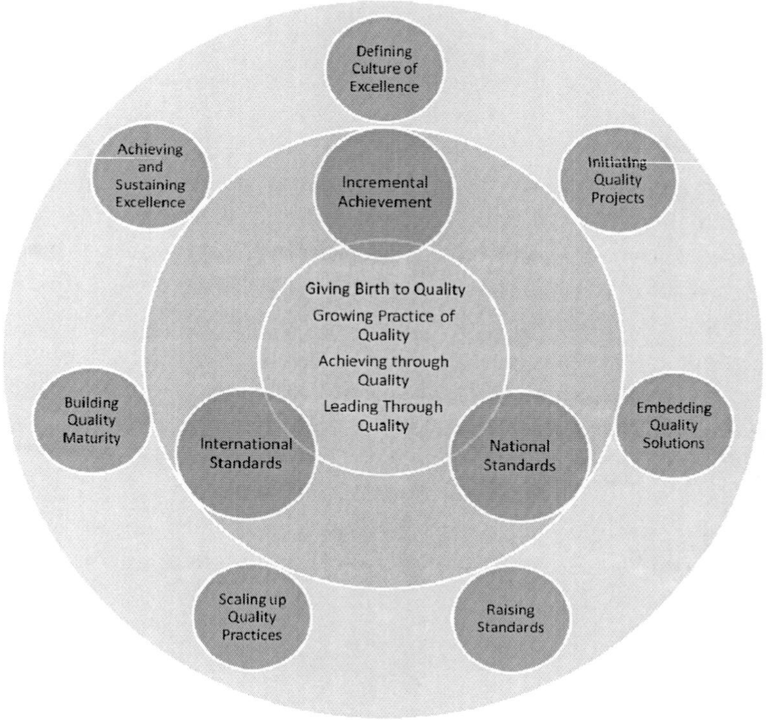

This model is premised on organisation's attempt to grow and nurture quality/excellence from three prongs:

- Core level – the focus at this level is on day-to-day activities, programmmes, tasks, events …etc. the organisation needs to improve both in terms of efficiency and effectiveness so as to cultivate and lay a firm foundation for quality principles and practices.
- Macro level – focuses on series of activities beyond the obvious day to-day initiatives that builds on the gains made at the core level to continue with improvements within the organisation.
- ***Micro level*** – stretches beyond the internal processes to involve adaptation of best practices from other organisations and departments within and without as well as adhering to industry and international standards to position itself for competitive advantage.

Thus, implementation of this model assumes to follow a triple loop approach (Fig. 21), whereby successful improvement in core level activities within an institution (programmes, activities, projects …etc) , serves as an impetus to focus on Micro –level activities within the institution (growing quality capabilities). Only when an institution has cultivated sufficient capabilities, and has sustained the gains made thereby can it then turn focus on sustaining excellence (Micro level). Thus incremental improvement and breakthrough innovations should be the fuel for excellence in HEIs. The triple loop is really a ramp of incremental improvements involving several Deming cycles (PDCA) cycles, where gains made at a lower level are sustained and used as springboard to catapult improvements at a higher and perhaps complex level.

Figure 21: The Triple Loop Approach

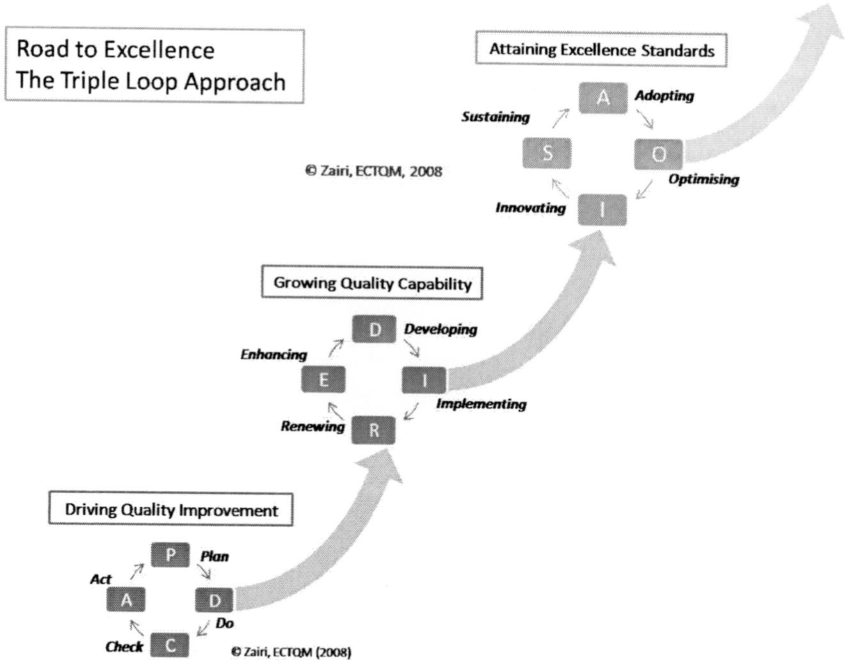

The Road to Excellence – A New DNA

A) CORE LEVEL – (Inner ring)

This is basically operating at the foundational level of inculcating the concept of quality in an organisation. Several approaches may be applied to imbed these concepts in an organisation namely:

1. ***Giving birth to quality*** – this basically refers to sowing the seeds of quality. Laying the firm foundations of quality from which to build on sound quality practices,
2. ***Growing practices of quality*** – once "seeds of quality" have germinated in an organisation; these must be supported to

generate desired results. Basically means propping up initiatives so as to deliver results.

3. ***Achieving through quality*** – ensuring that an organisations outcomes/offerings are screened or gauged using quality attributes to ensure superior performance,
4. ***Leading through quality*** – ensuring that organisation's leadership is focused on quality, leading the entity to deliver exceptional results to the delightment and satisfaction of all its stakeholders.

B) MACRO – LEVEL II (Middle ring)

Level II is characterised by a concerted effort by an organisation to harness its quality initiatives at corporate level rather than at unit or project level. This layer explains that institutions are involved in corporate wide initiatives to broaden its horizon through benchmarking against local, national and international standards in order to grow quality using initiatives, such as:

1. ***Incremental achievement-*** once an organisation introduces quality concepts, leaders need to develop a system where the organisation as a whole will thrive to achieve higher standards in a step by step approach.
2. ***National standards-*** ensuring that orgnasisation meet and thrive to exceed the national standards.
3. ***International standards-*** it is the highest level of achievement, where organisations set international standard as a benchmark and develop strategies for achieving and sustaining the highest level of international standards.

C) MICRO - Level III (Outer ring)

Institutions at this stage seeks to be more internally focused and develop short term mid-term and long-term strategy by taking a holistic view of the organisation and engaging all employees to achieve excellence in all the activities through the development of an effective assessment procedure of excellence. The initiatives that are used to enhance the quality movements are demonstrated hereunder:

1. ***Defining culture of excellence-*** ensuring that the philosophy of excellence exists in every corner of the organisation.
2. ***Initiating quality programmes-*** following a step by step approach for implementing quality in all the functional areas of the business.
3. ***Embedding quality solutions-*** ensuring that philosophy of excellence does not live in isolation. Quality becomes an integral part of all business practice through development and implementation of quality solutions.
4. ***Raising standards-*** leaders develop a procedure where everybody works with a common goal of achieving higher standards. Once the set standard is achieved, standards for all the future activities are automatically raised to a higher level.
5. ***Scaling up quality practices-*** making quality work in the organisation and setting standards for higher level of quality achievements and implementing through continuous improvement.
6. ***Building quality maturity-*** achieving through excellence becomes a habit and common practice of the organisation.
7. ***Achieving and sustaining excellence-*** ensuring excellence and operations blends smoothly in the organisation. The philosophy is not only to achieve excellence but also how to sustain it in the longer term.

The following sections will explain the 3 levels of the Assessment in Academic Excellence Model (see figure 20) in further details –

Level I – Core

Giving birth to quality

This is the very early stage of the quality movement of an organisation and the most difficult phase for the leaders. In this phase, leaders try to evaluate and understand different models and practices of quality management in order to investigate the strategic fit of the initiatives. Then leaders will introduce the quality concept and processes to the relevant stakeholders (Dale, 2003). This phase will involve more seminars, trainings, discussions groups, team building just to introduce the concept to the business. At this phase managers also inform the relevant stakeholders how it might change their way of doing things in the organisation. This is one of the most difficult phases for an organisation as it involves a lot of changes. And due to the basic human nature, employees are resistant to changes. Hence, the leaders have to have a very clear vision of how to implement excellence in every areas of the business. It is not only about taking quality initiatives but also about how to efficiently manage the changes that might drastically change the overall business. In some cases, leaders might have to think about business process reengineering (BPR) in this phase in order to efficiently implement quality initiatives in the organisation.

Growing Practice of Quality

Management for quality implies there is at least, a tacit understanding of the prescribed quality of the product or service that has to be delivered. For this to be effective, this tacit understanding requires articulation, strategies and actions. In the context of teaching it is transforming students through their attainment of the intended learning outcomes of a degree programme that illustrates the system of higher education for, management for quality (Greensted, 2002). The processes involved, include course design, the design of assessment, the shaping of student progress and student support will all require careful analysis.

Driving quality in HEIs is all about making sure that programmes, activities, tasks, initiatives and process within universities are all attuned to and focused on quality. The focus is on micro activities within the institutions that are geared towards solving day-to-day problems and thereby growing quality. There are three apparently simple questions that are central to management for quality and quality management within a university, namely (Elton, 2001):

- *What are we trying to achieve?*
- *How well are we doing?*
- *How could we do it better?*

The last of these three questions is the more important as it is concerned with enhancing quality or "prospective quality assurance". For if one has effective procedures for answering this last question then the answers to the other two questions, concerned with maintenance of quality, fall into place. Towards this end a variety of tools may be applied namely- PDCA, Kaizen and customer services which are discussed below (Biggs, 2001)-

PDCA (Plan, Do, Check and Act) Cycle

The PDCA (or PDSA) Cycle was originally conceived by Walter Shewhart in 1930's, and later adopted by W. Edwards Deming. The model provides a framework for the improvement of a process or system (Emiliani, 2005). It can be used to guide the entire improvement project, or to develop specific projects once target improvement areas have been identified (please see session/day 3 notes for a detailed description of PDCA/PDSA).

Kaizen philosophy - continuous incremental improvement

The Kaizen method of continuous incremental improvements is an originally Japanese management concept for incremental (gradual, continuous) change (improvement) that can also be applied in the HEIs. Kaizen is actually a way of life philosophy, assuming that every aspect of our life deserves to be constantly improved. The Kaizen philosophy lies behind many Japanese management concepts such as Total Quality Control, Quality Control circles, small group activities, labour relations. Key elements of Kaizen are quality, effort, and involvement of all employees, willingness to change, and communication (please refer to Session/Day -3 notes for the details on Kaizen Philosophy).

The foundation of the Kaizen method consists of 5 founding elements (ibid):

1. *Teamwork,*
2. *Personal discipline,*
3. *Improved morale,*
4. *Quality circles, and*
5. *Suggestions for improvement.*

Thus, by embedding and creating an amenable environment under, which Kaizen philosophy is applied, HEIs will rapidly reap the benefits of quality improvement. Kaizen's foundation and emphasis is really on the following core factors: (Emiliani, 2005)

- Elimination of waste (muda) and inefficiency
- The Kaizen five-S framework for good housekeeping
  1. *Seiri - tidiness*
  2. *Seiton - orderliness*
  3. *Seiso - cleanliness*
  4. *Seiketsu - standardized clean-up*
  5. *Shitsuke – discipline - standardization.*

When to apply the Kaizen philosophy?

Although it is difficult to give generic advice it is clear that it fits well in incremental change situations that require long-term change and in collective cultures. More individual cultures that are more focused on short-term success are often more conducive to concepts such as Business Process Reengineering.

When Kaizen is compared to BPR is it clear the K. philosophy is more people-oriented, easier to implement, requires long-term discipline. BPR on the other hand is harder, technology-oriented, enables radical change but requires major change management skills. Kaizen is a daily activity, the purpose of which goes beyond simple productivity improvement. It is also a process that, when done correctly, humanizes the workplace, eliminates overly hard work ("muri"), and teaches people how to perform experiments on their work using the scientific method and how to learn to spot and eliminate waste in business processes.

To be most effective kaizen must operate with three principles in place (Kanji, G. and Asher, G. (1993):

- *Consider the process and the results (not results-only) so that actions to achieve effects are surfaced;*
- *Systemic thinking of the whole process and not just that immediately in view (i.e. big picture, not solely the narrow view) in order to avoid creating problems elsewhere in the process; and*
- *A learning, non-judgmental, non-blaming (because blaming is wasteful) approach and intent will allow the re-examination of the assumptions that resulted in the current process.*

People at all levels of an organization can participate in kaizen, from the CEO down, as well as external stakeholders when applicable. The format for kaizen can be individual, suggestion system, small group, or large group. At Toyota, it is usually a local improvement within a workstation or local area and involves a small group in improving their own work environment and productivity. This group is often guided through the kaizen process by a line supervisor; sometimes this is the line supervisor's key role.

While kaizen (at Toyota) usually delivers small improvements, the culture of continual aligned small improvements and standardization yields large results in the form of compound productivity improvement. Hence the English usage of "kaizen" can be: "continuous improvement" or "continual improvement."

This philosophy differs from the "command-and-control" improvement programs of the mid-twentieth century. Kaizen methodology includes making changes and monitoring results, then adjusting. Large-scale pre-planning and extensive project scheduling are replaced by smaller experiments, which can be rapidly adapted as new improvements are suggested.

The Toyota Production System is known for kaizen, where all line personnel are expected to stop their moving production line in case of any abnormality and, along with their supervisor, suggest an improvement to resolve the abnormality, which may initiate a kaizen.

Hence, from the above discussion it can be summarised that the cycle of kaizen activity can be defined as:

- *Standardize an operation*
- *Measure the standardized operation (find cycle time and amount of in-process inventory)*
- *Gauge measurements against requirements*
- *Innovate to meet requirements and increase productivity*
- *Standardize the new, improved operations*
- *Continue cycle ad infinitum.*

Customer Surveys

Customer surveys are useful means of gauging customer satisfaction (Slater,1997). In the HEIs student surveys are common and these bring to the fore various issues universities need to attend to improve their offerings. The National Survey of Student Engagement(NSSE), the Canadian Undergraduate Survey Consortium(CUSC), and the *Maclean's* University Student Survey are the commonest national surveys in USA and Canada that HEIs have relied on to enhance their offerings. These surveys ask more than 100 questions about specific aspects of the undergraduate experience—inside the classroom and beyond—designed to provide universities with data to help them assess programmes and services (Woodruff, 1997).

The following section discusses the **National Survey of Student Engagement (NSSE)**[1]

The National Survey of Student Engagement (NSSE) obtains, on an annual basis, information from hundreds of four-year colleges and universities nationwide about student participation in programmes and activities that institutions provide for their learning and personal development. The results provide an estimate of how undergraduates spend their time and what they gain from attending college. Survey items on The National Survey of Student Engagement represent empirically confirmed "good practices" in undergraduate education. That is, they reflect behaviors by students and institutions that are associated with desired outcomes of college.

Institutions use their data to identify aspects of the undergraduate experience inside and outside the classroom that can be improved through changes in policies and practices more consistent with good practices in undergraduate education. This information is also used by prospective college students, their parents, college counselors, academic advisers, institutional research officers, and researchers in learning more about how students spend their time at different colleges and universities and what they gain from their experiences. More than 1200 different colleges and universities in the U.S. and Canada have participated in NSSE since it was first administered in 2000. NSSE's widespread use has spawned several other national used instruments including the Beginning College Survey of Student Engagement, the Community College Survey of Student Engagement, the Faculty Survey of Student Engagement, and the Law School Survey of Student Engagement, all of which are supported through institutional participation fees.

Canadian Undergraduate Survey Consortium (CUSC)[2]

---

[1] nsse.iub.edu/

[2] http://www.cusc-ccreu.ca/

The Canadian University Survey Consortium (CUSC) is a group of Canadian Universities working cooperatively to gain a better understanding of the Canadian undergraduate student population. Participation is open to any degree granting member university of the Association of Universities and Colleges of Canada (www.aucc.ca). Since CUSC's inception in 1994, universities across Canada have jointly implemented surveys of their undergraduate students. At that time 8 universities participated. The level of participation rose to a new high of 35 institutions in 2007.

The surveys provide comparative information on student characteristics and experiences. They target specific undergraduate sub-samples based on a three-year cycle, alternating between:

- *first year students,*
- *all undergraduates, and*
- *graduating students*

Maclean's National Reputational Ranking[3]

The Maclean's University Graduate Survey canvassed the opinions of a random sample of university alumni who completed their undergraduate degrees in 2002, 2003 or 2004. Universities contacted their graduates by email or mail, inviting them to take part. Nearly 15,000 did. Participants for the Maclean's survey were randomly selected from those who graduated from the undergraduate classes of 2002, 2003 and 2004. Universities contacted selected grads by email, surface mail or a combination of the two, inviting them to participate. Smaller universities, with fewer than 1,333 grads per graduating year, surveyed everyone. Larger institutions could elect to survey all grads or implement a sampling plan - developed by the Maclean's project statistician - to survey a minimum of 4,000 grads across the three years in question(http://oncampus.macleans.ca/education).

[3] http://oncampus.macleans.ca/education/

There are, however, several questions on NSSE, CUSC and the Maclean's survey that are broadly similar, asking survey-takers to assess their university experience. One of the key issues of these surveys is that, some universities that have taken part in CUSC and/or NSSE refused to disclose their results. For example, the most significant case is York: Canada's third-largest university, with 46,000 undergraduate students, participated in both CUSC and NSSE but has not made its results public[23]. It is due to the fact that these organisations realized that based on the survey report their standard do not match with the national and international institutes that they benchmark with. [ibid].

After reviewing the above agencies for student survey, the common themes that are used in all the surveys are summarized below-

- *Faculty*
- *Resources*
- *Student Support*
- *Library*
- *Student's academic programme and plans*
- *Student's study patterns and grades*
- *Student's perception of the university*
- *Student's involvement in activities*
- *Financing education*
- *Career/employment*
- *Students and classes*
- *Scholarship facilities*
- *Coursework*
- *Assessment policy*
- *Student counseling*
- *Communication with students*
- *Customer service, e.g. enrolment, registration etc and*
- *Diversity*

Hence, it is important for HEI' to continuously collect information from the students and other relevant stakeholders to evaluate the organisation's overall performance, so that they can plan to focus on their strengths and take corrective measure where necessary based on a right set of assessment criteria.

Achieving through quality

"To do the right thing, at the right time, in the right way; to do some things better than they were ever done before; to eliminate errors; to know both sides of the question; to be courteous; to be an example; to work for the love of the work; to anticipate requirements; to develop resources; to recognize no impediments; to master circumstances; to act from reason rather than rule; to be satisfied with nothing short of perfection."

Marshal Field

(Author: Give the Lady What She Wants)

Effective leaders communicate the values of the organisation to their employees by translating the vision and mission into day-to-day activities so that they can achieve their goal through quality. To do this effectively, leaders talk with customers, identify the organisation's critical success factors, and share this information about the things the organisation absolutely must do well in order to attract and retain customers. Creating alignment is essentially policy deployment, the step-by-step process of translating the organisation's vision and mission into strategies supported by goals and objectives that in turn become work activities for the employees. Leaders ensure that the organisation's vision, mission and strategies, goals and daily activities remain focused on these critical factors (Marshal, 1990).

The following example will give a clear idea, how one of the world class businesses have achieved their goal through providing quality product and service to the customer, what is rooted on the overall emphasis on quality in every sector of the business.

<u>Case study: Premier Department Store: Achieving and sustaining through quality</u>

Mr. Marshall Field was the premiere department store owner/manager during the late 1800s. Today, due in part to the fact that his stores still follow his management beliefs, Marshall Field's stores remains very successful. The following quote comes from Marshall Field's book *Give the Lady What She Wants*, written in 1900, based on his experiences.

> Mr. Field, while strolling through his store, came upon his assistant retail manager arguing heatedly with a woman customer.
>
> "What are you doing here?" asked Field.
>
> "I am settling a complaint," replied the manager.
>
> "No, you're not," snapped Field. "Give the lady what she wants!"

Later he sent the following memo to all employees:

"We wish," he advised all employees, old and new, "to make important the point of receiving merchandise that has been returned, without going through the unnecessary or unpleasant questions or remarks, which make the customer ill at ease and really accomplish no good. We would much prefer to be occasionally imposed upon than to feel that we have made any errors in the other direction. The employee is not the loser by the returning of goods, except in a very slight way. The house is the loser, and if we prefer to stand the loss cheerfully, please let us have corresponding cheerfulness from employees." (ibid)

Leading through quality

–"The aim of leadership should be to improve the performance of man and machine, to improve quality, to increase output and simultaneously to bring pride of workmanship to people. Put in a negative way, the aim of leadership is not merely to find and record failures of men, but to remove the causes of failure: to help people to do a better job with less effort."

W. Edwards Deming

Leadership is the ability to inspire people to make a total, willing, and voluntary commitment to accomplishing or exceeding organisational goals. Good leaders overcome resistance to change, broker the needs of constituent groups inside and outside the organisation, and establish an ethical framework. Good leaders are committed to both the job to be done and the people who must do it. They are good communicators and they are persuasive. Leadership for quality is based on the following principles: customer focus, obsession with quality, recognition of the structure of work, freedom through control, unity of purpose, looking for faults in the systems, teamwork, and continuing education and training.

Leaders get people to do what they have not done before thus leading to the organisation being more successful. Leaders provide direction and purpose for an organisation. It is leaders that provide the ultimate encouragement and reasoning behind why people would want to do their jobs. People perform on the job for a variety of reasons. They may perform for the financial incentives involved, the prestige, or the possibility of future rewards. Sometimes people even perform out of fear, fear of job loss, fear of retribution, fear of unpleasant consequences. The most effective reason why people work is because they want to. According to Dr. Deming, leadership's overall aim should be to create a system in which everyone takes joy in their work (Crosby, 1996).

In order to lead through quality leaders must describe how they set and deploy organisational values, steer the organisation toward its short and long term goals, how they create value for their customers, and how they set and monitor performance expectations. Senior leaders are also expected to describe how they create an environment supporting organisational agility, employee empowerment, and employee learning. Leaders should be reviewed in terms of their ability to translate priorities, strategies, and objectives into organisational improvement and opportunities for innovation.

Effective leaders provide guidance, often in the physical "walk the talk" type of format. These leaders make sure that their actions correspond with a written vision or mission statement. Effective leaders communicate the values of the organisation to their employees by translating the vision and mission into day-to-day activities. To do this effectively, leaders talk with customers, identify the organisation's critical success factors, and share this information about the things the organisation absolutely must do well in order to attract and retain customers. Creating alignment is essentially policy deployment, the step-by-step process of translating the organisation's vision and mission into strategies supported by goals and objectives that in turn become work activities for the employees. Leaders ensure that the organisation's vision, mission and strategies, goals and daily activities remain focused on these critical factors [ibid].

Effective leaders are also the first to realize that if any of these questions go unanswered, chances are, fault lies with leadership, not with the employees. To help create alignment, effective leaders carefully design employee policies supporting the links between the critical success factors identified by their customers and the employees' day-to-day activities. Effective leaders set realistic goals for their employees and give timely rewards to those who meet these goals. Leaders seek out employees' ideas and actively support the good ones. Very few people are truly good listeners, effective leaders have learned to listen to their employees. It helps to keep in mind that the same letters spell the words "listen" and "silent." Leaders also place a high priority on expanding employee capabilities and responsibilities through education and training (Chase and Stewart,1994).

Level II – Macro

Characterised by a concerted effort by an organisation to harness its quality initiatives at corporate level rather than at unit or project level. The institution is involved in corporate wide initiatives to grow quality using a variety of approaches, namely:

Incremental Achievements

Growing quality capabilities is essentially about improving performance and outcomes of the projects, activities, programmes and initiatives dealt with at level one, so as to generate superior outcomes and offerings. The assumption here is that the institution has excelled well at the micro level and is now daring to venture out at a macro level. The, process of growing capabilities in HEIs is aptly summed up by the acronym DIRE (Developing, Implementing, Renewing and Enhancing) institutions capabilities[28].

- *Developing – initiating quality programmes aimed at addressing day-to-day challenges the institution may be facing as well as customer satisfaction and competitive position in the market place,*
- *Implementing – Applying or committing institutions resources towards realizing the developments planned,*
- *Renewing – Revisiting programmes, projects and identifying opportunities for improvement and recommitting or reapplying institutions resources towards improvement,*
- *Enhancing – Making incremental gains is all the institutions sphere of activities and working towards robust programmes and efficiency in the delivery of university offerings*

Hence, improvement of quality, e.g. through dissemination of good practice or use of a continuous improvement cycle is more transformative and requires HEIs deliberate change of processes that are directly concerned with adding value, improving quality and implementing transformative change. In HEIs quality enhancement is given practical expression through staff appraisal and development, and the fostering of a culture of continuous improvement and innovation. Thus, towards realizing these capabilities, a university may engage in several initiatives namely:

National Standards

Organisations should have a clear understanding of the rules and regulations of a country to run their business smoothly in order to facilitate the aspiration for achieving highest standard of quality, organisations should first check the national standard and should develop a strategy to top in the list according to the national accreditation bodies. For example in the UK it is illegal to offer a qualification that is or might seem to be UK degree unless the awarding body is recognised by the Secretary of State, a Royal Charter or Act of Parliament to grant degrees. Prosecutions under the Education Reform Act are rare, as many unaccredited awarding bodies are based outside UK jurisdiction. It is also worth noting in this context that the Business Names Act 1985 made it an offence for any business in the UK to use the word "university" in its name without the formal approval of the Privy Council. Hence, there are many of these conformity assessment activities applied in today's marketplace including accreditation, certification, inspection, registration, supplier's declaration, and testing. Some benefits of accreditation include:

- *Signals a clear indication that an organization desires to have a competitive advantage by undergoing a voluntary evaluation*
- *Encourages marketplace confidence in HEIs by their undergoing regular impartial and independent audits by an internationally respected body*
- *Positively influences customer satisfaction with HEIs and their clients via greater quality awareness and enhanced communication*
- *Reduces liability insurance by the accountability and transparent aspects of the process*

- *Sustains continual improvement for the HEIs and their clients through the assessment of system effectiveness, efficiency and competence*
- *Promotes consistency and demonstrates equivalence of assessments via mutual recognition based on peer review*
- *Reduces multiple audits and removes barriers to trade in working towards the goal of "certified once – accepted everywhere."*

Some of the national agencies that accredit HEIs , Quality Assurance Agency

Quality Assurance Agency (QAA)[4]

In 1997, the Quality Assurance Agency for Higher Education (QAA) was established to provide an integrated quality assurance service for UK higher education. QAA is an independent body funded by subscriptions from universities and colleges of higher education (our subscribers), and through contracts with the main higher education funding bodies. QAA is a member of the International Network of Quality Assurance Agencies in Higher Education (INQAAHE), the UNESCO Global Forum Task Force and the OECD/UNESCO Working Group established to develop guidelines for quality provision in cross border education (www.qaa.ac.uk).

QAA ensures that each university and college of higher education is responsible for ensuring that appropriate standards are being achieved and a good quality education is being offered. It is QAA responsibility to safeguard the public interest in sound standards of higher education qualifications, and to encourage continuous improvement in the management of the quality of higher education. It achieves this by reviewing standards and quality, and providing reference points that help to define clear and explicit standards.

---

[4]www.qaa.ac.uk

QAA uses peer review processes where teams of academics conduct their audits and reviews. Some team members are drawn from industry and the professions. In England, universities and colleges of higher education are reviewed through an institutional audit [ibid]. Further education colleges that provide higher education programmes are reviewed through an academic review at subject level. Institutional audit aims to ensure that institutions are providing higher education, awards and qualifications of an acceptable quality and an appropriate academic standard; and exercising their legal powers to award degrees in a proper manner. The QAA followed a method of review for the period 1993-2000 which was based upon the notion of quality as fitness for purpose. It focused upon the match between the avowed aims and objectives of a subject provider (usually a School or a Department) and six aspects of provision. This method was primarily concerned with the quality of processes [ibid]. At its root was the question: Is this a good learning experience for these students in this School, in this University?

The National Consortium for Continuous Improvement (NCCI)[5]

The National Consortium for Continuous Improvement was formed in 1999 by national leaders in continuous improvement, organisational development, planning, quality, institutional effectiveness and related areas. Our mission is to advance academic and administrative excellence in higher education by identifying, promoting, supporting and sharing effective organisational practices among member institutions. Members of NCCI are involved in addressing critical issues by converting policies and ideas into action and results. NCCI enables HEIs to advance the effectiveness of their institutions through collaboration. Hence, NCCI's missing is to advance sustainable excellence in higher education by promoting the practice and discipline of continuous improvement across all academic and administrative functions (www.ncci-cu.org).

[5] www.ncci-cu.org/

The Leveraging Excellence Award Programm

There are outstanding examples of innovation and improvement throughout institutions of higher learning. Due to NCCI's decentralized and independent culture, many of these innovations or improvements lie in pockets where they were first developed. Too few are actively leveraged for maximum impact. Instead, NCCI reinvented.

"This award honors institutions and organisations that have created innovative planning and decision-making processes, and have leveraged their best practices in order to help other colleges, universities, and institutions become more efficient and improve their operational excellence. But this award also recognizes a new trend in higher education. It acknowledges higher education efforts that resonate with business leaders, legislators, and donors. Such relationships play an increasingly significant role in higher education today, as colleges and universities strive to build collaborative partnerships that add value to the various publics in which they serve. "

(University of Kentucky President Lee T. Todd)

Institutions and organisations that have planned and implemented academic or administrative improvements that extend within or across institutions, systems or organisations of higher education are encouraged to apply to the Leveraging Excellence Award Programme. The practice that is being leveraged [30]:

- *Is demonstrated to be an effective practice.*
- *Is having/has had broad impact, e.g. implemented by many units/institutions, disseminated broadly, achieved increased scale of impact.*
- *Has significant and measurable impact.*

Institutions and organisations have been immensely benefitted through this programme. Some of the examples of Leveraging Effective Practices are shown below [ibid]:

- *Development of coordinated curricula/coursework, assessment, or planning methodologies across campuses or institutions.*
- *Creation of service enhancement models and programmes, specifically designed to be used across institutions or throughout higher education.*
- *Establishment of a series of staff leadership or professional development programmes across institutions.*
- *Broad dissemination of a research finding beyond the original source of study, resulting in benefits to higher education or society.*
- *Implementation of a system for sharing resources across institutions.*
- *Implementation of collaborative administrative systems, such as purchasing, IT, libraries, etc. - reducing costs or creating efficiencies across units or institutions*
- *Collaboration across institutions to develop a compact with the state that results in improved systems, efficiencies, and services.*
- *Establishing a platform for sharing effective practices across institutions.*
- *Academic programmes using data to improve curricula and share approaches across disciplines*
- *Successful specialized accreditation practices shared within the discipline*

Some of the examples of award winning institutions of 2008 award ceremony and their contribution to knowledge and business practice is shown below:

Organisation	Indiana University - Purdue University Indianapolis (IUPUI)
Process	"Building a Culture of Evidence to Improve Learning"
Impact	IUPUI's centralized data and analysis services provide information resources for: • Outcomes assessment • Programme evaluation • Institutional research Extensive use of these services for evidence-based decision-making across the campus has contributed to: • Programme improvements at IUPUI • National awards for innovative teaching & learning initiatives • Adoption of these initiatives by other institutions in the US, Japan, Korea, and elsewhere in the world • Public demonstration of institutional accountability and student learning in an electronic institutional portfolio.
Organisation	Committee on Institutional Cooperation (CIC)
Process	"Strategic Collaboration"
Impact	Committee on Institutional Cooperation (CIC), a consortium of twelve research universities, developed strategic collaborations that saved over $29 million and impacted over 900 faculty leaders and 100 peer networks. This collaboration includes: • coordinated purchasing process – saved $16 million • shared fiber network that provides a faster network – saved $13 million • shared over 100 study abroad and course development efforts • best practice sharing and networking – 100+ peer networks • leadership development programme – 900 leaders
Organisation	Brigham Young University
Process	"Capital Needs Analysis"
Impact	Brigham Young University created a programme for managing capital assets in an integrated way. The project began as an innovative approach to managing capital assets and expanded to include: • capital funding, planning, needs projection

	• asset re-capitalization/life-cycle management • improvements/modernization and new asset planning of additional buildings/facilities and site/property needs • retrofits & renewals These efforts saved millions and have been adopted by other BYU campuses and by the Church of Jesus Christ of Later-Day Saints facilities division worldwide. Many educational institutions and governmental entities are introducing this design.
Organisation	Worldwide Universities Network
Process	"Leveraging Research through International Networks"
Impact	Worldwide Universities Network is an international alliance of 16 major research universities from 4 continents creating capability to address global challenges • Committed to large scale interdisciplinary research collaboration; enhanced graduate experiences; curriculum internationalization • Over 70 academic communities involving 3,500+ individuals, which have secured an additional $40 million in income. • 650+ research mobility awards and 4 collaboratively authored Master's programmes • Pump-priming financial, operational, and technical support aids faculty overcoming challenges & risks of establishing and sustaining substantive innovative international activities • First in an emerging trend, charting the course
Organisation	Tennessee Board of Regents
Process	"Academic Audit"
Impact	Tennessee Board of Regents focuses on continuous quality improvement of teaching and learning through auditing of "academic quality processes". With their excellent work Tennessee Board of Regents has leveraged the expertise of multiple institutions to maximize implementation of training and audit components in 19 universities and community colleges

International standards:

HEI's that want to excel in the field need to maintain international standards in order to gain world class reputation. Due to the globalisation, internationalisation of HEIs has become a common phenomenon. International standards is one way of overcoming the barriers in leading in the international market due to the differences among regulations and standards developed independently and separately by each nation, national standards organisation, or institutes. Operational barriers arise when different universities come together, each with a large user base, doing some well established thing that between them is mutually incompatible due to the differences in the basic structure of the curricula. Establishing international standards is one way of preventing or overcoming this problem.

International standards may be used either by direct application or by a process of modifying an international standard to suit local conditions. The adoption of international standards results in the creation of equivalent, national standards that are substantially the same as international standards content, but may have (i) editorial differences as to module descriptions, use of terms and assessment policies, and (ii) differences resulting from conflicts in governmental regulations or education sector-specific requirements caused by fundamental infrastructural factors, or the stringency of basic requirements that a given standard authority considers appropriate. Hence, HEI's that are driving towards excellence need to have key assessment criterion that satisfy the leading international standard bodies for their approval, what sets the stage for the organisations to operate globally with highest standard. Some of such international standard auditing organisations are discussed below for further understanding-

European Foundation for Quality Management (EFQM)[6]

European Foundation for Quality Management (EFQM) is a non-for-profit membership foundation. They have spent over 20 years sharing what works between our member organisations as a way to help them implement their strategies. Through their network of over 700 ambitious and active members comprising private and public organisations of every size and sector, EFQM applies its know-how and extracts outstanding approaches by engaging with executives and front-line managers. The EFQM Excellence Model is a practical tool that can be used in a number of different ways (www.efqm.org):

- As a tool for Self-Assessment
- As a way to Benchmark with other organisations
- As a guide to identify areas for Improvement
- As the basis for a common Vocabulary and a way of thinking
- As a Structure for the organisation's management system

The EFQM Excellence Model is a non-prescriptive framework based on 9 criteria. Five of these are 'Enablers' and four are 'Results'. The 'Enabler' criteria cover what an organisation does. The 'Results' criteria cover what an organisation achieves. 'Results' are caused by 'Enablers' and 'Enablers' are improved using feedback from 'Results'. The EFQM Model is presented in diagram form below. The arrows emphasise the dynamic nature of the Model. They show innovation and learning helping to improve enablers that in turn lead to improved results.

---

[6] www.efqm.org

Figure 22: EFQM Excellence Model

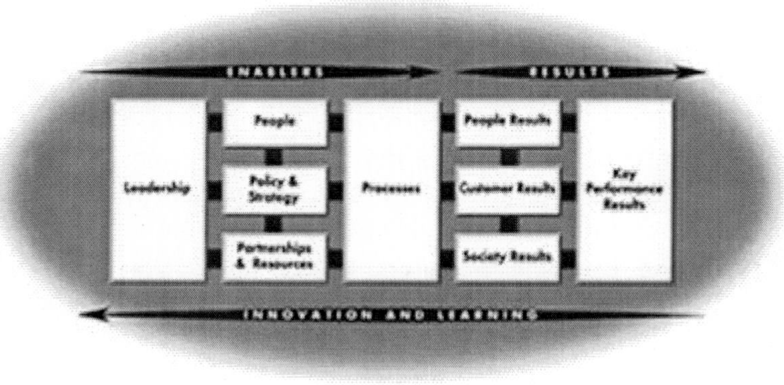

Source: http://www.efqm.org

While the literature suggests that only a small number of UK HEIs have formally adopted the EFQM model (according to the EQUIS website, fourteen business Schools have EQUIS accreditation at the time of writing) there has been a high level of adoption in UK schools and the further education sector. Unlike QAA this is more holistic framework. The Model, which recognises there are many approaches to achieving sustainable excellence in all aspects of performance, is based on the premise that, "Excellence in results, with the respect to performance, customers, people and society, are achieved through leadership drawing on policy and strategy, people, partnerships, resources and processes" (ibid).

The Fundamental Concepts for using EFQM assessment criteria are:

Results Orientation - Excellence is achieving results that delight all the organisation's stakeholders.

Customer Focus-Excellence is creating sustainable customer value.

Leadership and Constancy of Purpose- Excellence is visionary and inspirational leadership, coupled with constancy of purpose.

Management by Processes and Facts - *Excellence* is managing the organisation through a set of interdependent and interrelated systems, processes and facts.

People Development and Involvement- Excellence is maximising the contribution of employees through their development and involvement.

Continuous Learning, Innovation and Improvement- Excellence is challenging the status quo and effecting change by utilising learning to create innovation and improvement opportunities.

Partnership Development- Excellence is developing and maintaining value-adding partnerships.

Corporate Social Responsibility- Excellence is exceeding the minimum regulatory framework in which the organisation operates and to strive to understand and respond to the expectations of their stakeholders in society.

Figure 23: Relationship between EFQM attributes

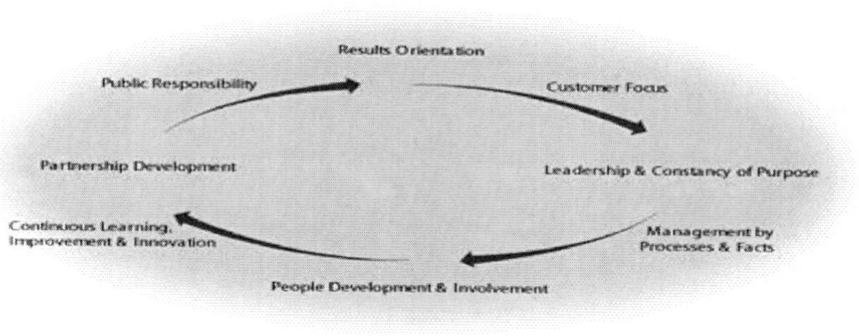

Source: http://www.efqm.org

However, a number of limitations have been identified in applying the EFQM model in an HE context (Oakland, 1999). The model is perceived as too prescriptive, too time consuming and requires adequate resources. Additionally, it requires prior knowledge and deliberate strategy for successful implementation. Finally, there is a high degree of "subjectivity" in scoring the EFQM criteria.

Malcolm Baldrige National Quality Award (MBNQA)[7]

Malcolm Baldrige National Quality Award was created in 1987 by U.S. Congress. It introduced new act in the legislation, Malcolm Baldrige National Quality Improvement Act, Public Law 100-107. The MBNQA was initially a National initiative to help industry and service organisations improve performance to become more competitive globally named after Malcolm Baldrige. It is now administered by the Baldrige National Quality Programme (BNQA) under the National Institute of Science and Technology (NIST), a division of the United States Department of Commerce (www.quality.nist.gov)

Baldrige Education Criteria for Performance Excellence provides a framework and an assessment tool for understanding organisational strengths and opportunities for improvement and thus for guiding planning efforts. It is an integrated approach to organisational performance management that results in [ibid]:

- Delivery of ever-improving value to students and stakeholders, contributing to improved education quality and student learning;
- Improvement of overall organisational effectiveness and capabilities;
- Organisational and personal learning.

This is a value based assessment for the education sector. The Core Values and Concepts of Baldrige National Quality programme are [ibid]-

- Systems Perspective
- Visionary Leadership
- Student-Centered Excellence
- Organisational and Personal Learning
- Valuing Employees and Partners

---

7 www.quality.nist.gov

- Agility
- Focus on the Future
- Managing for Innovation
- Management by Fact
- Emphasis on Results and Creating Value

Figure 24: MBQNA Model

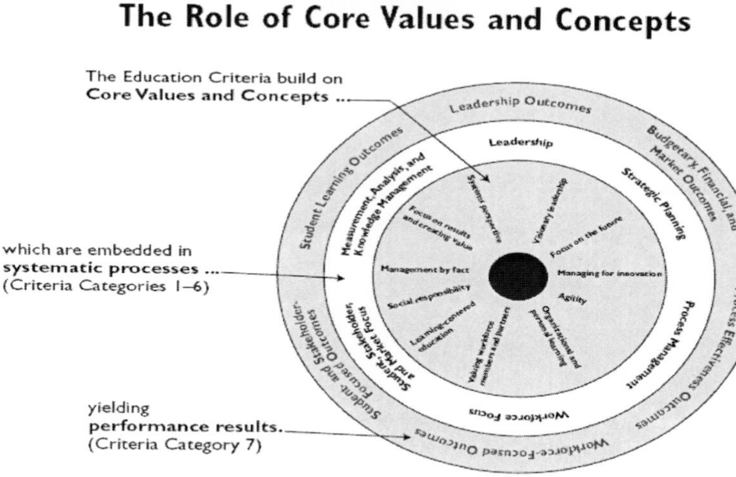

Source: www.quality.nist.gov

Figure 25: Criteria's Set to assess Excellence in Education

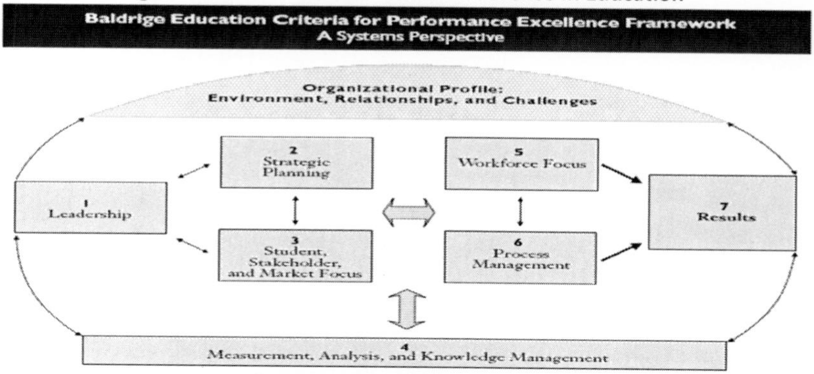

Source: www.quality.nist.gov

The Education Criteria for Performance Excellence in A Table below:

Malcolm Baldrige National Quality Award (MBNQA)	POINTS
1 Leadership	120
2 Strategic Planning	85
3 Student, Stakeholder, and Market Focus	85
4 Measurement, Analysis, and Knowledge Management	90
5 Workforce Focus	85
6 Process Management	85
7 Results	450
Total	**1000**

The above criteria for MBQA give a clear guideline to the HEI's where they can improve and what needs to be assessed to have a world class university. Both EFQM and MBQA provide self assessment pack on their website should HEIs like to do a self assessment in-house.

ISO in Higher Education[8]

ISO (the International Standard Organisation) head-quartered in Geneva, is a worldwide federation of national standard bodies (ISO member bodies, such as SIRIM, SISIR, etc) which is responsible for creating standard for each member country. The objective of setting up of this body is to encourage the formulation and practice of international standard. The creation of ISO 9000 standard is to assure the products and services offered by the member countries are globally recognized and accepted 10. ISO 9000 was initially published in 1979, and from a slow start it is now being implemented by a very large number of commercial organisations. The ISO 9000 deals with quality system requirements that can be used for external quality assurance purposes (www.iso.org).

[8] http://www.iso.org/iso/home.htm

The quality assurance models set out in this International Standards represent three distinct forms of quality system requirements suitable for the purpose of a supplier demonstrating its capability, and for the assessment of the capability of a supplier by external parties. Before any organisation achieved ISO recognition, it has to establish a quality system and procedure outlined in the models set out in the standard. ISO 9000 is divided into three basic sections: ISO 9001, for quality assurance system which includes design, development, production, installation and servicing, ISO 9002, for quality assurance system in production, installation and servicing, and ISO 9003, for quality assurance in final inspection and testing (ibid).

ISO created an education award in 2007 to encourage and recognize successful programmes in higher education on standardization. The ISO Award aims to raise awareness of the importance of standardization worldwide by supporting institutions of higher education that have developed and implemented successful programmes related to standardization as a tool to access world markets, transfer technology and promote good business practice and sustainable development.

The award comprises a certificate of appreciation and a cash prize of 15 000 Swiss francs. It is co-sponsored by ISO and the Japanese Industrial Standards Committee (JISC), the ISO member for Japan. ISO Secretary-General Alan Bryden commented: "Knowledge of the economic, technical and social importance and benefits of standards is becoming imperative in the curricula of future managers, scientists and technologists. Many universities and other higher education institutions have begun introducing their students to standardization. ISO is keen to support them in their efforts and to encourage them to share their knowledge, experience and expertise with other educational establishments." (ibid)

Benefits of Implementing ISO 9000

SIRIM carried out a survey on 536 companies, which have attained ISO 9000 certification and received 500 respondents. From the survey it is found that the two major advantages are improved quality (76.5%) and increased customer perception or improved advertising campaign (72.9%). Other than that, increased productivity (42.3%), reduced cost (36.7%), better staff morals (29.6%) and improved market shares (28.6%) are also gained when ISO 9000 is implemented. Others include [ibid]:

- *Enhance organization image with internationally accepted quality standard.*
- *Recognized globally as a centre of engineering education where quality is assured.*
- *Demonstrate documented quality management system.*
- *Satisfy customers and current market environment.*
- *Foundation for a total quality management program.*
- *Sets a baseline for continuous improvement.*
- *Reduction in customer complaints.*
- *Improve productivity and efficiency.*
- *Increase quality awareness, motivation, co-operation, workmanship and consciousness.*
- *Reduces time-consuming audits by customers and regulators.*
- *Focuses training and professional development.*
- *Reduce mistakes and rework (right first time).*
- *Improved communication internally.*
- *Prepare for future market requirement.*

Example ISO application in university libraries[9]

University libraries, both traditional and digital, are very important parts of the educational process, especially in terms of the 2010 horizon of the European Higher Education Area. As a service to the university community, it has to have mechanisms for measurement and evaluation of its activities in order to guarantee the quality of

[9] http://www2.ub.edu/bid/consulta_articulos.php?fichero=19balag3.htm

the services offered and the satisfaction of its users. As a result, one of the main challenges of libraries is to investigate and to decide upon the most appropriate mechanisms to improve and to ensure the quality of their services.

The ISO 9000 series has not been specially conceived to be applied in libraries and – as noted by St. Clair – a lot of work remains to be done to establish the value of implementing ISO standards in information services. Since the point when libraries began to adopt this standard, they have basically used two of the three editions that have appeared so far - the 1994 and the 2000 editions (www2.ub.edu).

ISO 9001:2000 has been applied to libraries in institutions of higher education of all sizes, regardless of whether the library system consists of a single library or a large network with many service points that is scattered across different campus locations. More than half the cases (50.8%) are library systems that consist of a maximum of three libraries, but the range is extended to fairly large library systems, with numerous points of service and 14.3% are systems consisting of 20 or more libraries. In the same way, the human resources of certified libraries vary from a library managed by a single person to library systems with a very large staff. 28.1% of the libraries have staffs of 15 people or less, 25.4% have staff of between 16 and 50 people, 20.6% have between 51 and 100 people, 20.7% have between 101 and 200 people and finally, 6.4% have more than 200 employees (ibid).

Consequently, from the above case study it can be summarised that the advantages of quality certification are, ISO:

- *Standardizes work processes*
- *Improves documentation procedures*
- *Facilitates data gathering for management*
- *Defines responsibilities clearly*

- *Promotes the dynamics of continuous improvement*
- *Reduces improvisation*
- *Provides management transparency*
- *Improves effectiveness of library services*
- *Provides a tool for promoting the library*
- *Acts as a catalyst for organizational change*
- *Increases user satisfaction*
- *Improves operational efficiency*
- *Creates improved understanding between the library and its customers*
- *Improves integration of the library within the university*
- *Improves communication within the library*
- *Improves the attitude of the staff*
- *Improves staff management*

The above discussion highlights the areas that need to be investigated in order for the HEIs having the right measurement tools to succeed as an excellent organisation in the field of academia.

Level III –Micro Level- Attaining Excellence

All of the top achievers I know are life-long learners... looking for new skills, insights, and ideas. If they're not learning, they're not growing... not moving toward excellence.
Denis Waitley

The institution at this stage seeks to be an international player in quality management and used different initiatives to enhance its visibility in the international forum. The key areas of level-3 of assessment excellence model are-

1. ***D****efining a culture of excellence,*
2. *Initiating quality projects,*

3. *Embedding quality solutions,*
4. *Raising standards,*
5. *Scaling up quality practices,*
6. *Building quality maturity,*
7. *Achieving & sustaining quality*

Once an institution has grown its quality capabilities, it then can be said to have attained excellent standard. The challenge for such an institution then is to build on the gains by adopting best practices from others optimizing its capabilities, honing its innovative capabilities and sustaining the gains made hence the acronym AOIS for (Adopting, Optimizing, Innovation and Sustaining) (Garvin, D.A. 1984).

- **Adopting** – institutions like people must be open to learn from others. However, such best practices need to be customized to suit the needs of the institution in line with its capabilities, otherwise the whole exercise will be a waste,
- **Optimizing** – having adopted best practices, then the institution should apply these practices to enhance or optimize its capabilities. The focus must be on the value chain and how to drive smart outcomes,
- **Innovation** – adoption of best practices must be combined by internal drive for innovation. Employee creativity within must be properly channeled and evaluated and harnessed. Funding is crucial here as is an amenable environment that does not stifle creativity,
- **Sustaining** – all incremental gains made ought to be quantified and upheld, to avoid sliding to non-performance. Robust leadership, structure, culture, approaches, systems and talent management are critical towards sustaining gains made.

Albeit it has been mentioned earlier in the discussion that the outer ring of the Assessment Excellence Model(see figure-1) are listed as level 3, these are the factors that will guide the organisation towards excellence as the factors are internally focused. Subsequently HEIs, need to focus on the following areas in order to have an correctly measured and rightly designed assessment procedure to achieve excellence in academia-

Defining culture of excellence

A quality culture is an organisational value system that results in an environment that is conducive to the establishment and continual improvement of quality. It consists of values, traditions, procedures, and expectations that promote quality. Attaining organisational excellence in assessment necessitates cultural change in an organisation, for the following reasons (Bryman, 1988):

- *Change cannot occur in a hostile environment.*
- *Moving towards excellence in quality takes time.*
- *It can be difficult to overcome the past.*

Change can be difficult because resisting change is natural human behavior. In any organisation there will be advocates of change and resisters. Sometimes advocates focus so intently on the expected benefits of change that they fail to realize how the change will be perceived by potential resisters. People resist change for the following reasons [ibid]:

- *Uncertainty*
- *More work*
- *Fear*
- *Loss of Control*

To overcome resistance to change, managers need to apply the following strategies- 1. involve potential resisters; 2. avoid surprises; 3. move slowly at first; 4.start small and be flexible; 5. create a positive environment; 6. incorporate the change. Provide a *quid pro quo; 7. r*espond quickly and positively; 8. work with established leaders; 9. treat people with dignity and respect and 10.be constructive(Richardson, 1998).

Strategies for establishing a quality culture include the following [ibid]:

- *Identify the changes needed.*
- *Put the planned changes in writing.*
- *Develop a plan for making the changes.*
- *Understand the emotional transition process.*
- *Identify key people and make them advocates.*
- *Take a hearts and minds approach.*
- *Apply courtship strategies.*
- *Support.*

At times it might be necessary to change an organisation's leadership team to ensure needed cultural changes. This situation arises when the organisation's senior executives have a great deal invested in the status quo and therefore are staunch defenders of orthodoxy (please refer to session / day 2 for further explanations on culture).

Initiating quality projects

In order to best fulfill customer needs, requirements, and expectations, effective organisations create and utilize quality systems. Within a quality management system the necessary ingredients exist to enable the organisation's employees to identify, design, develop, produce, deliver, and support products or services that the customer wants. Effective quality management systems are dynamic, able to adapt and change to meet the needs, requirements, and expectations of its customers. Effective organisations use standards such as ISO 9000 and QS 9000, programmes like Six Sigma, and awards like the Malcolm Baldrige National Quality Award to provide guidance for establishing their quality management system's structure, maintaining records, and using quality techniques to improve processes and systems (Bryman, 1988).

In today's highly competitive, global marketplace, a company that excels is one that continually strives to identify and focus on factors critical to its customers and improve its processes in order to provide the highest quality product or service possible. This task is far from simple. Companies have a variety of strategies that can be used to enhance their position in the marketplace; teams, quality assurance, just-in-time, total quality management, Six Sigma, lean manufacturing, and others. Like pieces of a puzzle that won't fall into place, many of these efforts have not created an overall alignment of an entire organisational system that focuses on the factors critical to the organisation's success. Instead, efforts are disjointed programmes that fail to reach their full potential, generating success in some areas and disillusionment in others. In truth, what is needed is an organisation-wide approach that improves and enhances the whole process of providing a product or service enabling the organisation to exceed customer expectations, each and every time through initiating quality projects.

Embedding quality solutions

Having excellent leadership and effective organisational culture might not necessarily help an organisation towards implementing a good system for assessing academic excellence. HEIs need to have the relevant and excellent solution tools for excellence through assessment. HEIs implement Six Sigma programmes which ultimately will lead to improved profitability; increased customer retention; reduced customer complaints and warranty claims; reduced costs through less waste, rework, and so on; achieve a greater market share; increased employee involvement and satisfaction; lower employee turnover; an increased ability to attract new customers, improve their competitiveness, and customer satisfaction; improved management-employee relations; improved focus on key goals; improved internal and external communication; and improved teamwork (Veal, 1997). This tool needs to be embedded in the system, what makes the management job easy for a systematic assessment of the organisation.

Raising standards

Whatever quality dimensions are being measured, it is necessary to consider whether a quantitative or qualitative approach is more appropriate given the purpose of a particular quality assessment. Powell et al.(1997) review of evaluation methods suggests that there is merit in both quantitative and qualitative approaches. While quantitative ratings facilitate performance comparability either internally or externally, they generally fail to provide any clear explanation as to why certain ratings are given. As such they may be more suitable for quality assurance initiatives. Using numerical ratings would enable assessors to establish that at least a minimum level of quality is attained. Qualitative data, on the other hand, provides richer or more "illuminating" (Blaxter et al., 2001) data that can more readily inform decision making for quality enhancement purposes. However, this type of data may prove to be less beneficial when benchmarking performance. A quality management programme that utilises a mixture of both types of data would seem most appropriate for both quality assurance and enhancement purposes (Brookes, 2003)

At the compliance end of the spectrum it is likely that quality audits might focus more on outputs rather than process, although inputs might be taken into consideration. However, in order to develop relevant enhancement initiatives, all three system components including processes should be assessed. While all of Harvey and Knight's (1996) dimensions of quality are important, it is quality as transformational that is most closely aligned with quality enhancement activities, particularly if qualitative assessments are used to inform change. Both snapshot and longitudinal approaches can be used for quality assurance and enhancement. However, it is the latter that is more in line with a continuous quality improvement approach. Any audit tool should therefore assess the provision for documenting and effecting change within quality management system. This will ultimately guide the managers how to raise the standard of the organisation. Ultimately, if the organisations do not keep on raising their standard on a regular basis, at one stage they will realize that they are sitting at the bottom of league table without lowering their standard.

Scaling up quality practices

All of the aforementioned criteria are relevant to the ultimate purpose of quality assessment. Traditionally, the focus within higher education has been to assess quality for assurance purposes often driven by external stakeholders. However, there is a greater emphasis today on assessing quality in order to inform change and enhance provision and there may be greater tendency for this when assessments are driven by internal stakeholders. This practice needs to be changed in the HEIs sector in order to survive in this highly competitive market of global education. HEIs needs to understand that it is not only implementing quality in their practices., they also need to move to the next phase of their management practice through improvement of their quality measures. As it can be seen in the following case of Vald Birn (UK) Ltd, how they achieved world class status through continuous improvement and scaling up their quality process.

Case: Vald Birn (UK) Ltd achieves international standard achieving team culture[10]

Vald Birn (UK) Ltd, leading suppliers of quality cast iron parts to the automotive and engineering industries, has announced dramatic gains as a result of a recent process improvement activity, facilitated by MICE (Metals Industry Competitive Enterprise). Through a structured five-month programme of MICE-led activities, Vald Birn has realised improvements such as cutting rework by 95%, reducing set up times on robotic finishing by 33% and gaining a 21% increase in overall equipment effectiveness. For the business, this

[10] http://www.allbusiness.com/primary-metal-manufacturing/foundries/248134-1.html

has generated major long-term financial savings that impact significantly on the company's bottom line. But as importantly, the MICE team-based approach used to achieve these results has sown the seeds for an entirely new workforce culture that has enabled Vald Birn to achieve the new ISO/TS 16949, putting the company amongst world class elite of manufacturers.

Building quality maturity

Maturity implies *knowing*. It has been discussed earlier how organisations can lead through excellence, how to create an excellent environment in academia, how to become an excellent HEI. However, it needs to be put in the discussion that it is not all about only working towards attaining excellence; the HEIs need to thrive to reach the maturity level of quality application. Philip Crosby was the originator of the concept of maturity in the area of quality, describing his Quality Management Maturity Grid in his seminal work, 'Quality is Free', where people go through five stages of maturity (Garvin,1984):

- *Uncertainty -- 'Quality problems are the fault of the Quality department.'*
- *Awakening -- 'Quality management might actually fix problems properly.'*
- *Enlightenment -- 'Management and quality people are working together to fix problems.'*
- *Wisdom -- 'Quality management integrated in to the way we do things.'*
- *Certainty -- 'We do not have quality problems because we understand everything.'*

HEI's leaders ought therefore to focus on quality improvement and quality capabilities to finally achieve the maturity level of excellence (see fig- 5 below). The model explains which tools needs to be used in different levels. It suggests that HEIs can initiate and drive the quality programme for improvement using tools such as Kaizen, Six sigma models, where PDCA will be used as a base model for all activities. Level indicates how HEIs can investigate the organisation's overall situation through internal and externally auditing in order improve their capabilities. Here HEIs will be focusing on the DIRE model and use EFQM or MBQA for self assessment or benchmarking as a tool for internal auditing and use ISO or accreditation agency services for externally auditing. Institutes can also contact EFQM or MBQA for externally audited. Finally, to rich the maturity of excellence, HEIs should further invest in improving the quality by following the AOIS (please see the next section for explanation) guidelines to compete in the international level. In this phase they will be benchmarking with the world class HEI and will focus on how to get accredited by most respectable accreditation global agencies.

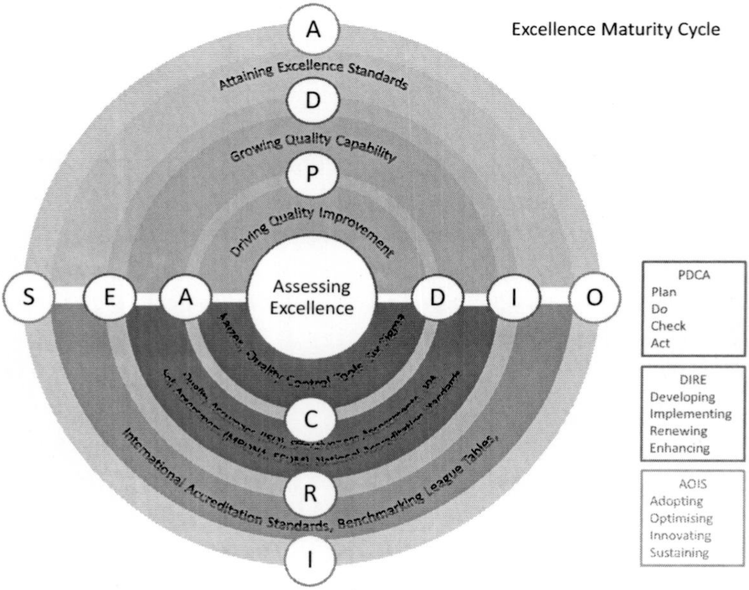

Achieving and sustaining excellence

Once an institution reaches the stage of academic excellence, the next logical question arises to the leaders is, whether they can sustain that excellence or not. It is much harder to sustain the academic excellence than achieving it for once. For HEIs, some of the approaches that may be applied to sustain excellence include:

- *International Accreditation*
- *Benchmarking*
- *Self Assessment*
- *Six Sigma in HE*

International Accreditation

International accreditation is an extensive quality control process normally carried out by teams of professional assessors assisted by senior management from high ranking Management Schools all over the world. The primary objectives of the world's leading accreditation bodies differ.

These accreditations are rigorous processes that involve assessment of numerous aspects of the school and its programmes. Typically, this involves the business school submitting an in-depth self-analysis report for scrutiny by these bodies, followed by a visiting panel and the consequent interviewing of current students, staff, alumni, corporate clients and employers. These bodies have no obligation to make an award - indeed; many business schools are unsuccessful in their application.

For example, there are at least 3500 MBA programmes worldwide, so for someone about to embark on one, choosing the right programme and business school can be a daunting task. Once a student have thought about the budget, preferred location and/or how the student want to study, can start to narrow things down a little, but thereafter it becomes difficult task to make the best choice. Accreditation of business schools and their programmes can help, as these official seals of approval offer a very objective way of measuring a school's credentials. For example, the quality of education on offer, the facilities, the student body and the faculty are all reviewed (Alstete 1996) .

The Association of MBAs (AMBA)[11]

With so many MBAs on offer, quality has become the key. AMBA was set up in 1967 to promote the MBA to institutions, prospective students and employers and to ensure the quality of programme produces professional managers. The accreditation process was established to secure these objectives. The process is market-driven and international in focus, and each business school offering an MBA are assessed against a set of criteria established by AMBA's Independent Accreditation Advisory Board.

For potential students, accreditation provides a reliable list of schools tested for quality. For business schools, it gives international credibility to their MBA provision and an overview of their position against international standards. For the MBA graduate, it gives reassurance of the degree's value at a time when the market risks saturation, and for the employer it guarantees the quality of the MBA. It confirms that to recruit an MBA from an accredited school is to recruit top talent.

European Quality Improvement System (EQUIS)[12]

EQUIS's fundamental objective is to raise the standard of management education worldwide. Its focus is not primarily on the MBA programme, but on all management programmes offered by an institution from a first degree up to the PhD. EQUIS provides recognition that the accredited institutions are not only attaining high standards in their national market, but are also credible in the international arena. Institutions accredited by EQUIS must demonstrate not only high general quality in all dimensions of their activities, but also a high degree of internationalisation. Deans of reputed academic institutions, managing directors and HR directors of major corporations, heads of national professional associations,

[11] http://graduate.mbaworld.com/content/welcome/index.htm

[12] http://www.efmd.org/component/efmd/?cmsid=040929rpku

consultants, and assessment experts form the pool from which the international peer review teams are drawn.

A school initially applies to enter the scheme, and then goes through a preliminary eligibility screening to determine whether there are major obstacles to eventual accreditation and whether accreditation is probable. Once declared eligible, the school carries out a self-assessment. This is submitted and a team of four peer reviewers visits the institution to establish whether it meets EQUIS standards. Their presentation to the awarding body is the deciding factor on accreditation.

EQUIS investigates the school's strategy, quality of resources, faculty, students, student services, programmes, research, the degree of internationalisation, and connections to the corporate world. In UK several top ranking business schools including the School of Management, University of Bradford have been accredited by EQUIS.

The Association to Advanced Collegiate Schools of Business (AACSB)[13]

AACSB accreditation is a process of voluntary, non-governmental review of educational institutions and programmes, reviewing entire colleges and universities. As a specialised agency, AACSB International grants accreditation for undergraduate and graduate business administration and accounting programmes.

AACSB International accreditation represents the highest standard of achievement for business schools, worldwide. Institutions that earn accreditation confirm their commitment to quality and continuous improvement through a rigorous and comprehensive

[13] http://www.aacsb.edu/

peer review. AACSB International accreditation is the hallmark of excellence in management education.
AACSB International accreditation assures stakeholders that business schools.

- Manage resources to achieve a vibrant and relevant mission.
- Advance business and management knowledge through faculty scholarship.
- Provide high-calibre teaching of quality and current curricula.
- Cultivate meaningful interaction between students and a qualified faculty.
- Produce graduates who have achieved specified learning goals.

Acknowledging the diversity within AACSB, all accredited members share a common purpose - the preparation of students to enter useful professional, societal and personal lives. The accreditation review focuses on a member's clear determination of its mission, development of its faculty members, and the planning and delivery of its instruction. Each institution must achieve and demonstrate an acceptable level of performance consistent with its mission while satisfying AACSB accreditation standards.

In the accreditation process, HEIs has to complete a self-evaluation report. AACSB evaluates the report, and a visit by the peer review team follows. For AACSB accreditation, a HEI must offer degree-granting programmes in business or management, and there must be continuing resources for these programmes [ibid].

Council for Higher Education Accreditation (CHEA)[14]

Council for Higher Education Accreditation (CHEA) is a national advocate and institutional voice for self-regulation of academic

[14] http://www.chea.org/default.asp

quality through accreditation, CHEA is an association of 3,000 degree-granting colleges and universities and recognizes 60 institutional and programmematic accrediting organisations. It is the largest institutional higher education membership organisation in the United States, with approximately 3,000 degree-granting colleges and universities. CHEA has sixty recognized institutional and programmematic accrediting organisations and is governed by a 20-person board of college and university presidents, institutional representatives and public members.

CHEA's commitment to the coordination and improvement of quality review is based on seven principles. These principles provide the foundation for the CHEA mission statement, the organisational functions described in the CHEA Bylaws and the CHEA Recognition Policy[ibid].

- Quality Assurance. CHEA applies its recognition standards and sustain ongoing review of its participating accrediting organisations to assure high quality of organisational performance.
- Leadership. CHEA provides thoughtful leadership to formulate issues related to quality assurance; to develop needed tools and strategies to sustain the value of quality assurance to institutions, accreditors and students; and to advance change and needed improvement in quality assurance in higher education.
- Advocacy. CHEA is a forceful and articulate advocate for voluntary accreditation of higher education to the public, government and other interested individuals, groups and countries.
- Service. CHEA consistently provides high-quality research, policy analysis and service to its member institutions, accrediting organisations, students and the public.
- Core Values. CHEA maintains the core academic values central to higher education and quality assurance. These

include, for example, the values of general education, collegiality and academic freedom.

- Independence. CHEA is an independent and authoritative voice for the strengthening of accreditation to strengthen higher education.
- Inclusion. CHEA will sustain an environment of active consultation and participation among its member institutions and participating organisations, as well as encourage cooperation and exchange throughout the higher education and quality assurance communities.

CHEA Recognition Standards criteria [ibid]	
Advance academic quality.	Accreditors have a clear description of academic quality and clear expectations that the institutions or programmes they accredit have processes to determine whether quality standards are being met.
Demonstrate accountability.	Accreditors have standards that call for institutions and programmes to provide consistent, reliable information about academic quality and student achievement to foster continuing public confidence and investment.
Encourage, where appropriate, self scrutiny and planning for change and needed improvement.	Accreditors encourage self scrutiny for change and needed improvement through ongoing self-examination in institutions and programmes.
Employ appropriate and fair procedures in decision making	Accreditors maintain appropriate and fair organisational policies and procedures that include effective checks and balances.
Demonstrate ongoing review of accreditation practice.	Accreditors undertake self scrutiny of their accrediting activities.
Possess sufficient resources.	Accreditors have and maintain predictable and stable resources.

Benchmarking

Benchmarking basically refers to learning from others and adopting best practices from such to improve own performance. Due to its reliance on hard data and research methodology, benchmarking is especially suited for institutions of higher education in which these types of studies are very familiar to faculty and administrators. Practitioners at colleges and universities have found that benchmarking helps overcome resistance to change, provides a structure for external evaluation, and creates new networks of communication between schools where valuable information and experiences can be shared (AACSB 1994). Benchmarking is a positive process, and provides objective measurements for baselining (setting the initial values), goal-setting and improvement tracking, which can lead to dramatic innovations (Shafer & Coate 1992). In addition, quality strategies and reengineering efforts are both enhanced by benchmarking because it can identify areas that could benefit most from TQM and/or BPR, and make it possible to improve operations with often dramatic innovations.

Benchmarking attempts to answer the following questions:

- How well are we doing compared to others?
- How good do we want to be?
- Who is doing it the best?
- How do they do it?
- How can we adapt what they do to our institution?
- How can we be better than the best?[55]

Application of benchmarking in HEIs?

Graduate business schools, professional associations such as NACUBO and ACHE, independent data sharing consortia, private consulting companies, and individual institutions are all conducting benchmarking projects today. The broad-based NACUBO benchmarking programme was begun in late 1991, and it seeks to provide participants with an objective basis for improved operational performance by offering a "pointer" to the best practices of other organisations. Today, nearly 282 institutions have participated in the study, and the current project analyzes 26 core functions at colleges and universities, such as accounting, admissions, development, payroll, purchasing, student housing, and others (NACUBO 1995). The Association for Continuing Higher Education (ACHE) and graduate business schools have also conducted specialized benchmarking studies that focus on the processes and practices concerning their particular institutional departments (AACSB 1994). A review of the literature finds independent benchmarking projects are currently in use, or have recently been conducted, by a wide range of institutions such as the University of the Chicago, Oregon State University, Pennsylvania State University, Babson College, and many others. These independent projects cover undergraduate and graduate teaching processes, as well as academic and business administrative practices.

How Can a HEI Get Started?

A HEI should decide if benchmarking is the correct quality improvement tool for the situation before starting a project. After processes are selected for analysis, the appropriate personnel, who have a working knowledge of the area undergoing the benchmarking analysis, should then be chosen to conduct the study. A college and university can take part in an externally sponsored benchmarking project with predefined objectives, or conduct a project on its own or with the help of consultants. It is recommended that, as a start, an institution new to benchmarking, begin with a more "grassroots" level departmental or administrative project that measures best practices internally, or with local competitors.

A HEI that is more advanced in quality improvement efforts can seek out world-class competitors better and implement the findings more readily than a benchmarking novice. Information on prospective benchmarking partners can be obtained from libraries, professional associations, personal contacts, and data sharing consortia. Once the benchmarking data is collected and analyzed, it can be distributed in a benchmarking report internally within the institution and externally to benchmarking partners for implementation of improved processes. The overall goal is the adaption of the process enablers at the home institution to achieve effective quality improvement. Benchmarking is more than just gathering data. It involves adapting a new approach of continually questioning how processes are performed, seeking out best practices, and implementing new models of operation. In HEIs, several benchmarking initiatives are conducted at individual, national and international levels.

University league tables

University league table is one of the most commonly used methods for assessing academic excellence. The top university league table ranks universities by measuring key aspects of activity. Examples of league tables in the UK include: Times good university guide, the Good university guide and Guardian university guide. The aspects considered in these rankings generally vary but include the following :

- **Student satisfaction**: a view of the learning experience at the university, taken from part of the National Student Survey in 2005. The survey It is a measure of student opinion, not a direct measure of quality. Scottish universities were not included and a small number of English ones had insufficient data.
- **Research assessment**: average quality of research by all staff at the university, from the 2001 Research Assessment Exercise.
- **Entry standards**: average full UCAS tariff score of new students under age 21, from the HESA (Higher Education Statistics Agency) in 2003/04. At A level, an A grade is 120 points, B 100, C 80, D 60, and E 40. AS grades are worth half as much.

- **Student-staff ratio**: average number of students per staff member at the university, taken from HESA data for 2003/04.
- **Library/computing spend**: average expenditure per student on library and computing facilities, from HESA data between 2001 and 2004.
- **Facilities spend**: average expenditure per student on facilities such as sports, careers services, health and counseling, from HESA data between 2001 and 2004.
- **Good honours**: percentage of graduates achieving a first or upper second class degree, from HESA data for 2003-04.
- **Graduate prospects:** the percentage of a university's UK graduates in "graduate" employment or further study, from HESA data for 2003-04. Only occupations that normally need a degree were included.
- **Completion:** the percentage of students at each university who are expected to graduate, including those who transfer to other institutions to complete courses, mainly from HESA data for 2003/04 and earlier years.

Hence, university league tables are not the only way to choose a University, but do give an indication of quality and reputation, both overall and in subject areas. This works for all the relevant stakeholders involved, eg, funding agencies, regulatory bodies, awarding authorities, business community, partners and strategic alliances etc.

Self-assessment

Self-assessment is the basic part of any assessment. An institution evaluating its own activities formulates its objectives and tasks, analyses its activities applying different approaches, reveals its activity problems and foresees the ways of resolving them. Self-evaluation is an integral part of any evaluation. The self-evaluation has a dual purpose; on the one hand, it should be used as documentation for the final report and its recommendations and, on the other hand, it should be seen as an inspiration for the evaluated educational programme or establishment for quality improvement. In the self-evaluation, the educational establishment has to describe and assess its own strengths and weaknesses. Normally, the participants will be the teachers and also the students or the pupils and management. The self-evaluation is based on guidelines prepared by the project group. Within the context of an audit, self-evaluation refers to the process by which an institution reviews the effectiveness of its quality management system for assuring, developing and monitoring the quality of teaching and learning, research and community engagement against the requirements of external audit criteria and any other quality criteria that the institution deems relevant. The self-evaluation process leads to the development of an audit portfolio by the institution for submission to a quality award.

Self-evaluation, in the right context, is useful for encouraging fundamental reviews of objectives, practices and outcomes. Owing to pressures from a range of stakeholders for a wider and improved range of services from the Higher Education (HE) sector , linked with a simultaneously increasing pressure on resource utilisation, universities are currently facing the challenges of reorienting their approaches to be more customer-focused and conducting their activities in a more business-like manner. A consortium of universities in Europe, America and Asia are currently implementing the European Foundation for Quality Management (EFQM) excellence model and MBQA models as a means for addressing these issues. The early signs of the implementation are that EFQM and MBQA excellence model self-assessment can help to produce a more customer-oriented culture in HE institutions, providing that the lessons learned from the wider public sector are put into practice.

Six Sigma in Education

In Higher education, Six Sigma pertains to improving the quality of matter taught, the character generated of the pupils, and the quality of study and school life. With the revolutionary usage of audio-visual devices, like projectors, video conferencing, etc., the students can also be asked to write papers on a particular subject and after the presentation of papers, a discussion can take place on the respective subject. Under this method of imparting knowledge of literacy with quality, the thinking, writing and presentation skills of the students can be kindled. In addition, the existing method of quality improvement through SQCC (Students Quality Control Circles) has created the value-based concept as a simile for the Six Sigma standards. It infuses a spike of excellence, emotional development, humaneness and self-discipline.

Culture of Six Sigma

The culture of Six Sigma suggests a work environment and quality of work life where everyone in the company desires to achieve the Six Sigma target, to increase customer satisfaction, to increase efficiency, to lower costs and to improve profitability. This culture provides an important and continuing focus to management. The Six Sigma quality concept penetrates -- applying to all processes within a company -- whether 'defective' means an out-of-spec time coming off a production line, the amount of 're-work' in a batch of a product, a document with a misprint, or a late delivery time. The implementation in the educational arena requires the teachers to be considered 'employees', or the workforce in general. The customers tend to be the parents who pay the fees and want quality in return of the good result of their wards .

Application of Six Sigma

The implementation or application of Six Sigma starts with the recognition of a problem, and the defining of a project to cure or alleviate that problem. The project is undertaken by a team using DMAIC, which stands for Define, Measure, Analyze, Improve and Control. These are defined further as :

- ***DEFINE****: This phase involves the definition of the project/assignment, using process map, application area,* *desired improvement, likely benefits, etc. The importance lies in having the chance of a high successful delivery of better quality and saving costs in totality. In the context of academic strata, the failures include identifying and defining the problem. Projects may include real life problems such as distractions in the classroom, for example.*

- ***MEASURE**: This phase involves the analysis of the process to determine its present state and the future, as obtained. Data collection is the main emphasis of this phase.*
- ***ANALYSE**: This phase involves the data analysis for identification of parts of process, which affect the quality of the problem.*
- ***IMPROVE**: This phase adds to the process to find a permanent solution to the problem. This may involve better forecasting, better scheduling, better procedures or equipment, specifying teaching techniques, work environment for the teachers, and school campus quality life.*
- ***CONTROL**: This phase involves the process of closing the problem by putting in the right procedures and management statistics.*

To sum up level-3, it is apparent from the above discussion that HEI's that want to excel in this level has to start with the basic question of how they can introduce the quality culture efficiently.

In conclusion, the literature suggests that even though the models of quality concepts are originated from the HEIs, there tend to be less implementation of these concepts in academia compared to the business field. One of the major reasons for this is the lack of interest in achieving excellence through quality implementation. It is due to the fact that in most of these HEIs they do not have the understanding of the importance of assessment and control issues in academia , hence do not have the right tools in place for assessing their performance and their future strategies. Therefore, it is vitally important that HEIs put more emphasis on developing an effective tool for assessing academic excellence to attain and sustain academic excellence. It can be seen from the case study below, how Oxford has achieved excellence through development of KPIs and focusing on them to sustain the academic excellence-

Case study: University of Oxford: Achieving international standards of excellence in teaching and learning[15]

Key issues:

- Distinguishing between the scholarships of discovery, integration, application and teaching
- Different strategies for linking R&T in different kinds of institutions
- Aligning research and teaching strategies
- Flexibility in academic contracts
- Equality of rewards: (Utrecht, Manchester)

How world-class universities develop teaching

- Increasing benefits to undergraduates of research strengths
- Curriculum-led change and 'constructive alignment'
- By-passing blocks
- Leadership of change
- Increasing pedagogic expertise
- Funding-led change
- Entrepreneurial management
- Management of 'complex organisational change'
- Research-informed change
- Discipline-led change

Teaching and learning at Oxford

- The tutorial, the tutor and the colleges
- Importance of undergraduates

---

[15] www.rektorkollegiet.dk/typo3conf/ext/naw_securedl/secure.php?

- The colleges: intensive residential experience
- Separation of teaching from assessment
- Separation of formative from summative assessment
- Extreme L:T ratios (4:1 in Science, 20:1 in Arts)
- Superb facilities, superb students
- Very limited Quality Assurance
- 4,500 doctoral students (u/g: g = 3:1)

Teaching and learning strategy at Oxford

- Change Academy and Corporate Plan
- Focus on graduate study
- Departmental and Divisional embedding and capacity building
- Research-informed
- 'Sharing good practice'
- Induction into academic practice at Oxford: learning to think about teaching

Importantly, in achieving excellence through assessment, HEIs leaders must always remember that:

"We are all faced with a series of great opportunities - brilliantly disguised as insoluble problems."

John W. Gardner

References

- Biggs, J. (2001) The reflective institution: Assuring and enhancing the quality of teaching and learning, Higher Education, 41,3: 221-238.
- Burke, J.C., and H. Minassians. (2003). Performance Reporting: "Real" Acountability or Accountability "Lite" Seventh Annual Survey 2003. Albany. N.Y.: Rockefeller Institute of Government.
- Crosby, P.B. (1996), "Thinking about excellence", *Journal for Quality and Participation*, Vol. 19 No.6, pp.70.
- Bryman, A. (1988), *Quantity and Quality in Social Research*, Unwin Hyman, London.
- Brookes, M. (2003), "Evaluating the 'Student Experience': an approach to managing and enhancing quality in higher education", *Journal of Hospitality, Leisure, Sport and Tourism Education*, Vol. 2 No.1, pp.22-31.
- Chase, R., Stewart, D. (1994), "Make your service fail-safe", Sloan Management Review, No.Spring, pp.35-44.

- Colling, C. and Harvey, L. (1995) Quality control, assurance and assessment – the link to continuous improvement, Quality Assurance in Education, 3, 4: 30-34
- Crosby, P.B. (1996), "Thinking about excellence", Journal for Quality and Participation, Vol. 19 No.6, pp.70.
- Cullen, J., Joyce, J., Hassel, T. and Broadbent, M. (2003) Quality in Higher Education: from monitoring to management, Quality Assurance in Education, 2, 1: 5-14
- Dale, B G (2003) Managing Quality (4th Ed), Oxford: Blackwell Publishing
- Elton, L. (2001) Quality Assurance through Quality Enhancement, Educational Developments. Issue 2.4 November
- Emiliani, M.L. (2005) Using Kaizen to improve graduate business school degree programs, Quality Assurance in Education, 13, 1: 37 – 52

- Garvin, D.A. (1984), "What does product quality really mean?", Sloan Management Review, No.Fall, pp.25-43.
- Greensted, C. (2002) Measure for Measure or a Pound of Flesh, (A comparison of quality assurance schemes), International Journal of Management Education: 3-10
- Harvey, L., Knight, P.T. (1996), *Transforming Higher Education*, SRHE and Open University Press, Buckingham,
- Hodgkinson, M. and Brown, G. (2003) Enhancing the Quality of Education: a case study and some emerging principles, Higher Education 45, 3: 337-352
- Kanji, G. and Asher, G. (1993), "Total quality management process: a systematic approach", Journal of Total Quality Management, Vol. 4, (Suppl.).
- Loh, L., Chong, C.L., Chang, Z.Y., Ho, Y.P. (1997), *Quality Management in Industries: Perspectives from Singapore*,
- Mizikaci, F. (2006), "A systems approach to program evaluation model for quality in higher education", *Quality Assurance in Education*, Vol. 14 No.1, pp.37-53.
- Osseo-Asare Jr, A. E. and Longbottom, D. (2002) The need for education and training in the use of the EFQM model for quality management in the UK higher education institutions, Quality Assurance in Education, 10,1:26 – 36
- Piper, D.W. (1993), *Quality Management in University*, Australian Government Publishing Service, Canberra.
- Porter, L. and Tanner, S., 1996. Assessing Business Excellence, Butterworth Heinemann, Oxford.
- Richardson, K.E. (1998), "Quantifiable feedback: can it really measure quality?", *Quality Assurance in Education*, Vol. 6 No.1/4, pp.212-9.
- Sallis, E. (1993), Total Quality Management in Education, Kogan Page, London
- Shafer, B.S., & Coate, L.E. (1992). Benchmarking in Higher Education: A Tool for Improving Quality and Reducing Cost. Business Officer, 26(5), 28-35.

- Slater, S.F. (1997), "Developing a customer value-based theory of the firm", *Journal of the Academy of Marketing Science*, Vol. 25 No.2, pp.162-7.
- Woodruff, R.B. (1997), "Customer value: the next source for competitive advantage", *Journal of the Academy of Marketing Science*, Vol. 25 No.2, pp.139-53.

Chapter 5
Creating a World Class University

Introduction

"... a world class university should have a forward - looking world - view, cutting edge research, lead scholars, drive, high aspiration and strategy in order to stay ahead in the academic arena. At the same time, it should nurture and uphold a learning culture and a spirit of cohesiveness and scholasticism among its campus community. Lest it being lapsed into becoming insular, it should always explore opportunities for synergistic alliances with other leading institutions"

Khoon et al., 2000

"... universities must never forget that they are very much embedded in their countries and their regions. The great universities become economic hotspots and play a huge role in their region. This is as true for Stanford University in the creation of Silicon Valley in the US as it is for Cambridge University in the creation of Silicon Fen in the UK. We are all very much part of where we live and, as we look to the future, managing the balance between the international and the local is one of the main challenges universities confront."

Prof. Alison Richard

(Vice - chancellor, University of Cambridge)

The Notion of a World Class University

As education sector enter an age of this high competitiveness through rapid advancement of communication and globalization, it is common for Higher Education Institutions (HEI) to have significant societal and educational aspirations. Among these are the quests to raise their existing status of universities to "World Class" stature or to establish "World Class"[16] university to dominate the global market. Although the term "World Class" has been used widely in conversations about academic institutions, there has been little attempt to define the term carefully. What does it mean to be a World Class University? Is this simply a public relations claim or does it have substance? What are the criteria for World Class status, and how would we know that a university has reached that lofty height? In order to provide some tentative answers, some explanations are given hereunder.

The definition of what makes a world class university is subjective. By definition, a world class university is one on which there is widespread agreement of a world class reputation—that it is one of the best in the world. Clearly, this a tautology in the sense that there is less agreement on what makes that reputation than the fact that there are a limited number of universities on which widespread agreement of "world class" is likely. The lack of an absolute set of performance criteria and measures may mean that world class will always be positional, referring to those universities that are at the top in terms of academic reputation rather than those that fit a class of standards (Tsarenko and Mavondo, 2001). Indeed, even when criteria are used to rank and measure university performance, they are incomplete and difficult to measure; and the ones that do exist are not very powerful predictors, especially for universities in non - English speaking countries. Some of the difficulties that institutions face to have a consensus on producing a list of world class universities that will be recognized worldwide are briefly mentioned below -

The subjective nature of world class status means that institutions will attempt to address those dimensions that are considered in

---

16 http://economictimes.indiatimes.com/Opinion/Guest_Writer/What_makes_a_world_class_university_/rssarticleshow/2679312.cms

assessing reputations and that are visible. In this respect, research activity, publications, citations, and major faculty awards are highly visible and measurable while the quality of the educational process is not. Thus, it is not surprising to see a focus on research criteria in the surveys and in the efforts of institutions to promote their importance and little or no attempt to measure and assess teaching quality or educational activities. Indeed, there is a tacit assumption that if an institution is highly competitive in its admissions that the educational quality is also very high, even without measuring that quality. Yet, student competition for admission may be based upon a prestigious reputation that is largely due to the research visibility of a university rather than its educational virtues.

Although teaching, service to society and research are all emphasized in the statements on what makes a great university, reputational ratings seem to be limited largely to the research dimension on the basis of our statistical analysis. With the exception of the reputational rankings of the top 10 - 12 institutions there is relatively wide disagreement on the status of other institutions.

English - speaking countries have an advantage in the reputational rankings of their universities by virtue of the fact that the leading international journals are published in English. English has become the *lingua franca* of worldwide academia. This has also led to an advantage in competing for talent on a worldwide basis for universities in English - speaking countries. To the degree that talent is widely distributed around the world, the top English - speaking institutions have an edge in attracting that talent internationally. The statistical determinants of ratings of universities in English - speaking countries do not appear to hold for those in non English speaking countries. Indeed, the ratings in non English - speaking countries appear to be almost random with respect to the criteria used to rank universities in international surveys (Tsarenko, Y. and Mavondo, F.T. 2001).

When viewing individual professional schools within a university or academic departments, it appears that the overall reputation of the university has an independent influence or "halo effect" beyond the attributes of the schools or departments. That is, a school or department in a prestigious university will be rated more highly than a statistically identical unit at a less prestigious university.

The above discussion gives a clear idea that it will be very hard if not impossible for accreditation institutions to develop a metrics to rank world class universities that will be broadly accepted across the globe. On the other hand, there is wide agreement in general that world class universities have three major roles: (1) excellence in education of their students; (2) research, development and dissemination of knowledge; and (3) activities contributing to the cultural, scientific, and civic life of society (Owlia, M.S. and Aspinwall, E.M. 1996). By excellence in education we refer to the resources and organization of undergraduate, graduate, and professional instruction and educational opportunities for students. Clearly, this goal requires outstanding faculty, high quality teaching and other instructional activities, and availability of good libraries, laboratories, and other pertinent facilities as well as highly prepared and motivated students who serve to educate through their peer influence. Research, development, and dissemination of knowledge refer to the embryonic identification, growth, and extension of concepts and ideas as well as their transformation into applications, goods, and services that enhance understanding and welfare. Activities contributing to the cultural, scientific, and civic life of society are many and varied, but include conferences, publications, artistic events and forums as well as provision of services (e.g. medical clinics and hospitals or museums) that engage and contribute to the larger community including the regional, national, and international communities.

Characteristics of a World Class University

Expressing similar sentiments, Niland (2000) argues that for universities, world - class standing is built on reputation and perception – often seen as subjective and uncertain – and it requires outstanding performance in many events, such as -

- **Quality of Faculty** - A world class university will be widely recognised as an eminent institution, as a place where top staff will wish to congregate. Given the chance, staff from other universities will migrate to the world class university, and top faculty attract top students. The process is auto - catalytic. This means such a university will almost certainly be a research - intensive university. It also must teach well. But first and foremost it is a place where people will want to spend time for the experience and to associate with the fame and respect that goes with this. Absolutely fundamental to building such a climate is the quality of the staff, especially the academic faculty members.
- **Research Reputation is Critical** - Although there is a general awareness in the wider community that university research delivers worthwhile outcomes, there is a particular need in medium - scale economies for the benefits flowing from research to be realised. It is largely through their research performance, and how this is carried through to excite and inform the learning process for all members of the university, which will most build reputational capital, and most put it at risk.
- **Talented Undergraduate Body** - As in the past, so into the future, universities accorded the tops spots will enrol the best of the brightest into their undergraduate programs. There is a special uplift effect from having thousands of really talented undergraduates and postgraduate students on the one campus sparking off each other.
- **International Presence** - Universities have long reached beyond their national borders to recruit staff, acquire knowledge and to

enrol students. But now, for universities, the world is shrinking even further through an array of developments increasingly familiar: the globalisation of economies, the revolution in international travel, both real and virtual and, most importantly, the opening of minds to a sense of an international engagement through networks that interlace study, work, consumption and leisure activity. One thing is certain the title of world - class will not come at a discount price, and without world - class funding the goal of reaching, and preserving, that high standard will be rhetoric alone.

- **The Leveraging Effect of Alliances and Networks** - The last decade has seen a literal explosion in the signing of exchange agreements between universities in different countries, primarily to facilitate study abroad programmes. Now with a new internationalism at hand and with a new competitiveness afoot, a new strategy on alliances is needed for universities pursuing the world - class goal.
- **Embraces Many Disciplines** - A world class university will accommodate a large number of disciplines and areas of study, to ensure cross - fertilisation of ideas and that frissance which comes from the gathering together of bright, higher - energy people from a variety of backgrounds and traditions. Some universities with a specific disciplinary focus such as in engineering or pharmacy or accountancy or even technology in a wider sense will draw international acclaim.
- **Technologically Smart Universities** - Primarily, are about the discovery and transmission of new knowledge. World class universities will have the fund and resources to introduce state of art technologies relevant to students learning. The cost of research equipment is now a major budget item that requires planning and special funding. Similarly, the technology of communications is a budget as much as it is a pedagogic issue, and no university of world class will hold that position without investing in it and making good use of it.

- **Practice the Art of Good Management** - It goes without saying that a truly eminent university will excel in teaching and research. But paralleling and supporting those core activities will be an excellence in management driving first - rate administrative systems. With continuing pressures on resources, every resource is reasonably saved and to be strategically spent. Without having an excellent leadership and management practice in place a university cannot attain world class status. Even if an organisation has a world class status, they will not be able to sustain it if there is a lack of good leadership and good management practices.
- **The Virtual Challenge** - Many in traditional universities view the "virtual university" phenomenon with some degree of anxiety, and that is not entirely an unreasonable position to take. One reason is that it throws open to all comers, both client and provider, the "knowledge economy". For better or for worse, knowledge is now bought and sold as a commodity. Research institutes, think tanks and consulting firms are all new competitors to universities in this knowledge economy. The virtual attributes, managed carefully, can breathe life into strategic alliances; can help bring institutions otherwise isolated beyond the critical mass to compete in the larger league. The possibilities are endless. So it really all depends on how it is done – on the nature of the strategic choices exercised. And this brings to the central point, which is that there are choices to be made, and strategies to be set, and while it once took centuries to build reputation as a university of renown, the timeline on this has been collapsed.
- **The New Internationalism** - Universities have long looked beyond national borders for the best qualified staff and the latest knowledge. But now the reach, the diversity and the intensity of international engagement is taking HEIs to a new level which universities aspiring to world - class recognition must heed. (ibid)

Echoing similar sentiments, Khoon et al. (2005) contend that the hallmarks of a world class university:

- **World - View** - It is imperative for a world class university or any university for that matter to have a forward looking world - view which is progressive and keeping abreast with the development of the world. Such invigorating self - images are certainly moral boosting to the institutions concerned. Inward looking will stifle academic and intellectual growth for no world class university should be an island, entire of itself.
- **Opportunity** - In this connection, a world class university seeks and explores every opportunity to forge networking with other premier universities and research institutions of the world. The close collaborations in terms of research and teaching will certainly bring about a win - win situation; it is synergistic in nature.
- **Research** - Doing cutting edge basic and applied research is a norm in a world class university. Excellence in terms of publications, patents and citations (all products of research) is the hallmark of a world class university. In the words of Derek Bok, the former President of Harvard University, patents offer universities an incentive to work harder to identify valuable ideas discovered in their laboratories. According to Ken Young, research in the university has never been more important to both individual and institutional fortune in view of the so - called 'audit explosion' and threats from competing pressure.
- **Learning** - All world class universities have traditionally a pervasive learning culture among their campus communities. In such environment learning is venerated and knowledge reigns supreme. Brandy Dahrouge of the University of Calgary opines that world class universities rely on a diversity of expertise to enrich the lives of professors, students and communities.
- Drive - A world class university constantly drives and pushes itself to scale greater heights such as increasing the number of

Nobel laureates among its rank of professors. Many unabashedly mention the number of Nobelists among its faculty members and alumni in their prospectus. Cohesiveness exists in a world class university. The esprit de corp among the campus community gives it a sense of shared mission and destiny. It also gives them a sense of belonging. Cohesiveness ensures that things are running smoothly in order to achieve success. Collegiality, part and parcel of cohesiveness, is also prevalent in a world class university. It includes faculty participation, through committees and senates, in the affairs of the institution, especially in educational matters such as admission of students, curricula, degree requirements, and faculty appointments and promotions. Lead scholars are the life - blood of a world class university. They provide vital academic leadership. World class universities have a coterie of prominent scholars who are also recipients of prestigious awards such as the coveted Nobel Prizes and Field Medals.

- **Aspiration -** Is another hallmark of a world class university. High aspiration will propel an institution to achieve greater success. The high aspiration is often reflected in the mission and vision statements of a university. Scholasticism in its purest and sublime form puts in place an academic culture that constantly strives for excellence. No world class university is found wanting in this respect. Strategic planning forms a blueprint for a world class university to maintain its pre - eminence. The competition among universities to attract the best scholars to their campuses is indeed a fierce one. No self - respecting university of a world - class standing wants to lose out in this respect.

Changing DNA For A World Class University Status

The future of universities in the 21st century thus, lies in imbedding a world class university culture that allows excellence to thrive in all forms of university processes, systems, programmes and deliverables. Towards this end a model is herein after suggested

(Fig. 1) to help universities transform themselves and create an enabling environment in which "*excellence*" is the medium of exchange. The components of this model are hereafter discussed in detail:

Figure 26: Sustaining World Class Status

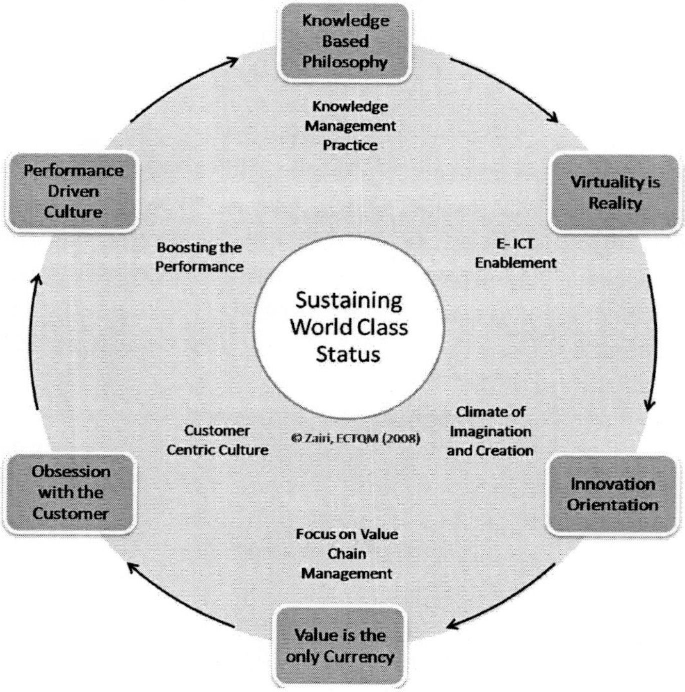

Adopting A Knowledge - Based Philosophy

"Intellectual capital is the sum of everything everybody in a company knows that gives it a competitive edge."

T.A. Stewart

"Of central importance is the changing nature of competitive advantage - not based on market position, size and power as in times past, but on the incorporation of knowledge into all of an organization's activities"

Leif Edvinsson

"The store of wisdom does not consist of hard coins which keep their shape as they pass from hand to hand; it consists of ideas and doctrines whose meanings change with the minds that entertain them"

John Plamenatz

Long before Knowledge Management became a term du jour, the industrialist giant, Andrew Carnegie, said, "The only irreplaceable capital an organization possesses is the knowledge and ability of its people. The productivity of that capital depends on how effectively people share their competence with those who can use it." The author of modern management, Peter Drucker,(1994) wrote, "The basic economic resource—the means of production—is no longer capital, nor natural resources, nor labour. It is and will be knowledge." Even the genius of Charles Darwin makes the point, "It is not the strongest of the species that survive, nor the most intelligent, but the one most responsive to change." In this age, the only constant is change. Beside the well known changes in technology, there are continuing changes politically, socially, and economically. The ability of an organization to stay current and stay relevant requires a core competence in Knowledge Management. Knowledge Management can transform an organization to new levels of effectiveness, efficiency, and scope of operation. Through advancements in technology, data and information are readily available. The modern business manager is able to discover and learn new measures, new technologies, and new opportunities, but this requires the ability to gather information in usable formats and disseminate knowledge to achieve the organization's objectives.

Knowledge Management is continually discovering what an organization knows—codifying tacit knowledge, Data Mining, and Business Intelligence; continually increasing what the organization knows—organizational learning and communities of practice, and continually organizing and disseminating explicit knowledge for use throughout the organization. There is a rapidly increasing and eclectic body of knowledge relating to knowledge management (KM) in regard to both practitioners and academics. Although definitions of KM vary widely, the following definitions are a reasonable summary of the contemporary thinking:

- *Knowledge management is... knowledge creation, which is followed by knowledge interpretation, knowledge dissemination and use, and knowledge retention and refinement (De Jarnett, 1996).*
- *Powerful environmental forces are reshaping the world of the manager of the 21 st century. These forces call for a fundamental shift in organisation process and human resource strategy. This is knowledge management.*
- *Knowledge management is the process of critically managing knowledge to meet existing needs, to identify and exploit existing and acquired knowledge assets and to develop new opportunities (Quintas et al, 1997).*

These definitions, and the bodies of knowledge they loosely represent, show that KM effects the organisation internally and externally. For example, Quintas et al. (1997) speaks of those "powerful external forces" which create pressure in organisations, in turn leading to the need for effective KM. Quintas et al(1997) and De Jarnett (1996), in their definitions, focus on the role of KM within the organisation and how organisation shape and operations can be effected by KM.

Knowledge is the fundamental basis for keeping sustaining competitive advantage. Knowledge–based view of the firm suggests that intellectual resources are key organizational assts that enable sustainable competitive advantage (Alavi et al. 2006). Many researchers have examined the linkage between knowledge management practice and organizational performance. Knowledge management has been an important issue for organization, strategy, and information technology. Thus, institutes should try to support knowledge processes evoked by employees. Schulize and Leidner(2002) address that organizations are implementing knowledge management practices on the promise of increasing their competitiveness. There are a lot of researches for knowledge management in organization. Organization - centric studies tend to focus on creating knowledge (Nonaka 1994). Some studies focused on knowledge flow; For example, (Malhotra, A., and Segars, 2001) suggested knowledge processes - creation, transfer, storing, and applying.

A recent survey indicates that issues such 'measuring the value of KM' and 'evaluating KM performance' are of great importance to managers (Chen et al. 2006). Knowledge management performance research examines the relationship between the organizational performance and knowledge management (Chen et al. 2006). Thus to gain and sustain competitive advantage, HEIs must capitalize their know - how and skills to achieve world class status.

The strategic value of the organizations resources and capabilities can be increased by the difficulty of buying, selling, imitating or substituting them. The invisible assets, like tacit knowledge or trust, can not be transacted or easily replicated by competitors, as they are usually founded in organizational history (Amit and Schoemaker, 1993). The human resources present a certain degree of mobility, but the capabilities they possess can be valuable to a firm and not so for another firm, or competitor. Certain capabilities, based upon the tacit knowledge of the firm, are only valuable when integrated with other individual capabilities specific to that particular firm, and that capacity of being complementary is immobile (Chuang 2004).

Knowledge management strategy

Organisations are facing ever - increasing challenges, brought on by marketplace pressures or the nature of the workplace. Many organisations are now looking to knowledge management (KM) to address these challenges. Such initiatives are often started with the development of a knowledge management strategy. To be successful, a KM strategy must do more than just outline high - level goals such as 'become a knowledge - enabled organisation'.

Instead, the strategy must identify the key needs and issues within the organisation, and provide a framework for addressing these. Taking this approach ensures that any activities and initiatives are firmly grounded in the real needs and challenges confronting the organisation. Each organisation will have unique issues and problems to be overcome. A KM strategy must address the real needs and issues, such as (Petty, R., Guthrie, J. 2000) -

Business managers - The volume of information available to business management has increased greatly. Known as 'information overload' or 'info - glut', the challenge is now to filter out the key information needed to support business decisions. The pace of organisational change is also increasing, as are the demands on the 'people skills' of management staff. In this environment, there is a need for sound decision making. These decisions are enabled by accurate, complete and relevant information. Knowledge management can play a key role in supporting the information needs of management staff. It can also assist with the mentoring and coaching skills needed by modern managers.

Aging workforce - The public sector is particularly confronted by the impacts of an aging workforce. Increasingly, private sector organisations are also recognising that this issue needs to be addressed if the continuity of business operations are to be maintained. Long - serving staff have a depth of knowledge that is relied upon by other staff, particularly in environments where little effort has been put into capturing or managing knowledge at an organisational level. In this situation, the loss of these key staff can have a major impact upon the level of knowledge within the organisation. Knowledge management can assist by putting in place a structured mechanism for capturing or transferring this knowledge when staff retire.

Supporting innovation - Many organisations have now recognised the importance of innovation in ensuring long - term growth (and even survival). This is particularly true in fast - moving industry sectors such as IT, consulting, telecommunications and pharmaceuticals. Most organisations, however, are constructed to ensure consistency, repeatability and efficiency of current processes and products. Innovation is does not tend to sit comfortably with this type of focus, and organisations often need to look to unfamiliar techniques to encourage and drive innovation. There has been considerable work in the knowledge management field regarding the process of innovation, and how to nurture it in a business environment.

Organisational environment

Thus, every organisation has a unique environment, defined by factors such as (Chase, R.L. 1997):

- *purpose and activities of the organisation*
- *overall strategic direction*
- *organisational culture*
- *size of the organisation*
- *geographic spread*
- *staff skills and experience*
- *organisational history*

- *available resources*
- *marketplace factors*

For this reason, each organisation has a unique set of needs and issues to be addressed by knowledge management. It is easy to jump into 'solutions mode', recommending approaches such as communities of practice, storytelling, content management systems, and much more. While these approaches may have widespread success in other organisations, they will only succeed in the current environment if they meet actual staff needs.

In practice, organisations are littered with well - meaning but poorly targeted knowledge management activities. In many cases, these failed because they simply didn't address a clear, concrete and imperative problem within the organisation. This is now recognised as one of the 'critical success factors' for knowledge management: identify the needs within the organisation, and then design the activities accordingly. Avoid jumping directly into 'solutions mode'

<u>Developing a KM strategy</u>

There are many approaches for developing a knowledge management strategy, each supported by a holistic model of KM processes.

Figure 27: Developing a KM Strategy

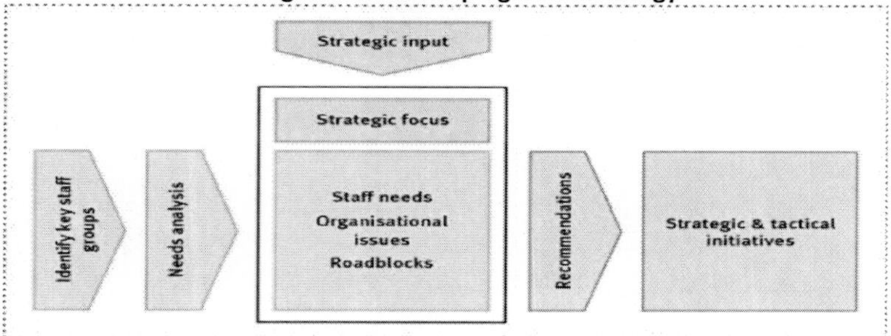

Source: Malhotra, A., and Segars, A.H.(2001)

Thus, developing a knowledge management strategy can be classified into two main approaches (Malhotra and Segars,2001):

- ***Top - down*** - *The overall strategic direction of the organisation is used to identify the focus of the knowledge management initiative. This is reflected in a series of activities designed to meet this broad goal.*
- ***Bottom - up*** - *Research is conducted into the activities of staff involved in key business processes. The findings of this research highlights key staff needs and issues, which are then tackled through a range of knowledge management initiatives.*

Each of these approaches has its strengths, and in practice, a success KM programme must encompass both. However, to follow either of the approaches, a needs analysis technique is strongly recommended. Historically, many knowledge management strategies have focused solely on the top - down approach, identifying high - level objectives such as 'become a knowledge - enabled organisation'. With little understanding, of the key issues and needs of staff throughout the organisation, these initiatives found it difficult to engage staff in the required cultural and process changes. As a result, many of these initiatives had little long - term impact on the organisation, despite initial efforts. Recognising these issues, this approach focuses much more strongly on the initial needs analysis activities.

Some of the activities that are needed to focus strongly on the needs analysis activities with staff, to drive a primarily bottom - up strategy, are shown below (ibid):

- *Identify the key staff groups within the organisation. These groups deliver the greatest business value, or are involved in the most important business activities.*
- *Conduct comprehensive and holistic needs analysis activities with selected staff groups, to identify key needs and issues.*

- *Supplement this research with input from senior management and organisational strategy documents, to determine an overall strategic focus.*
- *Based on these findings, develop recommendations for addressing the issues and needs identified.*
- *Implement a series of strategic and tactical initiatives, based on the recommendations. These will select suitable knowledge management techniques and approaches.*

Conversely, solution - independent approach is used to develop the knowledge management strategy which makes no assumptions about the solutions that might be implemented. As such, the approach is independent of any technologies implemented, or knowledge management techniques applied. Instead, the approach is to identify the need, and then determine the solution. Talking with staff is always enlightening (Morgan, R. 2004):

- **Simple** - The use of well - tested needs analysis techniques gives confidence that the true issues in the organisation will be identified. In practice, these simply 'fall out' of the research activities, with the key strategic and tactical recommendations becoming obvious in most cases. This simplicity makes the process easy to implement, and ensures that the findings and recommendations are well - understood throughout the organisation.
- **Efficient** - A modest amount of initial research will be sufficient to identify the most crucial problems within the organisation. These can then be tackled with suitable activities and initiatives. Once this first round of projects have delivered tangible business benefits, additional targeted research can be used to identify further issues to be addressed. This 'iterative' approach can then be repeated, ensuring that business improvements are seen even as the next round of research is initiated.

- **Targets resources** - There are many 'good ideas' that can be drawn from the field of knowledge management. The challenge is to identify those approaches that will have the greatest impact upon the organisation. By starting with the needs analysis, approaches can be targeted to address the most critical issues, or to deliver the greatest business benefits.

There are a number of sources of input that can be drawn upon when determining the strategic focus, including (Niland, 2005):

- *Senior management involvement, via interviews, facilitated discussions, or other interactions.*
- *Organisational strategy documents, such as the corporate plan or annual report.*
- *Results of other strategic research projects, such as 'staff satisfaction surveys'.*
- *External market research.*
- *Industry 'best practices', and other reports drawn from relevant industry or sector bodies.*

These inputs can then be synthesised into a strategic focus for the knowledge management initiatives. Use corporate documents as a key strategic input.

Example of IBM's KM strategy[17]

With a knowledge management history that dates to 1994, IBM certainly qualifies as an early adopter. Although its focus has shifted through the years, IBM's success with knowledge management continues to thrive through its enterprisewide knowledge exchange and collaboration. That strong history helped IBM earn KMWorld's KM Reality Award for 2005. Karen Ughetta, director, IBM Collaboration and Knowledge, leads 10 employees who focus on KM

[17] http://www.kmworld.com/Articles/Editorial/Feature/IBM's -KM -strategy - -16907.aspx

from a corporate perspective. The integration of collaboration and knowledge into portals and the way people learn is a major focus for IBM, she explains. It's very much an evolution to bring that learning right to the work experience.

Ughetta says they were already inundated as part of their daily jobs. After people realized that they could package questions and make a searchable FAQ before they were contacted, employees were more comfortable.

"I think the result of the expertise approach we've taken is people begin to realize that by declaring themselves an expert and posting usable and reusable content, it becomes a self - fulfilling prophecy in a positive way," says Betsy Stevenson, director, software group enablement. "They're actually going to get fewer calls and fewer requests for their expertise. You teach people to look there first and they don't necessarily have to speak to a live human every time they have a question."

IBM's business results from knowledge management initiatives are impressive. Yet it's efforts also impact the people side of the organization.

"When you have these virtual tools and capabilities, they've helped make IBM feel smaller," Martin says. "It's a place that feels like you're dealing with colleagues on a more personal level."

Stevenson agrees. "One more element that is driving productivity for salespeople is making information and experts more readily available," she says. "When those tools really work, our teams will tell you they're invaluable to them and drive productivity in the field."

Hence universities aspiring to be world class need to remember that:

"We live in a corporatist society with soft pretensions to democracy. More power is slipping every day over towards the groups. That is the meaning of the marketplace ideology and of our passive acceptance of whatever form globalization happens to take."

JR Saul – 2005
(The Unconscious Civilization)

Believing That Virtuality Is Reality

"Learning is more than just content or delivery software. It needs to be integrated into a broader learning process involving instructional support and collaboration, and designed with emphasis on the learning objectives. It also needs to be seen in the context of the broader strategy for training and skills development within a company and in many cases this means that it needs to be integrated into existing training delivery, creating a blended solution."

Sheila McGovern

"If we don't focus on the experience dimension of learning, we run the risk of mistaking the publishing of information for learning and training"

Elliott Masie

"The impact of information technology will be even more radical than the harnessing of steam and electricity in the 19th century. Rather it will be more akin to the discovery of fire by early ancestors, since it will prepare the way for a revolutionary leap into a new age that will profoundly transform human culture."

Jacques Attali, *Millennium: Winners and Losers in the Coming World Order* (1992)

Finding a common definition of e-learning—what it is and what it is not—can be a vexing problem in conversations about its regulation. Distributive (distance) learning in general encompasses a wide array of methods and has a long pre - Internet history. For our conversation, e-learning was defined as education that is provided *in substantial part* through the use of the Internet, or any other technology *du jour.* Many e-learning programs are not pure e-learning. We currently have pure Internet - based e-learning and hybrid models, (i.e., where there is both Internet - based instruction and face - to - face interactions among facilitators and students). The ratio between these two types of e-learning present in any one institution can vary significantly (Schultze and Leidner, 2002).

The basic distinction between e-learning and the traditional academic model creates complications when discussing quality. With e-learning, as one participant pointed out, there is the persistent notion that "different equals not good." This has generated a very one - sided approach, a wholly external evaluation of quality. The "extreme rationality, an extreme quantitative approach" to evaluating e-learning may be the result of uncertainty about exactly what is driving quality within e-learning. Campus - based teaching has historically depended upon autonomous faculty expertise, whereas with e-learning—at least in some courseware models (described more fully in the Finance section below)—the curriculum is developed by some person or a group of people, and has some level of standardization. This creates perhaps a false dichotomy between the individual (faculty) creation of instruction in the traditional models and a more corporate (or other entity) creation of instruction; the former is often presumed to be of high quality and the latter of lower quality, with virtually no data to support that presumption (ibid). And how do those perceptions of relative quality relate to questions of institutional prestige? Bill Durden asked further, "what makes prestige in educational institutions, be they e-learning or non - e-learning?"(ibid)

In order not to loose their market share universities and colleges have to gain and sustain the competitive advantage. There is a question if to realize this aim they, like enterprises, may use rapidly developing communication and information technologies (ICT). The answer is “yes” and HEI executives need convenient and effective methods to analyze the influence of ICT on their institutions competitive position and to implement winning strategies.

E-learning creates new sources of knowledge containing information not available before. The purpose is to increase the efficiency of learning and teaching. It also changes the way information is stored and transferred among students and their teachers and makes it available for them in any place at any time (e - course comes to student, not student comes to attend the course). The HEI physical resources or on - site availability of specialists are not the limitations to offer required number of courses any more. Also updating thein formation in e - book or e - course is easy what decreases the cost of such changes [18].

Thus, HEIs may make use of e-learning features by changing the activities it used to perform in order to improve teaching processes or answer the needs it was not able respond to before. There are many other ICT systems implemented in AHE like digital library, computer laboratories, office systems, portal or students' email accounts in academy domain. Like given above examples each of them has it position in the value chain where it causes that information is used to perform activities more effectively or do them in a new way.

Balanced Scorecard for ICT strategy

Defining value chain activities and analyzing how information may be used to make them more efficient and effective or performed in a way more attractive for students is not enough for decision

[18] http://insidehighered.com/news/focus/commission

makers as does not provide the way to control the effects of ICT implementation. There are many methods for measuring costs and benefits of ICT presented in the literature. Each of them has strengths and shortcomings and is suitable for specific situations. The one which is recommended in this paper for HEI is balanced scorecard (BSC) methodology as it has several features favourable for university or college competitive advantage analysis (Coimbra and Silva,2004).

Internal processes perspective

As it was often mentioned during value chain analysis ICT systems influence AHE operations and should make them more effective and efficient. Therefore the proposed CSFs for this perspective are as follows (Kaplan, D.P Norton):

- Improvement of teaching processes effectiveness The possible measures are: the number of contact hours or the number of students per one teacher which are necessary to sustain given level of teaching quality while the number of students and products increases. The quality should be evaluated with the same methods as institution used before.
- Improvement of administration processes effectiveness The growth of number of employees involved in administration operations linked with the growth of the number of students, teachers and products HEI offers may be chosen as KPIs for this factor.

If assumed KPIs values are achieved in this perspective it proves that the institution implemented proper ICT system and uses them effectively.

Client perspective

Students are the ones who should take advantage of the value created by ICT systems implemented in AHE and find its products more attractive. The CSFs which reflect this aim are (Porter and Millar,1985):

1. Increased student satisfaction and decreased total student study costs as the result of:
   a. *Simplified administration processes The possible KPIs are: the number of candidate visits in enrolment office and documents they had to fill in enrolment process, the average number student's visits in dean's office necessary to resolve the problem, the number of complaints students filed in the given period of time.*
   b. *Wide access to knowledge sources The proposed KPIs are: percentage of courses for which institution provides digital resources, number of places from which these resources are accessible (Internet = everywhere), percentage of students for which these resources are available.*
   c. *Personalizing product It may be measured by the total number of courses included in the curriculum linked with the minimal number of them which student must realize to get a degree and the number of courses in the curriculum for which student may choose among different forms of execution.*

2. New segments of clients This may be measured by analyzing students' profile (age, education, job and family status, place of living, nationality, other) and finding the number of students whose profile is different from one dominating in the past.

If institution succeeds in this perspective it proves that it was able convince students that they also the benefit from institution ICT systems and that HEI products are more attractive.

<u>Financial perspective</u>
The main aim of AHE strategy is to increase revenues while keeping the costs under control. Therefore the following CSFs are proposed for this perspective:

1. Effective expenses control It may be measured in a given period of time by the two numbers: growth of total administrative costs and growth of total didactic costs both linked with the total number of students and total number of products they have chosen.
2. Growth of total revenues This is measured by the total value of income in the given period.
3. Growth of revenues from the new products This is measured by the value of income from the new products the institution has offered.

The success in this perspective proves that all the benefits from implementing ICT systems were used to for HEI growth what means that it gained competitive advantage.

The choice of both CSFs and KPIs is subjective and the ones given above are the example proposals for the case study used in this paper. It illustrates that the institution after analyzing its activities in value chain and finding the ways in which information may be used to create value should use BSC methodology and perform the following steps: define CSFs which reflect this value in four perspectives, choose KPIs for each CSF, measure their values and compare them with planned values or observe the trends in order to find out if ICT strategy is implemented effectively.

Essentially, therefore HEIs should bear in mind the fact that:

"Companies will never have a truly sustainable advantage that's based on products or prices. You need to focus on the rate at which people learn. It's the learning speed of the slowest many, not the learning speed of the brightest few, that will set the pace for your company."

Jim Haudan

Developing An Innovation Orientation

"The milk of disruptive innovation doesn't flow from cash - cows"
David Isenberg

"Just as energy is the basis of life itself and ideas the source of innovation, so is innovation the vital spark of all human change, improvement and progress"
Ted Levitt

"Innovation is the specific instrument of entrepreneurship. The act that endows resources with a new capacity to create wealth."
Peter F. Drucker

The terms innovation and organisational change have become management buzz - words over twenty years. Innovation is the specific tool of entrepreneurs, the means by which they exploit the opportunity for a different business or a different service (Drucker, 1985). For more than half a century, research and development (R&D) has been closely associated with technological innovation (Miller and Morris, 1999). Invention is the narrowest definition of innovation. Drucker (1994) maintained that there are seven basic sources of opportunities to innovate. Only one of them is to do with inventing something new. Innovation is thus more than invention, and does not have to be technical.

There are numerous examples of social and economic innovations (Drucker, 1994). Innovation is a proposed theory or design concept that synthesises extant knowledge and techniques to provide a theoretical basis for a new concept (Sundbo, 1998; Bright, 1969). For the purpose of this session, innovation is defined broadly to include new products, new processes, new services (including new uses of established products, processes and services), new forms of organisation, new markets; the development of new skills and human capital and practice with the aim of improving the performance that is also commercially successful.

Scholars in higher education have expressed concern for survival in the midst of an ever - changing and turbulent operating environment. This environment, characterized by increasing competition, regulatory barriers, and decreasing enrollments faces pressure for innovation. World class universities are responding to such pressure by adopting innovations. In particular, institutions implement more technical innovations than administrative innovations.

Ducker's Principles of innovation

According to Drucker(1985), "Purposeful innovation - begins with the analysis of the opportunities. It begins with the sources of innovation opportunities. In different areas, different sources will have different importance at different times." He suggested several principles for successful innovation which are discussed briefly hereunder -

- *The first is simply not to try to be clever - Innovations have to be handled by ordinary human beings, and if they are to attain any size and importance at all, by morons or near - morons. Incompetence, after all, is the only thing in abundant and never - failing supply. Anything too clever, whether in design or execution, is almost bound to fail.*
- *Innovation is both conceptual and perceptual - The second imperative of innovation - is therefore to go out to look to ask to listen. This cannot be stressed too often.*
- *Don't diversify don't splinter; don't try to do too many things at once - This is, of course, the corollary to the "do": be focused! Innovations that stray from a core are likely to become diffuse. They remain ideas and do not become innovations. The core does not have to be technology or knowledge. In fact, market knowledge supplies a better core*

of unity in any enterprise, whether business or public - service institution, than knowledge or technology does. But there has to be a core of unity to innovative efforts or they are likely to fly apart. An innovation needs the concentrated energy of a unified effort behind it. It also requires that the people who put it into effect understand each other, and this, too, requires a unity, a common core. This, too, is imperiled by diversity and splintering.

- *An innovation to be effective - has to be simple and it has to be focused. It should do only one thing otherwise it confuses. Everything new runs into trouble. If complicated it cannot be repaired or fixed. All effective innovations are breathtakingly simple... Even the innovation that creates new uses and new markets should be directed to specific, clear applications.*
- *Don't try to innovate for the future. Innovate for the present! An innovation may have long - range impact; it may not reach its full maturity until twenty years later.*
- *Effective innovations start small. They are not grandiose. They try to do one specific thing. Why small? Frequent changes and adjustment are always as initial problems are ironed out and solved This is an trial and error process - involving lots of education and development. Such processes are inevitably slow. Especially so when the required knowledge and experience is being made in the process itself as it develops and cannot be acquired quickly through textbooks or experts. It is obviously better and more economical to do this on a small scale than risk big mistakes! Mistakes are inevitably a part of this trial and error process of continuous development and adjustment - Doing this on a large scale only invites large scale mistakes - and high unnecessary costs - a waste of precious resources*
- *A successful innovation always aims at leadership - all strategies aimed at exploiting an innovation - must achieve*

leadership within a given environment. Otherwise they simply create an opportunity for the competition."

- *Innovation starts when people convert problems to ideas. New ideas are born through questions, problems and obstacles. The process of innovation is indebted to the trouble that comes about when we are surrounded by that which is not solved, not smooth and not simple. Therefore, in order for the innovation process to flourish, it needs a climate that encourages inquiry and welcomes problems.*
- *Innovation needs a system. All organizations have innovation systems. Some are formal, designed by the leadership, and some are informal, taking place outside established channels. Informal channels are untidy and inefficient, yet innovation is always associated with them.*
- *Passion is the fuel and pain is the hidden ingredient. Ideas do not propel themselves; passion makes them go. Passion, in addition to talent and skill, is a valuable company asset. Passion is what transforms other resources into profits, but it never shows up on a balance sheet. Unfortunately, there seems to be some universal law that says when pursuing a passion or following a dream, pain is part of the process. Innovation leaders need to take the pain with the passion and learn to manage both effectively.*
- *Co - locating drives effective exchange. Co - location refers to physical proximity between people. It is a key for building the trust that is essential to the innovation process. It also increases the possibility for greater exchange of information, cross - fertilization of ideas, stimulation of creative thinking in one another and critique of ideas during their formative stage.*
- *Differences should be leveraged. The differences that normally divide people — such as language, culture, race, gender and thinking and problem solving styles — can be a boon to innovation. When differences are used constructively and people move beyond fear, suspicion,*

mistrust and prejudice, differences can be leveraged to enhance and sustain the innovation process.

Innovation Killers

While it's probably impossible to compute the exact percentage of business initiatives that fail, it is widely acknowledged that *most* do. After years of research and observation, it is clear that the same reasons for any change initiative failure tend to be the same culprits that make innovation initiatives fail. Here are the top ten reasons for innovation failure[19]:

- *Not creating a **culture** that supports innovation*
- *Not getting buy - in and **ownership** from business unit managers*
- *Not having a widely understood, system - wide **process***
- *Not allocating **resources** to the process*
- *Not tying projects to company **strategy***
- *Not spending enough time and energy on the **fuzzy front - end***
- *Not building sufficient **diversity** into the process*
- *Not developing **criteria and metrics** in advance*
- *Not **training and coaching** innovation teams*
- *Not having an **idea management system***

Some of the other issues that leaders need to plan very careful while managing innovation are discussed below (Keohane and Hoffmann 1991). -

- **Culture** – culture is the playing field of innovation. Unless the culture honours ideas and supports risk - taking, innovation will be stifled before it begins. Culture is like our immune system ... its job is to kill intruders before they can harm the body. Culture can change but it is a slow process.

---

[19] http://www.1000advices.com/guru/innovation_culture_sk.html

- **Ownership –** once great ideas have shown up, they have to be implemented somewhere. Generally that means a business unit manager has to take on the idea and devote scarce resources of time and budget to the new project. If that manager has not bought into the new project fully, it generally doesn't succeed. Business unit managers need to be engaged from the very beginning of an innovation initiative and they need to have the option of "buying" new concepts.
- **Process –** when organizations want to embrace innovation, they often hold a two - day kickoff to hype innovation and provide some training in tools and techniques. They set up a few innovation teams, schedule some brainstorming sessions and then are shocked to learn (about six weeks later) that "innovation isn't working." In today's world where people are already overloaded, a piecemeal approach to innovation just doesn't work, not if you want real, bottom line results. Innovation needs a process that focuses people on the right challenges and leads them through an organized process of releasing creativity and evaluating results so that the right concepts move into the implementation process.
- **Resources** – too often the CEO stands up at an annual meeting and says, "We need to be more innovative," and then goes on to the next topic. Innovation takes time, energy and money. People need some freedom and time to think and tinker around with new possibilities. They also need new skills and systems that support thinking and collaboration. Innovation is critical to the future; but it depends on the investment of today's resources.
- **Strategy** – somewhere along the line, as people were taught to "think out of the box," a false impression was created. People began to believe that there should be no rules, no boundaries, no constraints. This turns out to be a counter -

productive approach that produces popcorn – wild ideas bouncing around with no purpose in sight. Once in a millennium this might produce a breakthrough ... but it is not a cost - effective process. What is more effective is focusing creativity within the scope of a well - constructed company strategy. Of course, this requires a strategy that is both narrow enough to define the company's core competency and broad enough to allow exploration into related areas.

- **Fuzzy Front - End** – there are a lot of unexpressed ideas lurking in organizations. However, to find the truly new and different ideas ... the ones that could create a *breakthrough* , requires a process of looking outside and inside; at customers, suppliers and competitors; at changes in demographics, trends, economics, regulations, and political environments. Innovation that begins with an internal brainstorming session will seldom result in anything other than pale, incremental concepts.
- **Diversity –** diversity is the difference between "same - old, same - old" thinking and "Wow! I never thought of that!" possibilities. In the old days, cross - functional teams were a daring foray into diversity. Now they are standard fare and the true value of diversity comes when we deliberately focus diverse thinking styles, experiences, perspectives, and expertise on a challenging problem or opportunity. The process of innovation should include all functions; all genders, ages, races, all thinking styles, as well as all stakeholders, customers, suppliers, competitors.
- **Criteria & Metrics** – in a healthy innovation environment and process, more ideas will be generated than can possibly be implemented. This can lead to overload and frustration unless there is a mechanism for sorting and prioritizing. Developing criteria guides long before going into idea generation mode can provide the rational means for

evaluating ideas and prevent going over the edge on a seductive idea that doesn't fit.

- **Training & Coaching –** a mistake often made by organizations is assuming that innovation teams are the same as other project teams. In a recent survey by the InnovationNetwork, responses indicated that people participated on an average of 3.7 innovation projects per year. However, only 21% of the respondents had had some training on how to participate on an innovation team and less than 10% had actually had training *as part of the innovation team.* No wonder over 70% of all projects fail.
- Innovation requires new ways of thinking and new skills. Developing a just - in - time, active-learning training process insures that innovation teams develop the desired results effectively and efficiently. As with any new set of skills, innovation competency develops over time while working on real projects. Coaching is a critical piece of developing this competency.
- **Idea Management System –** Many innovation projects have died on a sticky - note covered wall as participants lost energy trying to figure out what to do with those yellow pieces of paper fluttering to the floor. Having an effective system that captures ideas and engages people in developing, modifying, enlarging and evaluating those ideas is just as critical to innovation as accounting systems are to the financial health of an organization.

Above discussion clearly shows that management of innovation is not a simple task. It requires a systematic approach to manage efficiently. Regrettably, majority of the higher education institutes lack an organizational culture and leadership for managing innovation within the institute. It is however, due to the several reasons -

First, in an era of decreasing public funding, universities are scrambling to respond to challenges like globalization, commercialization, and the increasing availability and capacities of information technologies (Taylor, 1998). Taylor (1998) continues, suggesting that responses to such forces within institutions have been energized primarily by lone rangers – individual staff members who are energetic, early adopters of innovation. However, innovation at the individual level often results in conflict with broader institutional practices, processes, values and structure. The challenge is to move beyond innovation at the individual level and turn attention to change at the institutional level – the reinventing of culture (ibid).

Second, institutions of higher education are potential users and producers of innovations. Colleges and universities function as suppliers of training, expertise, and personnel for industries, most of which have encountered the high - technology domain. In addition, changes in student demographics, the presence of high technology, and changes in funding are signals create forces for innovation for colleges and universities. Fourth, Rogers (1995) suggested that educational institutions, in one way or another, are involved in the adoption of innovations. Industries, including higher education, that have faced pressure for innovation have also faced fundamental changes in philosophy, values and operations. Some organizations appear to have resources, structures, processes and values that foster adoption of innovations while others do not. Technological innovations continue to hold vast opportunities for conducting operations in more effective and efficient ways. However, these same innovations place pressure on organizational resources, structures, processes and values for change.

Researchers of organizational innovation suggest that factors related to the "formal" organization such as, organizational size, structure and resources influence the ability of an organization to adopt an innovation. Christensen (1997) suggests that an organization's resources, processes and values – its organizational culture - contribute to its ability to adopt innovations. Kanter (1983) stresses the importance of a "pro - innovation" culture. Thus, the challenge facing HEIs is to identify organizational - level features that can be considered as enabling organizational innovation to attain or to sustain the world class status.

Hence, there is a need for understanding and developing a culture of innovation within higher education institutions. An example of Arizona State University is shown hereunder for further elucidation -

Example of Innovation Pipeline at Arizona State University[20]

Work is set to start at ASU on building an "innovation pipeline" for turning discoveries in nanotechnology into business ventures. Groundwork for the endeavor - teaching students how to construct and use that pipeline - is kicking off with support from a $39,500 grant recently awarded by the National Collegiate Inventors and Innovators Alliance to a group of professors in ASU's Ira A. Fulton School of Engineering and College of Liberal Arts and Sciences. The funding will help launch an undergraduate honours course in the fall on the emerging field of nanotechnology and its commercial potential.

"It's another step in expanding engineering education to include an entrepreneurship component," says Thomas Duening, director of the Entrepreneurial Programs Office at ASU's Ira A. Fulton School of Engineering. B.L. Ramakrishna, an associate professor in ASU's School of Life Sciences, is developing the course based on the proposal "From Discovery to Commercialization: The Greater Phoenix Nanotechnology Innovation Pathway and Pipeline."

Its aim will be to spark students' enthusiasm for the "enormous societal and economic impact" offered by nanotechnology science and engineering, and guide students in exploring ways of bringing

[20] http://www.asu.edu/news/stories/200604/20060424_pipeline.htm

technological advances to the marketplace, Ramakrishna says. Ramakrishna and Duening will work with Vincent Pizziconi, an associate professor in ASU's Harrington Department of Bioengineering. Pizziconi's extensive experience in teaching biomedical engineering product design and development will bring a valuable perspective to this hybrid nanotechnology and entrepreneurship course, Duening says. Titled "Nanotechnology: Perspectives and Entrepreneurial Opportunities," the course is designed to provide a model for a "real - word" educational experience by bringing together students, faculty, industry and the regional entrepreneurial community. Leaders of industry and small businesses will share their knowledge with students on commercialization prospects, global competition, regulatory issues and intellectual property rights.

Students will focus on two of the most promising areas in the field, nanobiob technology and environmental nanotechnology. They will explore the business potential of these emerging technologies, as well as the broad impacts on society. The course objective will be aided by the newly funded National Science Foundation Center for Nanotechnology and Society at ASU, which is charged with ensuring that "advances in nanotechnology bring about improvements in the quality of life for all Americans." Class members will form "E - teams" (entrepreneurial teams) to develop marketing and business plans that will be presented to panels of industry experts, attorneys and venture capitalists. The course will be offered as a pilot for two consecutive years - in fall 2006 and fall 2007 - and students will be encouraged to continue in following semesters to form E - teams. Some of the teams' activities will be funded through the grant.
Thus HEIs strategic innovations should be focused and be geared towards: quantum change balancing between incremental and breakthrough. As aptly summed up by Bill gates, innovation is the critical fuel for survival in the 21st Century.

"Never before in history has innovation offered promise of so much to so many in so short a time."

Bill Gates

"The key to achieving financial success today, or success in any field, for that matter, is being able to learn new things.... Things change so quickly that the most successful people in virtually every field are the people who learn new things fastest."

Paul Zane Pilzer

Focusing on 'Value' as the Main Currency

"If you are not managing your value chain, you are not managing your business."

Jack Welch

"...knowing what your value chain does well is difficult to identify but is most important in the face of rising competition. Value chain analysis is an excellent means of disentangling the complexities to reveal what is really going on between a company and its market."

Andrew Shepherd

Customer value is a strategic weapon in attracting and retaining customers and has become one of the most significant factors in the success of both manufacturing businesses and service providers (Zeithaml, 1988). Delivering superior customer value has become an ongoing concern in building and sustaining competitive advantage. As many researchers have suggested, firms should reorient their operations towards the creation and delivery of superior customer value if they are to improve their performance (Jensen, 2001). Driven by demanding customers, keen competition, and rapid technological change, many firms have sought to deliver superior customer value (Woodruff, 1997). Delivering superior customer

value is now recognised as one of the most important factors for the success of any firm now and in the future because it has a significant impact on the behavioural intentions of customers and because it has an important role in providing managers with insights into how to achieve sustainable competitive advantage.
The present - day university is an organization fragmented into academic specializations, primarily for the purpose of furthering knowledge in specific fields of study. Shortcomings of such an organization include isolation from society's real needs (hence the so - called "ivory tower"), hampering of interdisciplinary coordination, and the tendency to be task - instead of process - oriented. To complicate matters, the external environment presents a changing landscape characterized by heightened customer consciousness and demands, rising education costs, increasing competition in the form of new and alternative sources of learning and information (such as Internetbased distance learning), and the increasingly palpable presence of information - age technologies, particularly the Internet.

To define and analyze strategy – the way in which university is going to gain and sustain competitive advantage the value chain concept is recommended. M.E. Porter, its author, defined the generic value chain model for any industry and using it proved that organization may make use of information to win on the market. The model is primarily designed for the goods sector rather than service sector. The value chain of a modern university can be viewed as a network of activities centered on the functions of teaching, research, and community service, which, in turn, involve educational design, educational delivery, assessment, research and development, and outreach activities. Each of these processes add value to the total educational package provided to students, and supporting these processes are the activities of recruitment, admission, enrollment, academic service, and alumni support.

However, there are several ideas how to implement value chain model in higher education. The discussion below focuses on education and is based on given definition of HEI product and client. The explanation recommends to separate activities university or college performs to create value for the student and group them in the categories. Like in original Porter model "value" should be measured by the total incomes HEI gets from education. Its competitive advantage is the function of the value chain, as every separated activity is connected with efficiency (cost advantage) or realization of a specific student's need (unique value). The proposed generic university value chain for education is shown below and shortly described below.

Figure 28: Value Chain Model

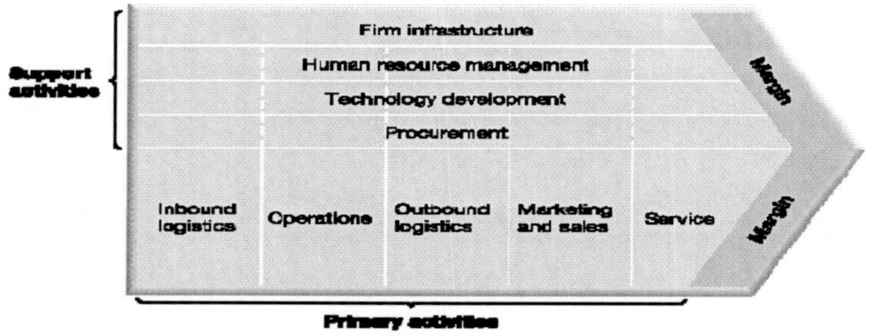

Source: M.E. Porter, *Competitive Advantage: Creating and Sustaining Superior Performance*, Free Press, 1985. Used with permission of The Free Press, a division of Simon & Schuster, Inc. © 1985, 1998 by Michael E. Porter.

The primary activities belong to the following categories:

Inbound logistics: This activity is concerned with receiving, storing and distributing the inputs to the product or service. In the case HEIs, it might include supplies from publishers to the library, technology, machineries, transport, visiting professors, guest lecturers etc. World class universities partner with right suppliers of knowledge providers. They also build relationship with the right suppliers for the day to day operations of the institute to reduce their cost in this activity and improve there performance and efficiency. A course (a module) is a basic educational unit, usually connected with one knowledge branch. After completing the course student should acquire given competences in this branch. University teachers create course by defining its content (course program) and the ways student is taught (course execution – kind of classes, number of hours and so on) to gain the competences, which are the output on course completion. Assembling all resources necessary to teach the course like labs or library collections is included in this category. As the result of all activities belonging to it HEI possesses a bunch of courses and a bunch of ways of their execution (one course may be taught in few different ways depending on students needs).

Operations: The operations activity transforms inputs into final product or service HEIs product is created from the courses and their specific executions. In this category curriculum, minimum requirements to get the degree, as well as all other regulations (for example time constrains) student should obey are defined. Also other activities like ones leading to accreditations are included. University academic staff, its authorities (deans, rectors) and its administration is involved in creating the product. The result of the activities in this category is the set of products consistent with definition and features given in previous section and offered by HEI.

Outbound Logistics: This activity is linked with collecting, storing and distributing the product or services to customers. This is the way in which the product - studies is delivered to the student. Many activities in this category are connected with courses execution for the given groups of students. The example ones are: scheduling classes (place, time, teacher, and students group), preparing. Universities of world class status adds the maximum value in this activity (eg. Knowledge dissemination through blackboard/ webct, arranging seminars, field trip/ company visit etc) with the minimum cost to differentiate tem from the competitors.

Marketing and sales: This activity provides the means whereby consumers/ users are made aware of the product and services and are able to purchase it in the best possible way. In this category, world class universities research the market and perform marketing mix operations like studies positioning, their price, promotion and the ways they are going to be "sold" either directly to students or to the parents, executive learners, businesses, state, local governments or donors. The whole enrolment process is also included in this category. The result of its activities is new group of students which start studies HEI has offered. The activities are performed by institution executives, administration and supporting staff as well as by academic staff especially in enrolment process to provide maximum support to the students.

Services: It includes all those activities which enhance or maintain the value of a product or service, such online resources, free training course, preparing for the job interviews, alumni facilities etc.

Each of these activities is linked to support activities (firm infrastructure, HRM, technology development, and procurement). The support activities may add value in the form of automation of value chain activities, or provision of tools that facilitate, if not make possible, the planning, organizing, and (performance) monitoring of activities in the value chain. To become world Class University a HEI value chain therefore has to incorporate a diverse pool of users: students, faculty, administrators, guidance counselors, student organizations, alumni, companies, the Office of Career Services, and feeder schools to add maximum value in each activity in order to gain sustainable competitive advantage. This can be further explained using the model hereunder, where HEIs are run with the philosophy of customer centric culture. The model also explains that the key activities of an excellent university are KM practice, ICT and Innovation where they should add maximum value in order to achieve and sustain a performance driven culture.

Figure 29: HEIs with a customer centric culture

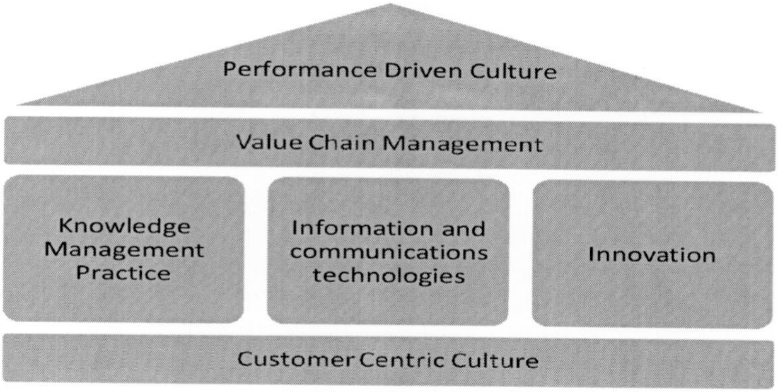

Source: Zairi,2008

Hence, the output of this activity may benefit society directly or may feed back into educational (re)design. From this perspective, the education activity may be said to consist of the different activities in an educator's professional life: educational design, educational delivery, research, professional development, and community service. The value chain model is a useful tool for defining a firm's core competencies and the competencies in which it can pursue competitive advantage for achieving world class status. As appropriately summed up by Johnson et al creating maximum value for the customers is the way forward to dominate in this global business world.

"A value - added activity or operation is one that accomplishes something that moves the process toward its final goal. There is a direct relationship between the Activity and the end result desired."

Johnson et al (2008)

Building an Obsession With 'The Customer'

"Being on par in terms of price and quality only gets you into the game. Service wins the game"

Tony Alessandra

"Research by the Forum Corporation suggests that 70% of the customers lost by 13 big service and manufacturing companies had scooted because of a lack of attention from the front - line employees. It's an emotional tie, not mere satisfaction that brings the customer back."

Tom Peters

"Service standards keep rising. As competitors render better and better service, customers become more demanding. Their expectations grow. When every company's service is shoddy, doing a few things well can earn you a reputation as the customer's saviour. But when a competitor emerges from the pack as a service leader, you have to do a lot of things right. Suddenly achieving service leadership costs more and takes longer. It may even be impossible if the competition has too much of a head start. The longer you wait, the harder it is to produce outstanding service"

William H. Davidow

"Companies can boost profits by almost 100 percent by retaining just 5 percent more of their customers."

Frederick Reicheld & W. Earl Sasser

"Those who enter to buy, support me. Those who come to flatter, please me. Those who complain, teach me how I may please others so that more will come. Those only hurt me who are displeased but

do not complain. They refuse me permission to correct my errors and thus improve my service."

Marshall Field

The current global business environment is extremely competitive. Today's consumers are more than willing to switch from supplier to supplier in search of better service or availability or courtesy or features or for any variety of reasons. To attract and retain customers, effective organizations need to focus on determining and providing what their customers want and value. Excellent organizations survive because they talk to customers, translate what their customers say into appropriate actions, and align their key business processes to support what their customers want.

Today's business world is experiencing important paradigm shifts in the direction of increased personalization of products and services. Certain paradigm shifts are transforming marketing and customer service. Because of advances in technology, one - to - one customer service will become the standard for businesses in the coming years. One - to - one marketing and personalized service are changing the face of commerce. The business landscape of the future will be affected by *technical trends* including unified messaging, Internet integration, near - infinite bandwidth, and natural language processing, as well as *operational trends* including virtual call centres, global outsourcing, and teleprofessionals. These technological changes are having a great impact on people in all segments of society. Therefore, organisations need to know some important facts about relationship marketing and service. Ultimately, customer loyalty will stem from the ability to use relationship marketing to gain a greater share of the customer. Customer relationship management (CRM) marries technology and customer service principles to build better relationships and create A - plus experiences for customers. Companies that fail to include today's technology run the risk of falling behind customer expectations and losing loyalty.

Perceived value and Customer Satisfaction

Customer perceived value is the result of comparing purchasing alternatives, allowing a customer to change its future product or service offerings to better suit its customers. Customer satisfaction, comparing past experience or expectations to the realities experienced, is reactive and retrospective. Organizations offer product or service features to their customers, but what the customers are really buying is the benefits those products or services offer. Perceived value is the customer's viewpoint of those benefits. Customer satisfaction, on the other hand, centers around how they felt the last time they bought a product or service from a company. It is a comparison between customer expectations and customer experience. Perceived value goes beyond customer satisfaction and concentrates on future transactions. Consumers' perception of the value they have received in the recent transaction will affect their future decision to purchase the same thing again. If they perceive their overall experience with the product or service as valuable, they will most likely purchase in the future, if they do not, they won't. Effective organizations realize that how the customer perceives the value of that transaction will determine whether or not they will buy from the same organization the next time.

Excellent organizations are always close to customers and service organizations should conduct their business on the basis of customer needs satisfaction (Parasuraman *et al.*, 1983). Customer - centered organizations or people are in a better position to identify new opportunities, set effective strategies, and serve the target customers (Kotler, 2000). Organisations that lead in the business understands the expressed as well as the latent needs and wants of customers need and fulfills so as to attend the desired level of service quality, customer satisfaction, customer retention, and loyalty.

Besides, customer relationships are claimed to be important in service quality management. Competitor orientation is another component needs to be investigated. Understanding of the competitors and responsiveness to them, so as to create continuous and superior customer value in service; the organization/employees gather, disseminate and respond to competitors' information for service excellence. As the competition intensifies worldwide, firms cannot afford to ignore the need to compete. The great reminder is that every company must try to understand and master competition (Porter, 1998). Authors like Day and Wensley, 1988; Morgan and Strong, 1998; and others agree that market orientation should also include the concept of competitive orientation. Garvin (1987) reminded managers that quality management should be rigorously moving towards understanding and meeting customers' needs and preferences so as to create competitive opportunities.

Customer Centricity in HEI

Seymour (1995) explains that the inability for higher education institutions to see themselves as customer - driven leads them away from the focused attention and common aim that it provides for business. Our disciplinary structure and organizational divisions create barriers within which the occupants see themselves and their supervisors as the customers—not the next person in line or the end user. The result is tremendous waste: duplication of efforts, needless complexity, and high overhead.

In the university environment, the concept of customer is not clearly defined, which makes these institutions difficult to manage from a marketing point of view. A review of specialised literature shows the existence of various groups that can be categorised as customers of university institutions: students, employers, families, society (Álvarez and Rodríguez, 1997). In spite of this diversity, one of the groups about which there is a consensus with regard to its consideration as a customer is the students of these institutions (Wilson, 1998).

Centring on this group of customers, we should consider the fact that universities are facing numerous challenges, and one of the most relevant is the need to take on the needs of students with a socio - demographic profile that is very different from the one of decade ago. The traditional classification of a student – youths of around 20 years of age who, after finalising their studies that provide access to the university, enrol in higher education studies and who are engaged full time in studying for a university degree – has changed, and among these students a much more varied classification has emerged.

Customer - driven quality, then, is a value that has low fit and high impact on a college campus. It is a problem that, properly dealt with, is a tremendous opportunity for our institutions. A strong customer focus can lead to greater morale, as people work together to achieve a common goal; greater productivity, as waste is reduced; and greater effectiveness, as the institution begins to deliver customer - pleasing services.

Customer loyalty

Who could argue about the idea that businesses, other organizations, and individuals enjoy their greatest potential for success when they build loyal relationships with their customers? At some level, every organization depends on customers—the people who rely on that organization for information, advice, services, products, or other value. Yet far too many employees in far too many organizations lack the foundation skills needed for building customer loyalty—despite the abundance of customer - service books available at any bookstore. The problem with many organizations' customer - service efforts, then, is not lack of availability of education or training about customer service. Rather, the problem may be that organizations lack the ability to translate the many customer - service tips, success stories, and ideas that they've found in abundance into useful, effective strategies for their organizations. The importance of measuring the satisfaction variable stems from its relationship to customer loyalty (Galloway, 1998). In current competitive environments, in order for organizations to be able to guarantee their survival, repeated purchases by their customers are necessary, which means customer retention. This situation affects most sectors, and higher education is certainly not beyond being affected (Athiayaman, 2000).

To a large extent, and given the characteristics of the current university environment, which includes a reduction of the potential number of customers, the need to guarantee the survival of university institutions justifies the importance of analysing the concepts of satisfaction and loyalty in this context. Student loyalty is becoming one of the key objectives of university institutions. Thus, prominent among the main motivations that lead universities to analyse the loyalty of their students are the advantages that this loyalty provides to universities, which include (Henning - Thurau *et al.*, 2001) the following:

- *Students constitute one of the main sources of university financing through enrolments. In spite of the fact that a lot of European universities are public, and therefore they should be financed through public resources, self - financing by these organisations is increasingly encouraged. In view of this situation, the retention of students as well as the attraction of other, new students means the input of economic resources.*
- *The theory of services marketing sets forth that a loyal student positively influences teaching quality through active participation and a committed behaviour (Rodie and Kleine, 2000). It is therefore an input of the service production process, and it conditions the quality management of the same.*
- *After leaving the university, students can continue to maintain a relationship with the institution through donations, through positive interpersonal communication and through co - operation, thereby offering internships to students, co - operating in research projects, etc.*

As with services in general, where satisfaction and loyalty are closely related and where satisfaction is a antecedent variable of loyalty (Dick and Basu, 1994), in the higher education sector, the concepts of loyalty and satisfaction are also closely related to each other, whereby the same causal relationship between them both can become established (Martensen *et al.* 1999; Gonçalves *et al.*, 2004). Thus, satisfaction is an antecedent of student loyalty. A student who is therefore satisfied with the service received may develop various attitudes and behaviours that are indicative of loyalty, among which is positive interpersonal communication with other potential customers about the university and/or students may show the intention to return to participate in other courses offered by the same university.

Moreover, excellent organisations understand that customers have come to expect a Web presence. Therefore, they also focus on Web - based customer service or "e - service" offers, a low - cost approach for routine customer transactions. The reasons why world class institutions implement Web - based customer service are mainly due to the advantages of (1) speed, (2) portals to other services, and (3) global 24/7 service. However, it has several disadvantages, such as - (1) added service costs, (2) the effect of the "bleeding edge," and (3) the potential for lost customers and poor reputation. Organisations can choose from one or a mixture of the four categories of e - service - (1) self - serve common answers (such as FAQs), (2) delayed answers (primarily email), (3) live answers (chat), and(4) self - serve personalized answers.

Exceed Customer Expectations

The core concept of exceeding customer expectation or customer delight is to continually working to anticipate customer expectations and then exceeding those expectations can bring great business and career success. Part of succeeding in that effort is learning to stay aware of how customer expectations may be changing so that customer - service strategies can continue to be effective in exceeding those expectations. A psychological theory called "equity theory" supports the importance of exceeding what customers anticipate (creating "A - plus") to keep customers and build their loyalty. Organisations can use equity theory to build relationships. When people believe they are getting more than they "deserve" from a relationship, they feel subtle pressures to rebalance the relationship by giving more to it.

Exceeding expectations works like magic. Consistently exceeding what customers anticipate is a powerful key to career success. Excellent organisations also must keep in step with changing expectations. Expectations change and evolve, forcing intelligent businesspeople to adjust and innovate. For innovating new ideas and exceeding customer expectation, they need to seek customer feedback so that they can achieve A - plus service through VISPAC. The six areas included in the acronym VISPAC provide the best opportunities for A - plus innovation: (1) Value, (2) Information, (3) Speed, (4) Personality, (5) Add - ons, and (6) Convenience. Everybody has great customer - service ideas. But the best A - plus ideas come from alert, innovative people at any level in the organization.

In summary, world class universities that lead in the business create a customer - focused management system and company culture that seeks to meet their customers' needs the first time and every time. These organizations analyze their customer's needs, wants, and expectations, translate them into technical specifics, and organize their key business operations accordingly. They also identify the gap between their current performance and what the customer requires in order to properly target improvement activities. They recognize the importance of studying both customer value perceptions and customer satisfaction. These organizations ensure that their leadership creates and implements strategic plans that focus on what is important to their customers and markets. The core issue here is the obsession with the customers by the world class universities to provide world class service by following a customer centric approach. As appropriately summed up by Sterne -

"The customer and the business together are now redefining what it means to participate in a commercial relationship. It is becoming a collaborative, interactive world. The new dynamic of competition is based on doing battle for one customer at a time."

Jim Sterne

Growing a Performance Driven Culture

"...the collection of values and norms that are shared by people and groups in an organization and that control the way they interact with each other and with contacts outside the organization. The culture dictates the beliefs and ideas about what kinds of goals members of an organization should pursue and ideas about the appropriate kinds or standards of behavior organizational members should use to achieve thee goals..."

Charles Hill

The culture of an organisation can facilitate the speedy achievement of its business plan and can be the major cause of its success. The careful design and shaping of the corporate culture should be the driving force enabling results to happen. It stands to reason that successful organisations focus their attention on creating the culture that will generate the desired outcomes. This is what should be the norm for all businesses, yet too many either fail to see the need to develop the 'culture' or have little idea how this could be achieved. In the majority of cases, the typical business culture that evolves is a largely matter of accident or luck. In many instances, the 'culture' may not fit the corporate plan or the institute's business intentions. It may even be counter to the needs of and the demands on their business! It is not unusual to witness a culture that is driving customers away simply because it is too internally, rather than externally, focused. Culture is the responsibility of the management or leadership team. It is within their control.

Whether the management team does nothing or does something, every business will have a corporate culture, which could be the result of numerous take - overs, mergers and acquisitions. 80% of organizational cultures exist by accident or default, rather than design (Risher 2007). Most are shaped through critical incidents or key events that have happened in the history of the organization. Many are shaped by key personalities moving through the business. It could be the result of key people impacting on the structure either through their 'joining' and or 'leaving' the business. It can be seen in certain businesses that the sheer presence of one character will shift the organisation forward. Their 'charisma' is good for the business. Everything they touch, influence and shape has far reaching consequences that create improvement. Conversely, in organisations the presence of another character in a key position proves disastrous! The impact of key people on the culture is a major issue. For good or bad, the leadership of an organisation and its key operations are paramount in shaping the business culture.

What is important to understand is that the relative health of the institution's business culture will either support the organisation in achieving results in difficult times or it can act as a brake on innovation or change. It can slow down the implementation of recovery plans. It can even hasten the demise of the business. Culture makes things happen. A strong and vibrant culture will enable new initiatives to flourish and grow. It will encourage 'high flyers' to be attracted to work within your business. A great culture will retain these high - flyers. It will enable speedy innovations to be introduced and will stand a better chance of holding onto its key staff. Conversely, a mediocre culture will not blossom. Results will be lacklustre. High potential people will pursue their careers elsewhere. Key vacancies will be difficult to fill. Even worse, a poor or negative culture will meander along aimlessly. Although some people will be focused and in touch with the real world, there will be no central rallying theme to provide any real focus, guidance or energy. Not surprisingly, these varieties of business will usually generate only average to poor performance. It should be unsurprisingly that staff who have difficulty moving on in the labour market will see out their days in this sort of culture.

There is a positive correlation between strong, positive cultures and corporate performance. A healthy culture creates healthy results. Knowing this positive relationship we would think that most management teams would probably commit to creating and designing their culture to generate superior performance. This is often not the case. In reality, creating a performance driven culture is the last thing to which most management teams commit their time, resources and energy.

Narver and Slater (1990) stressed on performance orientation in the original operationalization of service quality. It focuses on the organization - wide emphasis on superior performance in serving the target customers; different functional units having their own service performance oriented goals in line with the organization's mission; the organization/employees gather or measure, disseminate, and respond to performance related information for service excellence. Service management experts like Heskett *et al.* (1990) agree that the "service concept" should be results - oriented. Performance orientation is clearly seen in the definitions of Narver and Slater (1990) where the primary aim of market orientation is to create greater customer value. Service organizations must always seriously be thinking about excellence (Crosby, 1996), as there are many people and processes which need to be well managed for service excellence and be "fail - safe" (Chase and Stewart, 1994) at each and every service encounter. Garvin (1987) cautioned that quality market research is important as "shoddy market research can add quality features nobody wants". This indicates that a market orientation which emphasizes market research should be performance oriented. Professionalism is very much emphasized by market oriented service organizations especially higher learning institutions (Siu and Wilson, 1998), and this is also the case with quality cultures, especially service quality. Thus, organizations that value and emphasize performance will most probably be able to deliver quality service.

Therefore, universities that are aiming to become world class in the 21st century, the core activity of them should be building the culture for the future focusing on performance. This process will act as a major building block in developing a high performance business culture. The content inherent in each stage can help support building a resilient corporate culture supporting many functions and processes including different locations and geographies. The culture is the infrastructure, the fabric that binds together people and processes to generate results. The purpose of the culture change process is to enable much faster generation of a business culture that enables people to achieve results. If an organisation is adopting a logical approach to this process as it progresses, it will create 'small successes' that act as milestones along the way.

The culture change process makes that which was intangible, tangible, that which was assumed, the stable, and that which was practiced in some localities and unknown to others, open to debate and discussion. Much in culture change is focused upon diagnosing the current culture. It requires assessing the culture which is desired and then becomes a simple exercise or 'gap analysis'. What should be avoided is starting off to shape a culture in a format without knowing what positively or negatively the institution is upon. When managers/leaders designing a culture they should focus on the following -

- *Provide a 'visual map' of the building blocks of culture from vision to KPI's*
- *Highlight and identify the core values that drive behaviours.*

- *Enable the designers of the culture to focus upon a sequence of key stages and activities to build, rejuvenate or generate a desired culture.*
- *Provide a roadmap of activities to pursue, apply and implement within your own organisation.*
- *Identify the precise components of a business culture that will cause significant business improvement.*

However, Risher (2007) notes that while performance (or pay for performance) has been an on - going priority in the private sector, the public sector has been slow to adopt that priority for, among other reasons, fear of significantly changing the culture. A case in point is the U.S. Office of Management and Budget, which in 2001 initiated a program for performance improvement that was met with significant resistance by employees. To counteract such resistance, Risher (2007) recommends assessing the on - going culture as it impacts employee performance via surveys, focus groups or interviews. He also summarizes a multi - dimensional management practice, which fosters performance, and came via his own research and a study by the London School of Economics (LSE) and McKinsey & Co. (Dorgan, et al, 2005). The eight - pronged approach to performance involves:

- *Leaders as Champions - key people across the organization need to advocate and explain why the new strategy is needed and how it will affect people;*
- *Work Link to Mission - feeling their work is integral to the success of their employer and understanding the mission are general concerns of employees;*
- *Performance Tracking and dialogue - tracking it over time, taking corrective measures and broadly communicating results keep employees involved and attending to performance;*

- *Cascading Goals - being able to see the "big - picture" regarding goals at each level keeps employees engaged at all levels of the organization;*
- *Investment in Talent - investing in and promoting qualified personnel and development of individual talent support performance goals;*
- *Recognition and rewards - strategies that recognize and reward high - performing employees should be both fostered and evaluated now and then to ensure they are serving the needs of the organization;*
- *Manager Accountability - managers need to be committed, trained and reinforced in helping employees improve performance, and manager performance should be evaluated regarding these goals;*
- *Employee engagement - research performed by Gallup and others shows a correlation between emotional commitment to the success of the company and an employee's high - performance level; surveys help reveal employee engagement.*

In conclusion, the aforementioned discussion confirms the obvious: "Well - managed companies perform better." Thus, to attain and sustain world class status in academia, universities should focus on the day - to - day practices of middle managers and supervisors to foster a performance culture rather than the just the performance focus. The critical challenge for every organization is thus to create the culture and the climate that maximizes learning and innovativeness on both the cognitive - theoretical level and the practical level, in order to achieve superior performance and a competitive advantage.

Case study: The University of Illinois at Urbana - Champaign A World class university[21]

Since its founding in 1867, the University of Illinois at Urbana - Champaign has been committed to excellence in research, teaching, and public engagement.

- **Significant resources** - Among the University's most significant resources is its talented and highly respected faculty. Many faculty members are recognized for their exceptional scholarship, with memberships in the American Association for the Advancement of Sciences, American Academy of Arts and Sciences, the National Academy of Sciences, and the National Academy of Engineering; and as recipients of the Nobel Prize, Crafoord Prize in Biosciences, Japan Prize, National Medal of Science, Pulitzer Prize, and Presidential Early Career Awards for Scientists and Engineers, and MacArthur Fellowships; and by such organizations as the National Endowment for the Humanities, Guggenheim Memorial Foundation, National Academy of Education, and the Alfred P. Sloan Foundation.
- **Elite Scholarships** - Each year, Illinois students receive some of the world's most elite scholarships. The campus has a history of sending at least one student per year to Cambridge on a prestigious post - graduate fellowship. Other prestigious scholarships awarded to Illinois students recently include the Rhodes, Truman, Marshall, Gates, Goldwater, Churchill, Luce, and Fulbright Scholarships. And Illinois undergraduates who have studied abroad have earned National Security Education Program Boren Scholarships.
- **Alumni successes** - Another prime indicator of the University's excellence is the success of its alumni: 11 alumni are Nobel laureates, 158 Guggenheim Fellows and another 18 have won Pulitzer Prizes.
- **Academic Resources** - Academic resources on campus are among the finest in the world. The University Library is one of

[21] http://www.publicaffairs.uiuc.edu/facts/world.html

the largest public university collections in the nation, housing more than ten million volumes, over six million manuscripts, periodicals, and other non - print materials, and more than 65,000 journals. In addition to the main library, there are more than 35 departmental libraries and divisions throughout campus. The library's computerized cataloging system was the first in the world to serve as the primary access to a large academic library. More than one million users worldwide access the online catalog each week.

- **Leader in supercomputing** - A world leader in supercomputing design and applications, the University is home to the National Center for Supercomputing Applications, developer of the internet browser Mosaic(TM), which revolutionized the use of the World Wide Web. Students have access to over 3,500 computer terminals in classrooms, residence halls, and campus libraries. Seventy - six percent of classrooms and over 130 buildings allow wireless connectivity.
- **Interdisciplinary and multidisciplinary research** - Scholars, both faculty and students, find the University an ideal place to conduct inter - and multidisciplinary research. The most visible example of the University's commitment to such study is the Beckman Institute for Advanced Science and Technology, where 12 research groups from 30 University departments work within and across three broadly defined themes: biological intelligence, human - computer interaction, and molecular and electronic nanostructures.

The Institute for Genomic Biology houses up to 400 researchers in three broad Program Areas:

- **Systems Biology, Cellular and Metabolic Engineering, and Genome Technology**. The Energy Biosciences Institute, formed in 2007 is unique in both its scale and its partnership between BP, academia, and others in the private sector.

- **Undergraduate Education.** The University has a fundamental commitment to undergraduate education. Over 30,000 undergraduate students are enrolled in nine undergraduate divisions, which together offer over 5,000 courses in more than 150 fields of study. The divisions are the College of Agricultural, Consumer and Environmental Sciences; College of Applied Health Sciences; College of Business; College of Communications; College of Education; College of Engineering; College of Fine and Applied Arts; College of Liberal Arts and Sciences; and Institute of Aviation. Undergraduate admission is highly selective. In the 2007 Freshmen class, students in the middle 50 percent had ACT scores between 26 and 31 and 55 percent ranked in the top 10 percent of their high school graduating classes.
- **Graduate Enrollment.** The University enrolls over 11,000 graduate and professional students in more than 100 programs. It is among the top eight universities in number of earned doctorates awarded annually in the United States.
- **Public Engagement.** Also integral to the University's mission is a commitment to public engagement. Each year about 2.7 million Illinois residents participate in scores of conferences, institutes, credit and noncredit courses, and workshops presented on campus and statewide. The University of Illinois Extension provides 4 - H, nutrition intervention, and other programs in rural and urban settings. Research and class projects take students and professors outside their classrooms and laboratories to share expertise and technical support with Illinois farmers, manufacturing firms, and businesses. In a typical year, students log more than 78,000 volunteer hours in blood drives, day care centers, prisons, senior citizen centers, and tutoring programs through the Office of Volunteer Programs. The Osher Lifelong Learning Institute (OLLI) opens its doors to "curious minds over age 50" to attend intellectually

stimulating courses, small group discussion, and lunch time lectures.

- **The arts.** A major center for the arts, the campus attracts dozens of nationally and internationally renowned artists each year to its widely acclaimed Krannert Center for the Performing Arts. Designed by alumnus Max Abramovitz, an architect of New York City's Lincoln Center, the facility has four indoor theaters and an outdoor amphitheater. Together, they host more than 350 performances each year. The University also supports two major museums: the Krannert Art Museum and Kinkead Pavilion, second only to the Art Institute of Chicago among Illinois publicart museums housing over 9,000 works of art in its permanent collection; and the Spurlock Museum, a museum of world history and culture, which holds in its collections approximately 46,000 artifacts from diverse cultures and varied historical time periods.
- **Major facilities.** Other major facilities include the multipurpose Assembly Hall (16,500 seats), which hosts concerts, convocations, theater, and sporting events; Memorial Stadium (70,000 seats), site of Big Ten Conference football games; and the Campus Recreation Center – 470,000 square feet of recreational space between two newly expanded campus recreation and wellness centers, the largest recreational facilities of their kind on a university campus.
- **Location.** Located in east central Illinois in the twin cities of Urbana and Champaign (combined population 180,000), the University of Illinois at Urbana - Champaign is the state's flagship public university.

References

- Alavi, M., and Tiwana, A.(2002) "Knowledge integration in virtual teams: the potential tole of KMS," Journal of the American society for information science and technology (53:12) pp 1029 - 1037.
- Alavi, M., Leidner, D. (2001), "Review: knowledge management and knowledge management systems: conceptual foundations and research issues", MIS Quarterly, Vol. 25 No.1, pp.107 - 36.
- Allison, M. and Willmott, H. (1996), Making Sense of Management, Sage, London.
- Amit, R., Schoemaker, P.J. (1993), "Strategic assets and organizational rent", Strategic Management Journal, Vol. 14 pp.33 - 46.
- Andreassen, T.W, Lindestad, B (1998), "The effect of institutional image in the formation of customer loyalty", Journal of Service Research, Vol. 1 No.1, pp.82 - 92.
- Bright, J.R., (1969), Some management lessons from technological innovation research, Long Range Planning, 2, 1, 36 - 41.
- Chase, R., Stewart, D. (1994), "Make your service fail - safe", Sloan Management Review, No.Spring, pp.35 - 44.
- Chase, R.L. (1997), "The knowledge - based organization: an international survey", Journal of Knowledge Management, Vol. 1 No.1, pp.38 - 49.
- Chen, M. - Y., and Chen, A. - P. "Knowledge management performance evaluation: a decade review from 1995 to 2004," Journal of Information Science (32:1), February 1, 2006 2006, pp 17 - 38.
- Christensen, C. (1997). The Innovator's Dilemma. Massachusetts: Harvard Business School Press.
- Chuang, S. - H. "A resource - based perspective on knowledge management capability and competitive advantage: an

empirical study," Expert systems with Application (27) 2004, pp 459 - 465.

- Clarke, P. and Staunton, N. (1989), Innovation in Technology and Organisation, Routledge, London.
- Clegg, S., Barrett, M., Clarke, T., Dwyer, L., Gray, J., Kemp, S. and Marceau, J. (1996), "Management knowledge for the future: innovation, embryos and new paradigms", in Clegg, S. and Palmer, G. (Eds), The Politics of Management Knowledge, Sage, London.
- Coimbra, A.,. Silva, A.R (2004) "Value Chain: An interpretation for higher education institutions", Proceedings of the 10th International Conference of European University Information Systems, Bled, (2004).
- Cronin, J., Taylor, S. (1994), "SERVPERF versus SERVQUAL: reconciling performance - based and perceptions - minus - expectations measurement of service quality", Journal of Marketing, Vol. 58 pp.125 - 31.
- Crosby, P.B. (1996), "Thinking about excellence", Journal for Quality and Participation, Vol. 19 No.6, pp.70.
- De Jarnett, L. (1996), "Knowledge the latest thing", Information Strategy, The Executives Journal, Vol. 12, pt 2, pp. 3 - 5.
- Detert, J., Schroeder, R., Mauriel, J. (2000). A framework for linking culture and improvement initiatives in organizations. The Academy of Management Review, 25(4), 850 - 863.
- Diane Harley and Shannon Lawrence (2007) The Regulation of E - learning: New National and International Policy, Center for Studies in Higher Education, UC Berkeley, University of California.
- Dick, Alan S. and Basu, Kunal. (1994), "Customer Loyalty: Towards an Integrated Conceptual Framework", Journal of the Academy of Marketing Science, Spring, 1994, Vol. 22, Iss. 2, 99 - 113.
- Drucker, P. F. (1985), Innovation and Entrepreneurship. Harper & Row, New York.

- Drucker, P.F. (1994), Innovation and Entrepreneurship: Practice and Principles, Heinemann, London.
- Galloway, L. (1998). Quality perceptions of internal and external customers: A case study in educational administration. The TQM Magazine, 10(1), 20–26.
- Garvin, D.A. (1984), "What does product quality really mean?", Sloan Management Review, No.Fall, pp.25 - 43.
- Gold, A.H., Malhotra, A., and Segars, A.H. "Knowledge management: an organizational capabilities perspective," Journal of Management Information Systems (18:1) 2001, pp 185 - 214.
- Hamel, G., Prahalad, C.K. (1994), Computing for the Future, Harvard Business School Press, Boston, MA,.
- Henning - Thurau, T., Gwinner, K.P., Gremler, D.D. (2002), "Understanding relationship marketing outcome: an integration of relational benefits and relational quality", Journal of Service Research, Vol. 4 No.3, pp.230 - 47.
- Inside Higher Education, coverage of "A National Dialogue: The Secretary of Education's Commission on the Future of Higher Education." http://insidehighered.com/news/focus/commission.
- Jensen, H.R. (2001), "Antecedents and consequences of consumer value assessments: implications for marketing strategy and future research", Journal of Retailing and Consumer Services, Vol. 8 No.6, pp.299 - 310.
- Kanji, G. and Asher, G. (1993), "Total quality management process: a systematic approach", Journal of Total Quality Management, Vol. 4, (Suppl.)
- Keller, K.L. (1993), "Conceptualizing, measuring and managing customer - based brand equity", Journal of Marketing, Vol. 57 No.January, pp.1 - 22.
- Keohane, R.O. and Hoffmann, S. (1991). "Institutional Change in Europe in the 1980s", in Keohane R.O. and Hoffmann, S. (eds.),

The New European Community: Decision - Making and Institutional Change, Westview, Boulder, CO, pp. 1 - 40.

- Kotler, P. (1997), Marketing Management: Analysis, Planning, Implementation, and Control, 9th ed., Prentice - Hall, Upper Saddle River, NJ,.
- Kotler, P. (2000), Marketing Management, The Millennium Edition, Prentice - Hall Inc., New Jersey, NJ,.
- Lapierre, J. (2000), "Customer - perceived value in industrial contexts", Journal of Business & Industrial Marketing, Vol. 15 No.2/3, pp.122 - 40.
- Martensen, Anne, Gronholdt, Lars and Kristensen, Kai. (2000), "The drivers of customer satisfaction and loyalty: cross - industry findings from Denmark", Total Quality Management, 2000, Vol. 11, No. 4/5&6, 544 - 553.
- Miller, D. (1983). The correlates of entrepreneurship in three types of firms, Management Science, 29, pp. 770 - 791.
- Morgan, R. (2004), "Market - based organizational learning – theoretical reflections and conceptual insights", Journal of Marketing Management, Vol. 20 pp.67 - 103.
- Morris, M.H., Paul, G.W. (1987), Innovation in conservative and entrepreneurship firms, Journal of Business Venturing, 2, 247 - 59.
- Narver, J.C., Slater, S.F. (1990), "The effect of a market orientation on business profitability", Journal of Marketing, Vol. 54 No.October, pp.20 - 35.
- Narver, J.C., Slater, S.F., MacLanchlan, D.L. (2000), "Total market orientation, business performance, and innovation", Working Paper Series, Marketing Science Institute, Cambridge, MA,.
- Niland(2005) The challenge of building world class universities in the Asian region.
- http://www.onlineopinion.com.au/view.asp?article=997&page=0 accessed:04/06/2008 at 0200 GMT
- Nonaka, I. "A dynamic theory of organizational knowledge creation," Organization Science (5:1) 1994, pp 14 - 37.

- Nonaka, I. and Takeuchi, K. (1995), The Knowledge Creating Company: How Japanese Companies Create the Dynamics of Innovation, Oxford University Press, Oxford.
- Oakland, J. (1999), The "X" factor: winning performance through Business Excellence, European Centre for Business Excellence Press, Leeds.
- Owlia, M.S. and Aspinwall, E.M. (1996), "Quality Management, Vol. 7 No. 4, pp. 161 - 71.
- Parasuraman, A. (2000), "The impact of technology on the quality - value - loyalty chain: a research agenda", Journal of the Academy of Marketing Science, Vol. 28 No.1, pp.156 - 74.
- Petty, R., Guthrie, J. (2000), "Intellectual capital literature review, measuring, reporting and management", Journal of Intellectual Capital, Vol. 1 No.2,.
- Porter, M.E., Millar, V.E. (1985) "How information gives you competitive advantage", Harvard Business Review, July - August 1985, pp. 149 - 160, (1985).
- Porter. M.E. (1990)"Competitive Advantage. Creating and Sustaining Superior Performance", The Free Press, New York, USA (1985).
- Quintas, P., Lefrere, P. and Jones, G. (1997), "Knowledge management: a strategic agenda", Journal of Long Range Planning, Vol. 30 No. 3, pp. 385 - 91.
- R.S. Kaplan, D.P Norton. "The balanced scorecard: measures that driver performance", Harvard Business Review, January - February 1992, pp. 71 - 80, (1992).
- Ramsay, H. (1996), "Managing sceptically: a critique of organisational fashion", in Clegg, S. and Palmer, G. (Eds), The Politics of Management Knowledge, Sage, London.
- Risher, Howard. (2007). Pay for Performance: A Guide for Federal Managers, IBM's Center for The Business of Government.
- Rodie, A.R. and Kleine, S.S. (2000), "Customer participation in services production and delivery", in Swartz, T.A. and Iacobucci,

D. (Eds), Handbook of Service Marketing and Management, Sage, Thousand Oaks, CA, pp. 111 - 25.

- Rogers E.M (1995) Diffusion of Innovators, NewYork, Free Press.
- Rust, R.T., Zeithaml, V.A., Lemon, K.N. (2000), Driving Customer Equity: How Customer Lifetime Value Is Reshaping Corporate Strategy, The Free Press, New York, NY,.
- Sallis, E. (1993), Total Quality Management in Education, Kogan Page, London
- Schultze, U., and Leidner, D.E. (2002) "Studying knowledge management in information systems research: discourses and theoretical assumptions," MIS Quarterly (26:3) pp 213 - 242.
- Siu, N., Wilson, R. (1998), "Modelling market orientation: an application in the education sector", Journal of Marketing Management, Vol. 14 pp.293 - 323.
- Slater, S.F. (1997), "Developing a customer value - based theory of the firm", Journal of the Academy of Marketing Science, Vol. 25 No.2, pp.162 - 7.
- Sundbo, J., (1998) The Theory of Innovation: Entrepreneurs, Technology and Strategy, Edward Elgar, Northampton, MA.
- Sweeney, J.C., Soutar, G.N. (2001), "Consumer - perceived value: the development of a multiple - item scale", Journal of Retailing, Vol. 77 No.2, pp.203 - 20.
- Taylor (1998) L. Taylor, Denver public library's adaptation of messaging technologies, Journal of Interlibrary Loan, Document Delivery and Information Supply 8 (1998) (4), pp. 49–58.
- Tsarenko, Y. and Mavondo, F.T. (2001), “Resources and capabilities as determinants of student satisfaction: do foreign and local students differ”, Proceedings of the Conference ANZMAC, Auckland, 1 - 5 December.
- Webster, F.E. (1988), "The rediscovery of the marketing concept", Business Horizon, No.May - June, pp.29 - 39.
- Wilson, R. J. T. (2001). Transitional issues in e - education: Re - engineering organizational culture, ICEE Conference, October, Kuala Lumpur.

- Woodruff, R.B. (1997), "Customer value: the next source for competitive advantage", Journal of the Academy of Marketing Science, Vol. 25 No.2, pp.139 - 53.
- Zeithaml, V.A. (1988), "Consumer perceptions of price, quality and value: a means - end model and synthesis of evidence", Journal of Marketing, Vol. 52 pp.2 - 22.
- Zeithaml, V.A., Berry, L., Parasuraman, A. (1996), "The behavioral consequences of service quality", Journal of Marketing, Vol. 60 No.2, pp.31 - 46.